CW00409240

BOGNOR BOY

How I Became an Anarchist

PETER MARSHALL

London

First published
2018 by Zena Publications
www.zenapublications.co.uk

ISBN
978-0-9511069-7-6

© Peter Marshall 2018

All rights reserved. No part of this publication may be reproduced or transmitted in any form or by any means, electronic or mechanical, including photocopying, recording or any information storage or retrieval system, without permission in writing from the publishers.

The right of Peter Marshall to be identified as author of this work has been asserted by him in accordance with the Copyright, Designs and Patents Act 1988.

Design, layout and typesetting by
Jonathan How
www.coherentvisions.com

Cover design by
Jonathan How
inspired by Ronald Brett's 1950s 'Bognor Regis' poster
for British Railways

Printed and bound in Great Britain by
Lightning Source UK Ltd, Chapter House, Pitfield, Kiln Farm,
Milton Keynes MK11 3LW
FSC® Certificate Registration Code: RA-COC-004900
FSC-C084699

Distributed by
Central Books Ltd, 50 Freshwater Road, Chadwell Heath, London
RM8 1RX
www.centralbooks.com

By the same author

William Godwin

Journey through Tanzania

Into Cuba

Cuba Libre: Breaking the Chains?

William Blake: Visionary Anarchist

Demanding the Impossible: A History of Anarchism

Nature's Web: Rethinking our Place on Earth

Journey through Maldives

Around Africa: From the Pillars of Hercules to the Strait
  of Gibraltar

Celtic Gold: A Voyage around Ireland

Riding the Wind: Liberation Ecology for a New Era

The Philosopher's Stone: A Quest for the Secrets of Alchemy

World Astrology

Europe's Lost Civilization: Exploring the Mysteries of
  the Megaliths

The Theatre of the World: Alchemy, Astrology and Magic in
  Renaissance Prague

Poseidon's Realm: A Voyage around the Aegean

'It is propitious that Peter Marshall's *Bognor Boy* appears at the 50th anniversary of the momentous revolutionary year of 1968. The book is valuable for many reasons, but not least of all as a major document of the generation of 68 and its living legacy. It is an important work, not only of biography, but of social history. It has a rich sense of time and place, and paints a vivid picture not only of Bognor, but of the culture of post-war England, continuing through the 60s. Marshall, a gifted story-teller, tells a compelling tale of personal and social evolution.

The narrative progresses through careful attention to the details of everyday life, exemplified perhaps most strikingly in Marshall's exploration – perhaps demolition – of the worlds of education and work. Throughout the book, he depicts brilliantly how the dialectic between large institutions and small personal incidents leads to insights and awakenings, and thus shapes character, values, and political evolution.

At the outset, we discover a young man who is naturally sensitive to the injustices, cruelties, brutalities, prejudices, and absurdities of society. At a certain critical point in history, the facts of personality converge with the facts of history. New possibilities for personal freedom, liberated imagination, and radical social transformation emerge. The springtime of freedom becomes the springtime for Peter Marshall. He becomes what he was always becoming. He becomes an anarchist.'

John Clark, Emeritus Professor,
philosopher and author

'Peter Marshall found a silver lining in growing up in a philistine, one-parent, middle-class family that exiled him to boarding school. He discovered the right books, listened to jazz, took to the sea, and thought for himself. His autobiography will chime with freedom-lovers everywhere.'

Max Farrar, Emeritus Professor,
sociologist, author and photographer

'Peter Marshall is a rare soul: writer, philosopher, poet, sailor, and a man with an unusually developed social conscience defined by his long interest in history and radical politics beside his grasp of the esoteric as essential to our personal and spiritual development. His work in every sense is the 'bigger picture' and is absolutely of our time. I was fascinated to see how all this came into being in this beautifully written memoir.'

Jay Ramsay,
poet and author

"'I wanted my life to be an open field of unexpected opportunities, not a closed future," Peter Marshall writes in his inspiring chronicle of a boy's progress from a small seaside town in Sussex to a career at sea to the beginnings of a new life as a writer, thinker, traveller, and anarchist. *Bognor Boy* gives us, in beautiful detail, the experience of growing into a young rebel while the world races to catch up with you.
That the world he describes is the sixties – in the UK, the US, post-colonial Africa, and the Paris of May 1968 – only underscores the fact that the inheritance of that amazing decade was built out of the brave lives of the people who came of age then. Like Peter Marshall.
Bognor Boy charts one soul's path to freedom, not to mention the yearnings that produced one of the finest radical historians and philosophic speculators of our time.'

Eric Laursen,
activist, organizer, and author

Peter Marshall

is a philosopher, historian, biographer, poet and travel writer.
He is the author of 16 highly acclaimed books which have been
translated into many languages. His circumnavigation of Africa
was made into a British TV series and an Italian TV series was
based on his book on alchemy. He has a doctorate in the History of
Ideas and is an elected fellow of the Royal Geographical Society.

www.petermarshall.net

Dedication

For my children Dylan and Emily
and grandchildren Charlotte, Jonathan Peter, Rose and Theodore

Acknowledgements

I would like to acknowledge the help of Louise Weston, née Payne, and Rhoda Cowley, née Payne, for the background of the Payne family. My half-brothers Tom and Harry Marshall have provided details of our father and his family. My mother Vera has given many delightful particulars of our family and my childhood. I would like to thank my brother Michael for his insights into our youth. Peter Dawson and Jeremy Gane have read and corrected my memories of boarding school and college. My first great love and the mother of my children Jenny Zobel has kindly read the relevant sections. Emily Zobel Marshall, Max Farrar, Eric Laursen and John Clark have all given their incisive comments. Jonathan How has beautifully done the design, layout, typesetting and editing of the book. Above all, I would like to thank my partner Elizabeth Ashton Hill for her continued and valued support, for her careful editing and proofreading of the text and the selection of photographs.

CONTENTS

ILLUSTRATIONS

PROLOGUE

I hope I have been true about my earlier life. As a philosopher, historian and biographer, I have always tried to distinguish between truth and falsehood, history and myth. But the memory plays tricks and in important areas often fails, especially as we grow older and the events of our life become more distant and faraway. The unconscious can weave its own idealised version of our life and protects and promotes its own desires and fears which occasionally break through into the consciousness in a disguised form in dreams, reveries and unguarded moments.

Am I guilty of distorting the truth in writing these autobiographical fragments, impressions and reflections? Indeed, is not all autobiography a form of myth-making, a kind of mythopoesis (to use a word from Greek for the poetry of myth)? Is not all reality ultimately a constructed or imagined story? Inevitably, certain events and experiences stand out after the passage of years; these are the most important in childhood which largely make us what we are.

As my son Dylan – who is a psychologist – tells me, we can easily have many false memories. I think this is particularly true of early childhood when we actually think we experienced something directly when, in fact, it was only related to us later by members of our family or seen in early, faded, black and white photographs. We can also have certain 'light bulb' memories of key events in our lives, both public and private. I suppose this is what Wordsworth calls 'spots of time'. Like poems, they often involve intense feeling recollected in tranquillity, although they can make the adrenaline still pulse through the arteries. They can even create acute pleasure in the present where the original experience may have been dull and fitful.

Memory plays tricks. That is well known. It has lapses, makes unconscious demands, and can change the past record to suit the owner. It has flashes which come and go and can be quite wrong. When Memory and Imagination get together, they can play havoc with the past – they embellish, erase, exaggerate, distort and invent. But apart from the memories of others, some letters and photographs – and in my case notes and books – what else can a writer of a memoir, the teller of the story of one's own life, rely on?

As a writer, I have tried in other books to describe things as they are and things as they might be, to portray existing society and culture and how they could be changed for the better. Thinking against the ideas, beliefs and feelings I inherited and had been taught, thinking against myself, I eventually became an agnostic and a social anarchist.

So in autobiographical fragments and reminiscences of my childhood and growing up, I have tried to be as reliable and accurate as possible. Clearly, I have chosen to write about certain experiences and events while I have passed over others in silence. Much of the editing of my life is done inevitably in an unconscious way. I am writing mainly in my 60s, before, I hope, dementia settles in. As my half-brother Harry says: 'when you leave the island of truth it is difficult to get back'.

Why do people write about themselves? My brother Michael asked about my early autobiography bluntly: 'What is it for?'

Some wish to 'put the record straight' which usually means justifying themselves against adverse criticism or a sense of having done wrong but wanting to present it as right. Others wish to promote and publicise themselves, to show how brilliant they are. Most, I suspect, want to create some order in the chaos of their life and experience and make something permanent out of the fleeting years. We are all born astride the grave and in a flash our lives are over. A beautiful young man looks up and explores the world; he then looks down and sees in the mirror an old man with a grey beard and balding hair.

In my case, it is trying to discern a pattern in my life after the event and to see what kind of meaning emerges. To what extent have I managed to live up to my ideals? How far have I achieved my childhood ambitions? Can I share with others any knowledge or wisdom from my experiences and studies?

To talk of success or failure seems inadequate for who defines the terms? There is no success like failure, some say, and no failure like success. They both are intertwined, like good and bad, night and day. Apparent success in one area can mean failure in another. I am not interested in judging whether I did right or wrong, or trying to justify myself, but to explain how I came to be what I am and to record what took place in the life of a young man of average abilities but considerable perseverance. Whether it can enlighten or entertain, it is for others to decide.

1
WHY I AM HERE

We had just loaded another batch of Post Office mail sacks on to the express train for London. I was scattering some sawdust on the floor at the depot in Paignton before brushing up the dust, when the foreman, a middle-aged Irishman, said casually:

'I'm off to Newton Abbott races tomorrow – I go there every year and help out in Bill Marshall's stables.'

'Bill Marshall?'

'Yes, Bill's got a real way with horses. He's a real character, quite a lady's man. Come to think of it, he's got the same surname as you; he even looks a bit like you...'

'Actually, he's my father. But I don't know him. He left my mother just before I was two and I've never heard anything from him since.'

'Your father! You know, he's one of the top trainers at the moment; he's been having a string of good luck. They say he was an ace pilot too during the war, in Spitfires. He's a real character, that's for sure! Never a dull moment with Bill!'

I had heard it before but it always seemed as if people were describing somebody who should be important in my life but who wasn't.

I was nineteen at the time, having spent nearly two years as a Purser cadet with the P&O-Orient shipping company, during which time I had gone around the world on a luxury cruiser. I was earning some money as an Assistant Foreman at Paignton Railway Station in order to pay for the boat fare to go to West Africa in order to teach English for a year.

'I'll tell you what, perhaps I could arrange for you to meet him. I'll ask around the stable and see what can be done.'

I wasn't sure if I wanted to see him. Yet it seemed a good time if there ever was going to be one. I had grown up in the seaside resort of Bognor Regis in West Sussex and had left boarding school in the Sussex Downs to train in London for a year before going to sea – anything to get out of Bognor and the staid and boring professions my family were urging me to take.

Bognor Boy

I knew from conversations with my mother and from photos and yellowing articles in an old laundry box at home that my father had been a fighter pilot during the war and had become a successful race-horse trainer. Yet characters who took to the air in war films at the time were more real to me than he was. I nevertheless decided to take the sudden opportunity to meet him before I disappeared into Africa.

My older brother Michael, who was working at my uncle's grocer's shop in Ardingley (while being ashore from the Merchant Navy to take his mate's certificate), also encouraged me to see our father despite the 'subtle nature' of the arrangements.

'I would go ahead Pete and if possible arrange a meeting with him,' he wrote in a letter in July 1966. He recognised that, however, 'it certainly does feel rather strange.'

Soon after I had the odd experience of meeting my father for the first time as a teenager. A couple of years after the war, when he left my mother, he was living for most of the week in a caravan with a few horses to his name near his parents' farm in Runcton near Chichester. It was a situation which could not last long and my father soon became involved with a young farmer's daughter who was helping out in the stables.

After my parents separated, my older brother Michael and I never received a letter, a birthday card, a note or a present from our father. Complete silence. My mother never received any alimony from him and did not bother to pursue it through the courts. It would have been too painful. So she left it at that.

However, it was not particularly distressing to me. Growing up with my grandparents, mother and older brother in a large sunny house a stone's throw from the sea, for some reason I never missed him. When people asked me what my father did I would nonchalantly reply:

'I don't have a father.'

This was invariably followed by an awkward silence and the words: 'I'm sorry about that; it must be very difficult for you!'

But it wasn't; since I didn't know him I didn't miss him. If anything, I was rather proud of the fact that I didn't have a father; it made me feel rather special and made me stand out from the other boys at school who were always going on about what their dad did and owned and said. I could see later that many boys painfully carried their fathers around on their backs – even when they were men – constantly worried about what they might think of them.

My mother's older brother, Uncle Al, a failed accountant who took over my grandparents' hotel, tried to become an authoritarian father figure, but not with great success. Once when I was about nine and he was looking at Saturday afternoon sport on television in Bognor, he suddenly said:

'That's your father! He's won another race.'

I was about to say that I didn't have a father, but then I noticed the beaming face of a short man wearing a hat and a dark suit with something flapping in his lapel on the small black-and-white television screen. He was saying how he had expected his horse to win despite the odds against him and how the jockey had done his best. It was all over in a flash and I never thought any more of it. He seemed to me at the time as remote as the horses running on the screen.

On the rare occasions he was mentioned at home, my uncle would say:

'He was a real rotter leaving you boys and your mother like that.'

My aunt, on the other hand, clearly had a soft spot for him and spoke warmly of him; I wondered later whether they had had an affair.

So it was with strange feelings that I entered the Queen's Hotel opposite the Railway Station in Newton Abbot one sunny July day and asked the receptionist for Bill Marshall.

She said: 'Who shall I say it is?'

'His son Peter,' I replied.

The word 'son' felt decidedly odd. I had never used the word before.

She went to the bar and out came a small, stooping man in a short-sleeve shirt with silver hair swept back. He gave me a hard hand shake with a gnarled fist. He had a boyish grin and his deep blue eyes looked for a brief moment in mine. I noticed a crude anchor tattooed on his forearm.

'Peter! What a surprise! How good to see you after all these years!'

He had obviously decided that bonhomie was the answer to the difficult situation.

'Hello, Bill,' I replied, unable to use the word 'dad.'

We went into the dark gloominess of the bar which was bustling with men shouting and laughing. Rolls of notes flashed. Bill introduced me as his 'son' to his 'great pal', a large, red-faced man with a vast belly who turned out to be a bookmaker and one of his owners.

'I didn't know you had any boys other than Tom, Dick and Harry,' the man said, ignoring me and calling for more drinks.

'I did by my first wife during the war.'

'You never told us about that, you sly old bugger!' he said, turning back to the bar. At that point a girl in a short mini skirt turned up, not much older than I was. I didn't fancy her; she was too plump. Bill introduced her to me as Liz, saying that she was helping out in the stables. She was Swedish and embarrassed to meet me and to be in the company of so many boisterous men. She sidled up to Bill; she was clearly helping him out, I thought, in more ways than one.

The conversation at lunch was dominated by beery jokes and racecourse chat. Afterwards, Bill suggested going for a walk in the small park next to the hotel. We walked round and round, the trees and flowers whirling in my head. I had had too much drink and the situation was totally new and unexpected.

'I loved your mother, you know,' Bill said. And looking at the path, he started to cry.

I did not know what to do. I felt numb, no emotion. Boarding school and years of not knowing him had hardened my heart.

'I loved her,' he went on, 'but we couldn't have stayed together.' He blew his nose and pulled himself together. I recalled that my mother used to say he could be very sentimental at times and easily cried.

'Your mother lived such a sheltered life growing up in the Bridport Hotel in Bognor. She was completely dominated by her mother Nelly. Her father was too. Vera just didn't understand what I was going through during the war. I would return from Tangmere aerodrome after a dogfight in my Spitfire, seeing my pals shot down over the Channel and just escaping myself, and all she would offer me for supper was a boiled egg! I had to go round to the Little Vic to get something half-decent to eat! She was very beautiful and I loved her but she just had no idea what I was going through.'

He went on justifying himself. He didn't ask what I felt about it all. As he talked, I felt that I was better off without him. If he had stayed with my mother, my life would have been completely different. I would have grown up amongst horses and stables in the country, not by the sea.

'But why didn't you ever contact us?' I suddenly interrupted.

'I thought it was best all round. I married Diana and we had four more children. I had to get on with my life and my work. I thought it was best for all of us if you got on with yours.'

I didn't mention the fact that he had never paid any alimony after the decree nisi – an incomprehensible term to me but loaded with meaning when my mother used to talk about it. She was lucky as a single mother in the late forties and fifties to have her parents to fall back on.

We eventually stopped our padding around the park. Bill said that he had to get back to the racecourse to see his horses which were running that afternoon. I too had to return to my mother's house at Elbury Cove near Brixham to pack my bags.

The next morning I had all my wisdom teeth taken out and my mother drove me to Newhaven to catch the ferry to France. I was spitting blood all the way. Not surprisingly, we chatted about my recent meeting with Bill. She had a very different story to tell. In the past, she had rarely talked about him but when she did, she inevitably said:

'I cannot understand why he never contacted you two boys. I blame that girl Diana who was helping him with his horses. You know, I once went over there and knocked on their caravan and when she came out I hit her on the bottom! I said: "How can you take Bill away from his boys?" She was so shocked she didn't reply. I just turned around and left. It was very unlike me to do something like that!'

Our house in Bognor had been named after Chideock which is a small village in Dorset where my grandfather had been born in Ruin's Lane. As we passed through I asked her how she had met my father.

'It was during the war. His mother Hatty was the secretary to the Bridge Club that Nanna used to run at the Bridport Hotel. She would often appear in her slippers, with a whisky in one hand and a cigarette in the other. Her husband was a real gentleman, very polite; they had a farm out at Runcton where they grew vegetables.'

'What happened to the Bridport Hotel during the war?,' I asked.

'It was taken over for the pilots from Tangmere. We had a great time; the pilots made sure that we were never short of food and drink which were rationed at the time. We had lots of parties. I know it's not a good thing to say when so many were being killed, but it was the best time of my life. Many of the officers courted me. There was an older RAF officer called Reg who smoked a pipe – he was very keen on me but not my cup of tea. When I said I didn't want to marry him, he threatened to kill himself. Dear old Pop had to take his gun away from him!'

'What about Bill?'

'When I first saw Bill I hardly paid any attention to him. He was short and not very good-looking. It was only one day when he turned up with a new uniform with his wings that I took any notice! Soon after he asked me out for a ride in a racing coupé which had been left to him by a friend who had been shot down over France. We were driving along the promenade when the steering wheel came off in his hands!'

'I can't say that I really loved Bill but he was very keen,' my mother continued as we sped through the New Forest. 'When he asked me to marry him just before he was going off to North Africa, I agreed. He was allowed a week's leave and on our honeymoon we went to London and stayed at the Dorchester Hotel in Mayfair. He was very attentive, always having a posy of flowers delivered to the bedroom before we went out; he also made sure that there was an Orchid for me on the table at breakfast. We went dancing in night clubs and to the theatre. But he drank too much. I was shocked to see him spend a penny in the basin. Then he got up in the middle of one night, opened the wardrobe and relieved himself all over my trousseau! It was quite a shock. While we were in London, he got a letter from the Air Ministry saying that he could have another week's leave but by that time we had spent all our money so we came back to Bognor.'

A photograph taken at the wedding shows her in a full veil holding a large bouquet of roses with Bill in his RAF uniform and silk handkerchief up his sleeve. Another portrait shows them together taken in Oxford Street during their honeymoon with my mother wearing a large stylish hat and fur collar and Bill in his uniform. My mother was very beautiful – a chain of photographic shops used her image in their display windows. They looked a handsome couple together, however short their union.

My mother Vera and my father Bill on their honeymoon

My mother was almost certainly a virgin when she married and was no doubt put off by the roughness and messiness of it all. She was never very tactile – apart from tucking us up in bed with a cursory kiss. I suspect that she was something of a 'cold fish', as she once called a friend of hers. Anyway, my parents clearly did not have much of a relationship of passion, however desultory. My mother was twenty-five when she got married – about eighteen months older than Bill. She was no doubt worried about being 'left on the shelf', as she put it.

As she talked on, I continued to spit blood in my handkerchief – my gums were still very sore after the dentist.

'Why did it go wrong then?' I asked as we approached the outskirts of Southampton on our way to Bognor.

'It was the war – and we didn't have a decent place of our own. When Bill went off to North Africa, I stayed at home with Nanna and Pop. I can remember Bill and his squadron flying over the nursing home in Bognor.

'Where did you live?'

'I stayed at the hotel because Bill was always away and I only saw him on leave. He asked me to go and stay with him in the gardener's cottage on his father's farm at Runcton. It was tiny and there wasn't a bath. Having grown up in the hotel, how could I look after a baby without a bath? I had to cross the lawn in the rain to take Michael up to the house. I eventually asked Pop to come and get me and I went back to live at the hotel. It was no place for a baby!'

My mother remained silent for a while and then said:

'I could never have kept up with Bill. And I wasn't keen on horses. I remember one day at Arundel, he thundered past me on a horse with his sister not far behind. I could never have got on a horse like that! They gave me asthma too; I was allergic to their hair.'

We stayed that night in a damp caravan in the forecourt of Bridport Hotel in Bognor which was then managed by my Uncle Al and his wife Barbie. I felt very sad saying goodbye to my mother; it was like saying goodbye when I used to return to boarding school, leaving the comfort and security of the home. I didn't know when I would see her again or for how long I would stay in West Africa. I felt tired with the physical and emotional upheaval. My wisdom teeth had not only been torn out but the deep roots of my early childhood had been tugged roughly. It seemed that I had gone through some sort of rite of passage.

The next day, my mother's last words to me were:

'If you can't be good, be careful!'

2
THE LOVELY HAIRMESSER

I was born at tea time on 23 August 1946 in a nursing home in Nyewood Lane in the west end of Bognor Regis in the county of Sussex. This apparently means I was just in the star sign of Leo. My birth certificate gives my mother's profession as 'hairdresser' and my father's as 'horse dealer'. My entrance into this world seems to have been reasonably easy. My brother and I were both circumcised for reasons never explained.

Having been born in a nursing home, I returned with my mother to a small dark, two-bedroomed flat above the kitchen of Bridport Hotel which her parents ran. It was a large 'private' hotel, made up of two connected houses with about fifty rooms, a large staff and a lounge and dining room at the front. It was on the north side of Stocker Road in the West End, the fashionable part of Bognor,

facing the south and the sun as it crossed the sky. It was one road back from the promenade, the shingle beaches, the golden sands and the sea.

But our flat was a dismal place: cold, poky and never got the sun. It looked out on to an overgrown hedge and the long abandoned gardens of a row of shops in the local high street. A large mouse once fell out of a packet of cornflakes into my breakfast bowl. In the back garden, where the sun never shone, I played in a damp sand pit with my brother, our cousin Lindsey who was a year younger, and a pretty girl called Irena who was the daughter of the Polish cook.

The kitchen below smelt bad and was full of noise, steam, red arms, rushing figures and my grandmother Nelly (Nanna) with her ample bosom and heavy arms overseeing it all. She was as regular and reliable as the hotel's meal times. I never saw her get excited or annoyed. My grandfather Alfred (Pop), by contrast, kept out of it all, remaining steadfastly in his small office – with its brass door handle – opposite the entrance to the hotel, shuffling papers and worrying about the slates and guttering falling off.

We are told that it is rare to remember anything before the age of four. It is difficult to pin down first memories because they often become confused with stories told to you later about when you were young. Photographs too make you feel sometimes that you were there. There's one story, supported by a photograph when I was nine months old, which I feel is right.

I was left by my mother in a pram, tied in with straps, in the forecourt of my grandparent's hotel in Bognor Regis. I can imagine myself looking at all the life going along the street and at the passing clouds in the sky. I feel sure that at one point I had the sun directly in my eyes from which I could not escape and that large faces of strangers loomed into my pram with their insane grimaces. But then the sun began to disappear. Dark shapes moved in the street and a white moon rose in the sky. I was frightened. I cried and cried but no one heard my cries. I tried to wriggle out of my straps but the more I struggled the tighter they became. I shook the pram from side to side but it would not fall over. I got colder and colder.

My Aunt Barbie tells me that she came across me by chance, whimpering exhausted in the pram. My mother had been having a good time with some guests of the hotel and had simply forgotten me, still stuck in the pram in the cold and the dark. And apparently it happened on more than one occasion. Perhaps it was this experience that gave rise to my love of freedom, of free movement, of not being held back by anyone. I've always hated being tied down, whether by boys at school or by commitments as an adult.

When I later saw a photograph of myself tied down in the pram, my mother would say:

'It was such a beautiful pram, very expensive.'

For me, it had been a torture chamber.

My mother had been very beautiful as a young woman but because of severe asthma was unable to have a formal education. She had a very sheltered life and was totally dominated by her mother who also ran her own husband on a tight string.

She wanted to learn photography and work in a photographic shop with a studio but there was no opening at the time. Instead, she worked for a short while for a local jeweller and then was apprenticed to a hairdresser. Her parents thought she should do something before she was married off rather than stay at home.

She remembered doing very menial jobs at the hairdressers, such as brushing down the stairs and taking off and putting on the coats of the clients. On one occasion to her horror she cut the ear of a woman who soon had her white dress covered in blood. Nevertheless, she became a good hairdresser although she liked to joke and undermine herself by describing herself as a 'hairmesser'. She cut my hair and constantly pushed my hair out my eyes, much to my annoyance as a boy. She was meant to have even curled my blond hair when I was baby.

My mother had her own 'Doodlebug' story – the first German unmanned missile during the war. She would hear Doodlebugs flying over Bognor from France. On one occasion, the engine of one of them cut out. It fell on a house on the seafront about a hundred yards away from ours. She said:

'It was when the engine stopped that you started worrying; as long as you heard the engine, you knew it was going overhead. Pop was sleeping at the time in the afternoon by a window and all the glass fell over him, just missing him. I can remember throwing myself under a table over Michael in case the house fell in.' When I grew up there was still the waste lot near our house – the empty space of the fabled German 'Doodlebug'.

When she did get married to my father Bill Marshall she had no sense of what he was going through. In the Battle of Britain, in which he claimed to have participated, life-expectancy of a fighter pilot was six weeks. The day that my brother was born in 1944 (in a nursing home in Bognor) he flew out over the house with his squadron. Only four men returned safely from Normandy.

He tried to get my mother to break the tie with her mother and move into the cottage on his father's market-gardening farm at Runcton near Chichester. But she soon returned to her parents' hotel in Bognor. Eventually, in 1949, he had had enough and left my mother with two small boys still living in the flat above the kitchen in the hotel.

My mother had been born in a nursing home in 23 Shaftesbury Road, Islington, London on 12 December 1917, a couple of years after her brother Allen. She returned to her parents' house in Marlborough Road, quite near Holloway, a prison for women which once took in the suffragettes. Her name was Vera Ida Payne, one of her aunts being called 'Ada Payne'. She later joked that it meant 'I had a pain' or that she was a 'V.I.P.'

The family then moved to Leicester Road, East Finchley. She

remembers playing as a young girl in Cherry Tree Park by the underground station and going with her older brother to the local church at the end of the road. Her parents would sometimes leave the two children alone in the house. My mother remembered waking up one evening and finding herself alone. She was terrified and tried to wake up her older brother Allen but he just turned over and slept. She waited in a nightdress clutching her teddy bear in the cold landing and dark until her parents returned.

Vera as a child

They moved to Bognor when she was twelve. This was partly because of her severe asthma. London still suffered from smogs and it was felt that the fresh sea air and 'ozone' would do her good. At thirteen, she was sent away to a boarding school run by nuns in Surrey because the pine trees there were said to be good for her breathing. She hated it and it did not last long. The nuns caught her cheating in an exam, writing answers on her hand and looking at them in the toilet, which she never forgot. She then attended a small private school at the end of our road until she left at 16. Her school career was remarkable for being so undistinguished. As she liked to joke, 'I was always first at school – with the list turned upside down!'

My mother once had another serious escapade when she was young. She drove a car under-aged on the promenade in Bognor Regis. She not only failed to slow down at a pedestrian crossing but nearly ran down a policeman. Not knowing how to stop in gear, she only came to a halt when the young man she was with pulled on the handbrake. The magistrate let her off with a warning and a small fine of two shillings and sixpence, no doubted charmed by her youthful innocence, blushes and her middle-class accent honed by elocution lessons. She was moreover the daughter of a well-known and respected hotelier; the magistrate also probably

belonged to the same Freemasons' Lodge as my grandfather.
The local weekly rag *The Bognor Post* reported the story with the
headline 'Too Chivalrous to Refuse', referring to her willing car
companion.

She did her best to make my young life agreeable but not always
with the desired results. She gave me a party on my third birthday,
with one of her photographs to prove it. It shows me looking
somewhat bemused in high-up shorts and a silk white tie and shirt
with white socks and shoes. My hair has been carefully fixed by my
mother. I am sitting on a swing surrounded by twelve friends and
family. My right hand is on the knee of my first cousin Lindsey, a
year younger. My brother Michael is sitting at the end of the swing
holding the chain and frame.

   My mother was undoubtedly absent-minded. When I was about
four I got separated from her in the crowds of a Bank Holiday
weekend. For me to venture out of the west end of Bognor was,
at first, like entering a foreign country. In my disorientation I
started to walk in the wrong direction – towards the pier. I felt
increasingly desperate as I waded through a sea of naked legs in
frocks or shorts. Eventually a lady found me crying.

   I was saying: 'I've lost my mummy! I've lost my mummy!'

Guests at my third birthday party

She took me to a St John's Ambulance centre opposite the pier where I dangled my legs over a high seat and a nurse with a large bosom like my grandmother's leaned over me. It seemed an age before my sweet-smelling mother turned up. She had walked home, forgetting that I had been with her.

Abandonment was clearly becoming a traumatic theme of my early childhood. At about the same age, I can remember being left in a hospital in Brighton with no explanation. My grandmother later told me that I had been crying for a week with a terrible earache and they had contacted our family doctor several times. During this period, I was obsessed with tidiness and put my shoes together and cried even more if someone disturbed them. Since I did not stop screaming, the doctor eventually sent me to the emergency department in Brighton, an hour and a half drive away. I did not know what was going on as I had never been in a hospital before. My mother put me in a bed with sides like a cot and left. She did not explain anything. I can see her leaving through the door of the brown-painted children's ward into the corridor. I screamed after her and then the men and women in white moved in on me, holding me down. The rest is blank.

In fact the pain was caused by a severe mastoid infection in the right ear, so severe that I was told later that the infection could have gone on the brain within twenty four hours and killed me. I used to joke later that perhaps a little did and that explains everything! The operation involved cutting away the bone behind my ear and sucking out the pus. More formally described, it was the surgical removal of the 'mastoid process', a nipple-like piece of temporal bone behind the ear. I have a long scar there behind my ear to this day which feels strangely delicate. I was left with a perforated eardrum and impaired hearing in my right ear.

In the long run, the experience of being dumped in hospital, aged four, without explanation, has left an irrational horror of hospitals and dislike of 'experts' in white coats who think they know what is good for me. I was very pleased to come back to my home with all the familiar smells of the house and garden and the murmur of the nearby sea.

In general, I found my relationship with my mother always easy-going. She was rather like an older sister to my brother and me, especially when faced with our grandparents. When she tried to hit us with the back of a hairbrush we just ran away and laughed.

We would lay traps for her in the back breakfast room, by putting cushions on top of a door so that when she opened it they would fall down on her. She wouldn't get angry but laughed at our playful antics. We would often fight each other and at one time – to our great surprise – we split an old armchair in two; her main concern was what her mother would think of it all. But again, she just laughed.

As I grew up however I found her constant chatting to strangers and her praise of me increasingly irritating. She hated what she called 'pregnant silences' and always said the first thing that came into her mind to break a pause in the conversation.

We were materially well off in Chideock, 10 Stocker Road, which my grandfather and grandmother had built a few houses down from the Bridport Hotel when they retired. It had well-furnished rooms on three floors, a large garden and middle-class aspirations. But we were culturally poor. We had no library. In the dark breakfast room at the back of the house, where the canary rarely sang in a corner, there was only the shorter Pears' Cyclopaedia with a girlish boy blowing bubbles on its front cover, a small prayer book, sellotape, bits of string, drawing pins, tacks and other bric-a-brac which might or might not one day come 'in handy'.

The only newspapers were the *Evening Standard*, which came down on the London train for my grandfather and was delivered around tea time, and *The Bognor Post*, which fell on the mat on Saturday morning.

My mother's reading consisted almost entirely of women's magazines such as *The Lady*, *Woman's Realm* and *Woman's Own* which were full of recipes, household hints and knitting patterns. When she took us, against the wishes of her parents, to a holiday camp at Roedean near Brighton my brother won for her an annual subscription for the upmarket *She*.

She had no qualms about beauty contests. My mother was proud of once being chosen before the war as 'Miss Hopton' and kept a red sash and a photograph to prove it. Her portrait taken by a local photographer was to be found in a string of shops as far as Brighton.

During the same holiday, I, aged nine, won third place in 'What a Smasher' Competition. I was pictured in woollen swimming trunks grinning embarrassingly and flexing my pimple biceps – the first and last of such exploits. I was given a model hand gun as a prize. Fortunately, I never became a body builder, despite this initial encouragement. *The Bognor Post* carried the article 'Marshall Family Takes All.' It is not clear who leaked the story to the press, but I suspect it was my mother.

She, as usual, won the Table Tennis Championship at the holiday camp. She claimed that she had honed her skills with one 'Neil Dias', a Ceylonese student at Oxford who came down to the hotel with a friend – a photograph shows him in his white 'Oxford bags.' He asked my mother to marry him but she refused; he later became an arch Singhalese nationalist and fought for Sri Lankan independence.

Despite her prowess on the dance floor and her weekly visit to the local cinema with a friend, my mother did not manage to find a husband during my childhood. We did however have a string of 'uncles' who did not last very long; the best I thought was a man with curly hair who had a large motorbike which he allowed my brother and me to sit on. He once gave me an orange.

The main cultural icon was the black and white television. It arrived when I was seven years old for the Queen's Coronation. We were the first in the street to get one. I found the whole event excruciatingly boring. My uncle insisted on us listening to the Queen's speech after every Christmas dinner. I associated the Queen with a droning accent, a tiara, and a seat too large for her. When she had finished the television was switched off and the distribution of presents began. It felt like a true liberation.

My mother followed in her magazines the stories about the royal family, especially Princess Margaret who was her own age. But she said on more than one occasion: 'They might have all that wealth but they are no different to us. We all have the same blood.'

Unwittingly, she sowed the seeds of my later republicanism. She always treated my brother and I equally, whether it was in cutting a banana or giving pocket money. She thus first gave me a sense of fair play which later crystallized into the principles of justice and equality.

We were allowed one hour of TV per night between 5 and 6 p.m. My preferences were the exciting Westerns such as *The Cisco Kid* (who galloped away at the end of the show) and *Buffalo Bill* (whose horse reared magnificently). I had had enough of *Listen with Mother* or *Bill and Ben the Flowerpot Men* or *Lassie*.

I was terrified out of my wits on two occasions while viewing television outside the children's hour. One was seeing a clip from an episode of the 1950s *Quatermass* series. Worried men in white coats gathered around a great hole in the ground and suggested that an alien species might have landed and might take over the world. I thought it was real news.

The other programme was even more frightening about a doomed ship. One of the first steam ships, on its maiden voyage all sorts of disaster befell it: the mast toppled and killed some passengers; the engines broke down; and many were mysteriously lost overboard. Each time one of these incidents happened, the steady sound of hammering could be heard on the ship's metal hull like a doom-ridden bell. They eventually broke open the first layer of the hull and found beneath it a skeleton with a hammer in its hand. Apparently, a worker had been riveted inside the twin hulls of the ship when it was being built. The strangest thing was that the bones of the skeleton had not fallen into a pile but were still connected together. I thought that it was still somehow alive, exacting its revenge.

The world of music was confined to an ancient wind-up gramophone with a steel needle (His Master's Voice, with a small dog listening to a vast trumpet) in the cupboard of the front room. My grandparents had a stern patriotic record of *Red, White and Blue, What does it Mean to You?* while my mother had the silky sounds of Glen Miller's *In the Mood* and *String of Pearls*. By the time my brother and I were old enough, we were buying our own records, first the rock & roll records of Bill Hailey's *Rock around the Clock* and Buddy Holly's *Peggy Sue*. Soon after we experienced the heady freedom of jazz. Later my brother made a double bass from a tea chest at school and with a couple of friends formed a skiffle band. I bought a banjo but having no musical training did not get on with it and soon discarded it in a cupboard.

Art was represented by two coloured engravings in the sunny front sitting room of the house by the Royal Academy artist William J. Phillips, the husband of a distant great cousin. One was of a fishing boat pulled up on to the shingle beach with the chalk cliffs of Golden Cap at Seatown near Chideock in the distance (Chideock was where my grandfather's family came from and was also the name of our house). The other painting was of a cobbled courtyard of an old hotel in Bridport with some chickens. In the sunless backroom, there was a small reproduction of Constable's 'Hay Wain' crossing a stream; I liked to imagine that I was the boy as they approached the water among the trees.

Although we were baptised and christened in the nearby St Winifred's Church in Victoria Road, no one in our family was particularly religious or went to Sunday service. The nearest we got to a religious Easter was buying delicious hot cross buns from a local baker and eating them for breakfast on Easter Friday.

For me, film-going, first introduced by my mother, was a great liberation and meant adventure and excitement in an otherwise dull life. She loved the romantic Hollywood films and during my childhood would go once a week with a girl friend to the cinema. It was an escape from dealing with two unruly boys, a single bed, hairdressing in a dark back room, and two demanding parents in whose house she lived.

My brother and I had our own experience of children's cinema at the Saturday morning 'flics' at the Odeon Cinema in the centre of town. It was very noisy and unruly before the show began. We would sit in the better seats in the balcony but did not flick chewing gum at the 'kids' in the dark cavern below us. I preferred the lollies rather than ice creams at the intermission.

The best time was when my mother managed later to smuggle my brother and me to see films which were meant for older children accompanied by adults. She would buy the cheapest tickets at the front and then once the film had begun, always to my intense embarrassment, get us to creep, heads down, many rows back. In this way, we saw the great war films *Reach for the Sky*, featuring the fighter pilot Douglas-Bader with whom my mother had once danced at Tangmere after he had lost both legs; *The Colditz Story*, about the great escape from a German POW camp; and *The Dam Busters*, telling the story of bombers going at low level to destroy a Germans arms factory. These black-and-white films all showed plucky Britishers, against all odds, pulling one over the superior force of the Krauts. Nothing like the doughty Brits, one was encouraged to think, who built the Empire, kept a stiff upper lip and faced up to any foreigner. The most harrowing film was *The Bridge over the River Kwai* in full technicolor, showing the brutality of the Japs forcing Commonwealth prisoners to build a railway in Burma.

We would march along the promenade and streets of Bognor and sing like them:

'Hitler, he only had one ball; Goering had two but very small; Himmler was rather similar but poor old Goebbels had no balls at all.'

My mother had, of course, lived through the Second World War ten years earlier. The war was an invisible shadow cast over my childhood and Britain in the fifties which still suffered from austerity and food rationing. I could even remember having powdered egg and concentrated orange juice on rations which did not end until 1954 when I was eight years old.

3

THE MAN WHO
SPITS FIRE

When I was young I hardly knew my father Bill Marshall directly but as an absentee father he figured inevitably in my life. He was born on14 August 1918 in South Shields near Newcastle upon Tyne to Cyril Charles and Harriet Marshall. He was named William Cyril Marshall.

The Marshalls had lived at Barnham, north of Bognor. Cyril's grandfather, Ebenezer James (1832-1899), had been headmaster of Brighton Grammar School but had a house in Barnham. It was even visited in an Old Boys' Reunion by the aesthete artist Aubrey Beardsley. His poems, drawings and cartoons appeared in print in *Past and Present*, the school's magazine. Ebenezer, unorthodox in his views at the time, believed in educating the whole person, not just helping his pupils to pass exams. He presumably brought up his children in the same way.

His sons Richard (Harry) and Sidney Skelton (Sydney) set up a market garden with the help of Ebenezer when they were young. At the outset, they employed 14 men and a boy. The brothers soon split up, however, and Harry traded under the name of H.R. Marshall Ltd. He had three sons, including my grandfather Cyril Charles, born in 1891, and two daughters. As a well-known local family, they even had a 'Marshall Close' in Barnham named after them.

Cyril had been an officer in the Merchant Navy on the Indian run before First World War. He then became a sub-lieutenant in submarines, only to be promoted to a temporary acting lieutenant, in the North Sea and Baltic. He was appointed to the *Titania*, a J2 submarine, at the beginning of 1917. On 17 July, he torpedoed and sank the German submarine U-99 between the Orkney Islands and Norway. He was mentioned in dispatches for his 'long and arduous service in submarines in the third period of the war' (*Gazette* 2.11.17).

Conditions on board the J2 class submarines were very basic and cramped. Three officers shared one bunk and the heads or lavatory was often a bucket. The weather in the Baltic was extremely cold too with much of the submarine's superstructure freezing as soon as it surfaced. In 1918 Cyril almost choked to death from fumes from batteries when his submarine was hit by a depth charge. He was eventually invalided out of the Royal Navy as unfit for service on 6 January 1926.

He married Harriet Hunter at the registry office in Harwich. She was a much younger woman from Tipperary in Ireland who had been his nurse while he was in hospital. They moved soon after Cyril left the Navy to a farm in Runcton near Chichester and not far from Bognor. He followed his father by running a market garden where he could breathe more easily in the open air. He bred shire horses and was keen on hunting. His wife 'Hattie' had, during the Second World War, been a member of my grandmother's Bridge Club at Bridport Hotel in Bognor and through them my father and mother met.

My father Bill undoubtedly had an extraordinary life before he met my mother. It is the stuff of boys' adventure novels. All I knew then was that he had been a bit of a tearaway as a boy, had become a Spitfire fighter pilot during the war, and afterwards a racehorse trainer whom I occasionally saw on television. From what I could glean from my later conversations with Bill, my half-brothers and my brother as well as from what Bill told his biographers, my father had – to say the least – lived a very colourful life.

Horses had been the great love of his life. He had his first – a New Forest pony – when he was five years old and rode him bare back with a head collar. His father still used carthorses on their farm to plough the fields for vegetables but always had a few racehorses in training.

He had a younger sister, but he was largely left to his own devices. He taught himself how to swim and to fish and would jump on his pony to explore the countryside around the 250-acre family farm called 'Saltham', which was down a long drive at Runcton. He said that he preferred the company of the hedgers and ditchers to his teacher. They taught him about the foxes, badgers, rabbits, and birds in the tangled banks. Looking at a dormouse dangling from a leaf, his favourite hedger – a Mr Ted – explained in his broad Sussex drawl: 'They sleep eight months of the year. They never leave the hedgerow. It's like it's their road and their home all in one.' Back in his room at night, Bill would make up stories about the creatures living on the edge of the fields, imagining himself to be one of them setting forth from the safety of the hedgerow. He became good at telling stories, particularly about his own life.

He went to a prep school – a five-mile bike ride away – but when it was time to send him off to boarding-school, he would have none of it. He wanted to be a jockey but his father had put him down for Rugby – his grandfather and great-grandfather had apparently all gone there. But he didn't like school – with the initials WC (William Cyril), the boys called him 'Shithouse Marshall' – and he never learned how to spell properly. But he was so passionate about riding that he once wrote to the headmaster of his prep school saying that he wasn't going to school that term because he had broken his leg. Instead, he went hunting every day. He was only found out a couple of months later when his father ran into the headmaster. There was, understandably, 'one hell of a row.'

By the time he was thirteen, he was already riding and winning in point-to-point races. He was so keen on horses at this time that he asked the manager of a knacker's yard for a horse's leg so he could see how it worked.

Lying about his age, he cycled nineteen miles to Portsmouth on his bike in his school grey flannels and blue pullover and joined at fourteen a ship in Portsmouth, having told a shipping clerk that he wanted to go to Australia. He signed him on a tramp ship which took cargoes wherever it could. As it was, it took eighteen months before Bill reached Sydney Harbour.

His first ship, the SS *Harmattan* of the Harrison Line, was a steam ship run on coal. It first sailed up the east coast of England to South Shields where Bill had been born fourteen years earlier. Having signed on his tramp ship as a deckhand, Bill soon learned how to cope with the rough banter of the other sailors who must have been amused by the short, wiry lad with his blond hair, deep blue eyes and posh accent.

'Almost right away,' he recalled, 'they started making fun of me, but after a while I took a swing at one of them. I couldn't do much but I wanted to show that I wasn't a namby-pamby. They left me alone after that. But I can tell you, you learned your manners in a hurry.'

He quickly took to the life at sea. In Hamburg, an old sailor called Ken took him ashore, advising him: 'Stick with me, my boy. The rest of them will rush and get drunk, then go to a whorehouse. That's the wrong way round. You'll enjoy it a lot more if you go to the whorehouse first, when you're sober, and then go on the piss!'

From there, it was to Buenos Aires via Havana and Rio. Some of the seaman's ways always remained with him. He would call someone 'skipper' if he liked them, whether a barman or a boss. He may have been at the bottom of the ladder on board ship, but he could not escape from his privileged background. He may have been a schoolboy rebel by running away to sea, but he had great respect for authority and became intensely patriotic. When he read in a newspaper about of the abdication of Edward VIII for an American woman, he was deeply shocked.

It was at Rosario, a town up the River Parana from Buenos Aires, that Bill first fell in love. He had kissed a few girls at home and one of them even took her clothes off but he didn't know what to do. He was eventually seduced by an older girl and then of course there had been the brothels on the way. But when he became besotted with the pretty daughter (about his own age) of a pistol-packing, legless owner of a bar, her father told him that all he would get was a farewell kiss.

He eventually was signed on a vessel to Australia and, after eighteen months at sea, he jumped ship in March 1936 in Sydney – cramming his few possessions in a sea bag. He had travelled from Latin America to South Africa and then up the east coast of Africa through the Suez Canal to the Adriatic; thence back to India, Canada and finally across the Pacific to Hong Kong.

'I got myself some shirts and suits made in Hong Kong,' he told me later. 'But I was a bloody fool. I got drunk with the lads and when I woke up I had that on me!' He pointed to a crude tattoo of an anchor on his forearm. 'I was 16 at the time.'

Having arrived in Australia, he started riding, won a few races and with the proceeds bought a caravan and three horses. In the company of an Aborigine called Namitjara, he began to travel from one country meeting to another in what was called 'Bush Racing.' They slept rough most of the time, and if Namitjara wasn't around in the morning he would catch him up later. They would usually walk about twenty or thirty miles a day. Bill was not a hard-line racist but his attitude to his companion was typical of the time:

'Namitjara was his real name, but no one called him that. We used to call him "Hey man". He wasn't very talkative, unless he had a few brandies inside him, and then he couldn't stop. It was hard to tell his age – anything from 18 to 25. He was a strong sort of fellow and a good rider. I used to give him a few dollars a week.'

There were however few women in his life at this stage and those were mostly whores. He told me however that he travelled to Fiji when he was sixteen and lived with an islander:

'We lived in her hut by the beach. She really looked after me but after six week's she threw me out. She did me a favour for I could easily have stayed on there and done nothing with my life.'

After a couple of years, he realised that life as a vagabond trainer cum jockey in Australia was not leading him very far. He took a cattle-herding job for six months in the Outback west of Brisbane. When he had delivered the cattle to an abattoir in Darwin, he got drunk and started to play 'Two Up' which consisted of tossing two coins on a blanket and calling heads or tails. Forever a gambling man, he lost his entire six months' wages. He then fell asleep in a drunken stupor on the beach. 'I remember feeling awful and hearing a dog bark. It kept bloody well barking and I woke up. There about fifteen yards from me was the first alligator I had ever seen in my life. I almost shit myself.'

Fortunately, the alligator was not hungry for they gorged themselves from the offal in the river coming from the slaughter house.

It was the last straw. He decided to sign on a ship bound for South Africa. Being broke on arrival in Cape Town, he immediately signed on a whaling ship and was gone for six months working amongst the blood and guts of a factory ship down in the freezing wastes of the Antarctic. He claimed that although he was only seventeen he was promoted to become a 'chaser', in charge of one of the small motor boats using harpoons with powdered charges to kill the whales. 'No one had a feeling for the whales back then,' he observed. 'It was just business.'

One voyage on a whaler was enough and he travelled north to work as a rigger in a gold mine near Johannesburg, operating the cage which dropped men a mile below the surface. Although the whites got the best jobs, Bill mixed freely with all races in the bars. The pay was good and he managed to buy half a dozen horses to train and ride. He also said he started to learn how to fly and bought himself a Tiger Moth, a biplane built by de Havilland which cruised at a speed of 110 mph at a maximum altitude of 12,000 feet.

When the Second World War broke out, he claimed that he decided to fly back to England in order to enlist in the RAF. He told me that he had no proper maps or any weather forecasts and had to land at unknown airstrips to refuel every 300 miles or so. He flew his Tiger Moth across to Walvis Bay in Namibia and then up the west coast of Africa via Luanda (where a Portuguese woman 'entertained' him in a hotel before he left at five in the morning). From there it was Libreville, Lagos, Abidjan, Freetown, somewhere in Spanish Morocco (where he pretended to be a Boer from South Africa) and Casablanca. He had hoped to land at Tangmere near his home in West Sussex but ended up in Biggin Hill, east of London. Ironically, so close to home, it was his biggest navigation error in his 6000-mile journey.

Bill arrived back in England a rich young man, with 6,000 South African pounds in his money belt. It is hard to verify this story – and it seems unlikely – but if true it must be one the great voyages of early aviation. It also shows that he had little fear and was highly skilled as a largely self-taught pilot.

He was twenty one and had been away from home for seven years. He had never been in touch with his parents. 'When I entered our kitchen,' he told me, 'I saw my mother leaning over the oven. I slapped her on the backside and said "How are you Ma?" She got up and said: "What do you want for breakfast?" – and burst into tears. I could never understand why. I then sat down with my father and got drunk. There were no recriminations.'

When he was later stationed in the RAF at Tangmere, not far from his family home in Runcton, he would go out drinking with his pals after flying all day and then in the early hours would wake his mother up and she – without complaining – would cook bacon and eggs for them until 'blue in the face'. His father always kept a barrel of gin and another of whisky in the kitchen and everyone would just walk up and help themselves.

The pilots led a life which was dashing, carefree and short. They could not expect to live a long time. Bill certainly looks the part in photos taken at the time, with turned down hat, spotted silk scarf and fur boots.

It is strange that my father, given his experience as a pilot, did not go straight away into the RAF but told me later that he first joined the Commandos.

'They sent me on a clandestine mission into Calais in France to blow up an arms dump,' he told me. 'As we were going through the docks, someone grabbed me from behind. I pulled out my knife and stabbed him in the stomach. I killed him immediately. It was a young German soldier.'

'What did you feel about killing someone of your own age who was fighting for his country just like you?' I asked him.

'Nothing. It was either him or me.'

It was strange to look at my father's hands which he claimed had killed a man so readily in hand-to-hand combat. It was even stranger that he should never have felt any remorse or regret. But there was no mention of becoming a commando in his ghost-written autobiography; it says that he went straight into the RAF on his return from Africa. Was this Commando episode in his life a tall story, the dream of an old man who had drunk too much?

Bill told his biographers that he was posted to a squadron of Spitfires early in 1940 as a Flight Sergeant but saw little action until after the fall of France in May 1940. If this is the case he would have participated in the Battle of Britain. Mysteriously, his log book is missing for the first part of the war; he said it was burnt in a fire at Cranwell College on 18 March 1942.

Although – according to the official records – he was not made a pilot officer until May 1942, he told his biographers that his first battle came in early 1940: 'I was a Flight Lieutenant then.' He also told them that in July or August 1940 he was flying Spitfires from the fighter base at Biggin Hill during the Battle of Britain.

The Battle of Britain began in June 1940, a month before Bill's 22nd birthday, with a German attack on airfields and radar installations. There were only 1400 British pilots trained at the time. The life expectancy of a British fighter pilot was about three weeks or, for inexperienced pilots, about ten sorties. It was very lonely in the air, for you lived or died alone.

The height of the Battle was in the last week in August and the first week in September, with the Luftwaffe constantly pounding the airfields. On 7 September an invasion alert was given. It was very quiet until the late afternoon when the heaviest attack so far began but this time the Luftwaffe did not go for the airfields but to London – the Blitz had begun. As far as Air Force Command was concerned, it was a great relief for the airfields could hardly take any more.

It was during the Battle of Britain that Bill told his biographers that the he was first shot down.

'I was flying along and all of a sudden the plane blew up. I wasn't paying enough attention. That didn't happen again. The tail must have come off. It wasn't spinning. It was going straight down. Luckily, the hood wasn't jammed so I got that back and as soon as I got halfway out I was sucked clear. I'd forgotten to take my oxygen mask off. Almost broke my bloody neck.' Landing by parachute for the first time, he said he was confronted by an old man of the Home Guard poking a rifle at him.

Yet despite these reminiscences in his eighties, it is not clear what role, if any, he played in the Battle of Britain in the summer and autumn of 1940. According to my mother he was at this time an airman and not a pilot officer. In fact, *The London Gazette* records that William Cyril Marshall (126834) was only promoted from Leading Airman to Pilot Officer on 26 May 1942. According to the *Gazette* again he was then promoted on 26 November 1942 'from pilot offs (prob) to be Flg. Offs on Prob (War Subs.)'.

What I have learnt about my father was mainly from my mother, from our meeting when I was about to go to sea, and from a lunchtime drinking session later at Cardigan Yacht Club. I have also drawn on the interpretation of events by my half-brothers Tom and Harry, from my brother Michael in his book *The Art and Science of Racehorse Training: The "Bill" Marshall Guide* and from Bill's memoirs *You Win a Few, you Lose a Few*. The latter was taken from conversations with my father in his eighties and ghost-written by a couple of sports journalists. All arranged, paid for and published privately by his third wife. There is in this book a photograph of my brother Michael and me with Bill taken in 1984 in Barbados in which we are called his 'brothers.' In the text, there is no mention of our mother Vera, his first wife.

Many of Bill's later stories about his life do not tally with the known facts collaborated by reliable sources. Perhaps he just got the dates wrong, due to a few drinks, a fading memory and a vivid imagination. Or was there something else at work? Did he feel the need to make out that he was more than he was? Was he simply a great story teller who embellished his stories in the telling? There was really no need as he had certainly led a colourful youth, had been a very brave pilot and was a great race horse trainer. Lester Piggot was the champion jockey who rode Raffingora to win in a then electronically timed world-record (53.89 seconds) over five furlongs at Epsom in 1970. Piggot said of my father: 'He was an extraordinary man because he did so many things besides training horses.'

4
WAR AND PEACE

My mother told me that she did not take any notice of Bill until he got his wings on 26 May 1942. They got married on 6 October 1942 at the Parish Church of St John the Baptist, in London Road, Bognor. Bill was aged 24, my mother, 25. The certificate gives Bill's rank or profession as simply 'Air Force.' It was just before he left to fly Hurricanes in North Africa. Their courtship must have been short.

A photograph taken outside Bridport Hotel shows my mother with an elaborate veil and holding red roses and my father beaming in his new pilot's uniform. They went to the Dorchester Hotel in Mayfair for their honeymoon. It seems to have been a happy time.

My mother recalled that Bill kept sending her notes during their courtship saying how much he loved her. No letters have survived – Bill rarely wrote – but on the back of a small photograph of his RAF pals next to a Spitfire kept in my mother's laundry box are the words: 'Cheerio dearest. Couldn't wait any longer, see you to night,

Bill and Vera on their wedding day

lots of love, Bill.' He's not in the photo and probably got it from his wallet. Another torn photo shows Bill leaning against the wing of his aircraft, gun in holster and cigarette in hand with the caption written on the back 'Me looking "brassed off" before it started raining.' They are the only words of his that have survived in our family archives from the war years.

Yet a series of snaps little larger than a thumbnail show my mother having fun with Bill's uniformed pals in the Walnut Tree pub out at

Bill as a fighter pilot in World War II

Runcton. My mother in one is sitting on a bench outside with Bill, his father and friend with pints in their hands. Another shows Bill being held upside down by a mate – something you had to do to get out of a Spitfire which had been hit. They must have gone back to his parents' house for they are shown later sprawled on the lawn playing cards in a circle or larking about climbing on chairs. In one my mother and another woman are surrounded by nine pilots with probably Bill's mother Hattie looking on.

Whilst fighting in North Africa, Bill flew Hurricanes which were adapted with four cannons for desert warfare and for attacking the tanks and armoured troop carriers of Rommel's Panzer force. The pilots were issued with gold coins to buy off the locals in case they were shot down behind enemy lines. What Bill didn't tell his newly married wife when he saw her next time was that he had spent three days on 'relief' leave with some young French girls in an 'upper class' brothel in Phillipeville, just out of Algiers. 'They looked after us because we treated them like ladies and we got on very well,' he recalled.

On his return to England, he was soon having affairs with other women. He told his biographer, repeated in *The Daily Telegraph* obituary and Wikipedia, that he had arranged to meet a girl in the Compleat Angler pub on the River Thames in Marlow in Buckinghamshire in the summer of 1943, almost a year after his marriage and about six months before my brother was born. His squadron had done a couple of sweeps over France and lost about five pilots. Bill had arranged to meet the girl at two o'clock in the pub. He should have headed 100 miles further south to Tangmere, but since he knew he would be late he decided to go to Marlow, fly under the bridge by the pub and do a roll.

'She was in the bar and came running out when she heard the plane coming over – she thought it might have been an attack. She was happy when she saw it was a Spitfire and she figured it was me.'

Unfortunately, as he recounted there was also an Air Commodore having a lunch with his wife in the pub who reported him to his superior officer. It could have meant a court martial in peacetime; in the circumstance, it was ignored.

But is this true? The headway of Marlow Bridge was 3.86 metres; the height of a Spitfire was 3.86 metres.

What is true is that from 1943 after returning from North Africa, Bill was flying regularly over occupied France. Pairs of Spitfire pilots would 'go on a rhubarb', that is, follow a flight pattern which was straight across the Channel and then a long sweep around looking for the enemy. It was a hunt for anything which they considered fair game, whether in cars, lorries or trains. They would inevitably contain French civilians but the pilots worked on the erroneous theory that only Germans drove cars. On one day in the summer of 1943 Bill and a pal left Tangmere and after shooting up a car and a goods train, they flew over a rise in the ground near the Somme to see thousands of men on a beautiful Sunday morning parade. They emptied all the shells they could spare into the packed ranks.

'It was like a Sunday church parade,' observed Bill. 'We were just lucky to find them.'

On another occasion during that summer, he was not so lucky. Over a long lunch in Cardigan Yacht Club, he later recalled his terrible predicament. He told me that he was returning from escorting some bombers on the Atlantic coast of France:

'I was hit by flak off the north coast of France,' he told me, 'but managed to turn my Spitfire upside down and bail out with a small inflatable dinghy which was not much bigger than an inner tube. I got into the tiny dinghy which had about a foot of water in it. The fog soon came down and in the next few days I drifted in and out with the tide. At night, I could hear voices and see the lights and the silhouettes of the German soldiers walking up and down. As I drifted in with the tide, I thought I would be caught and shot – it was said at the time that the Germans were shooting captured British pilots. As I drifted out with the tide, I knew I would eventually die of exposure. Even though it was late summer, I was cold and wet. On the third day I thought I was done for. Then around midday a seagull landed on my life raft. I made a grab for it and caught it by the leg; I drunk its blood and ate some of its flesh. It was still warm. I felt a little better afterwards but I still thought I wouldn't be able to make it that night. Then just before dusk the fog lifted and a seaplane spotted me, landed and bundled me on board. One of my pals had seen me go down in the water and they had been looking for me up and down the Channel all that time.'

Bill told his biographers almost twenty years later that a fast motor boat spotted him and that he had drifted in his dinghy for four nights and five days. If so, he would have been seriously dehydrated.

'Were you all right afterwards?' I asked him.

'I had been so huddled up against the cold that it took hours in hospital before they could straighten me out. But I soon recovered and went back to flying duties.'

'What happened next time you were shot down?'

'We had being doing a long sweep over France and I ran out of petrol and bailed out over some fields – some flak or a bullet must have hit my tank. As I came down I could see the Germans rushing everywhere in a nearby village, jumping in trucks and tearing down the narrow lanes in motorbikes with side cars. But as I came down in a small field, some French fellows got there first and grabbed me and put me into a beaten-up van. They were working for the Resistance. They got me out of my uniform and dressed me like a French peasant with a pair of clogs. They took me into a café right in the middle of the village square where the Germans were rushing around in all directions. They gave me a beer and a cigarette and I quickly got the idea that I had to pretend to be dumb.'

'How did you manage to escape?'

'Well, when all things had quietened down I was taken home by one of my rescuers in Abbeville and then passed from safe house to safe house all down through France to Spain. Some of them were brothels. It took me about six weeks, travelling by train, cart and on foot. When we got to the Pyrenees I joined a group with a guide and we walked over the mountains. I eventually got to Barcelona where I was taken out by night to a British frigate waiting to pick us up.'

His biography gives a rather different story as well as further details. Although late spring, the weather was foul and apart from the eggs they could steal on the way, they had very little food. Bill linked up with a Polish pilot – 'a tough bastard.' It took ten days to walk over the Pyrenees and only a third of his group managed to complete the journey. Once in Franco's Spain, he was arrested and put into a jail.

'There were about eight of us in a cell, crapping in the corner and peeing in a bucket, with very little food and no exercise or washing.'

After a month, he was bailed out by the British Consulate and taken to Barcelona where he flew back to England in a RAF plane. On his return to England, he said he was interrogated for about ten days.

I wanted to learn more about this epic journey, worthy of a book or a film, but the conversation swirled on after more drinks. We were having a lunch time session alone in Cardigan Yacht Club. I never again had the opportunity to ask him about his experiences with the French Resistance. It sounded too familiar and dramatic to have happened. My mother recalled him being reported missing on one occasion but it seems that he never mentioned it to my mother for I'm sure she would have told me if he had.

The next near miss Bill experienced was over south east England in August 1944, a couple of months after D-Day and the invasion of Normandy. My brother would have been about eight months old at the time. He was based at West Malling near Maidstone. He told me:

'Hitler was sending over Doodlebugs – VI flying bombs. We called them Divers. We had orders to try and shoot them down safely, into a field or the sea. Well, some of us liked to fly alongside them and tip them with our wings. But with this one the engine suddenly cut out over Lydd in Kent. When I hit it I must have been too close. The last thing I remember was a big bang and I blacked out. Then I found myself in a parachute coming down to earth. I must have been blown out of the cockpit. God knows how the parachute opened. I couldn't believe my luck. You can be sure I spent a few days on the piss!'

He gave more details to his biographers: 'It almost blew me up too. I managed to land but there was a huge hole in the radiator.' This seems to be the correct version. His entry for the day in his surviving log says: 'Shot down a diver N.W. of Dungeness. Diver exploded in the air. Landed with a hole through radiator.'

The story was collaborated by a yellowing cutting in my mother's box of family photographs. There was a letter from the Mayor of Lydd on 15 August 1944 thanking him for his 'excellent shooting' for having 'finished off the flying bomb by exploding it in the air' over the centre of the town at 'about 2213 hours' on 9 August. He was given the freedom of the town. A plaque was even mounted in the Royal Mail pub in Lydd in 2006 to commemorate the event.

If these close shaves were not bad enough, the closest Bill came to death was probably in late March 1944, a couple of months after my brother was born. He did not tell me this story but he told his biographers. He was apparently stationed in Scotland east of Edinburgh and doing reconnaissance flights over German-held Norway – at 42,000 feet, it was 'quite chilly'. The Allies were concerned at the time that the Germans were making 'heavy water' there for a potential atomic bomb. On his way home, his Spitfire was hit by flak – a piece of metal went through his left thigh, missing the bone but cutting the artery. He tied a tourniquet around his leg and managed to make it back to base, but not without a great loss of blood. The scar was on him when he lay in his coffin 62 years later.

One of his last brushes with death, again told to his biographers but not to me, was at the end of the war in the latest Spitfire XXI against two German jet-propelled Me 262s which were very fast but not easy to handle. His long experience got the better of the new technology:

> We were escorting bombers to Berlin. The German jets jumped us and then flew right through us. I followed them down in a dive. They were just out of range and every time I shot my plane slowed a bit. Heading down, I went past the point where the airframe was meant to come apart. I pulled up at the last minute. I blacked out from the G-force and when I came out of it all I could see was the sky up above as I was heading almost straight up. When I managed to get back to base we saw I had bent the titanium screws holding the wings on.

Now stationed at Ludham in Norfolk, one of his last actions was shooting on 16 April 1945 a midget submarine along the Norwegian coast. For this, he with another pilot was mentioned in dispatches. My mother kept a copy of an article about the incident from the *Bognor Post* among the photos in her treasured laundry box which she kept in her room until she died at ninety. It must have been unique for father and son to have both destroyed a submarine in two World Wars.

During the war, Bill lost most his friends. In combat, nothing lasted very long – five or ten minutes were considered a long time. Bill would try and get behind an enemy aircraft and swoop down on it or if he took them straight on, he refused to give way first. Although it is difficult to confirm, since several pilots often counted the same aircraft, he claimed to have downed five German fighters during the war.

Bill was undoubtedly a skilled pilot; he would not have survived otherwise. He was also a so-called 'Diver Ace.' To be a 'Fighter Ace' you have had to have shot down five planes whereas he shot down either seven or nine 'Divers' or Doodlebugs. This is all documented in the book of his Squadron Nigeria 91. He also bravely flew straight at two Messerschmitts. One swerved and hit the other one, resulting in two 'kills' for which he was officially accredited.

He told me that he was a good pilot because he had developed sensitive hands as a rider. He was also exceptionally brave. 'You got used to death,' he said. 'You'd say "bit of luck, I'm still alive". Seeing a fellow going down in flames, you'd say "poor bastard". Then you think, "thank God it's not me" and you look behind immediately in case someone's up your arse.'

When I asked him whether he ever thought about the young German pilots and soldiers he killed, he replied: 'Never. They killed my pals. It was a question of them or me and I was going to make sure, it wasn't me.'

Bill liked later to call himself a wing commander ; he was in fact promoted to Flight Lieutenant on 26 May 1944 and on 8 June 1945 had his name included in a list in the *London Gazette* commended by the king 'for valuable services in the air.' On 14 August 1945 he was also awarded the Distinguished Flying Cross (DFC) which was the third-level decoration awarded to personnel of the Air Force. The citation, signed by the future Prime Minister Harold Macmillan, declared:

> Throughout numerous operations, including reconnaissance patrols, escorting bombers against heavily defended targets on the Continent and low-level attacks against railway targets, mechanical transports and gun positions, Flight Lieutenant Marshall has displayed outstanding skill, courage and a fine fighting spirit. He has destroyed two enemy aircraft, damaged another, destroyed seven flying bombs and shared in the destruction of one midget submarine. This officer's fine leadership has been largely responsible for the success of many missions.

A series of posed photographs taken around this time shows Bill visibly older, with a slight moustache and a band for his medal under his RAF wings. In some shots taken outside, he wears a poker dot silk scarf around his neck and looks heroically up to the skies. In others taken in the studio, he wears a collar and tie with

his uniform, wings and ribbons, and insignia on his arm denoting
Flight Lieutenant.

The motto of his last squadron No 91 was 'We seek alone' which
seems very apt for him. It had the word Nigeria on its badge,
reflecting its imperial origins. Its heraldic devise was a spring with
two upturned triangles – an alchemical symbol of Solomon's seal
which would have meant little to him. For the Nigeria squadron
there were about 20 DFC's awarded and 40 pilots killed in action
during the war, and many others injured and maimed. A squadron
consisted of about 12 to 14 pilots.

The squadron was so-called because of the contribution of
Nigeria to its cost and was manned by a diverse band of pilots
from across the world. It apparently achieved exceptional
results employing new low-level interception tactics along the
south coast of England. It
used the latest Spitfire planes
available.

Bill as Flight Lieutenant

The last time my father
ever flew in the RAF was on
November 14, 1945, six weeks
before I was conceived. About
sixty years later, he wore his
medals when he was welcomed
on board the ss. *Britannia* as
a 'Wing Commander' and
successful race-horse trainer
by the Queen and Prince Philip
in Barbados. It was a long
way from his first tramp ship
ss. *Harmattan*.

When my father came out
of the RAF, aged 27, he had
already led an extraordinary
life, travelled around the world while he was still very young,
faced death on a daily basis and acquired a wife and two
children. But he had no property and only £150 to his name.
There was talk of taking over his local pub The Walnut Tree
with my mother out at Runcton but it came to nothing. He was
determined to realise his childhood ambition to become a jockey
and racehorse trainer. My mother had long realised that she was

not made out to be a jockey's wife. No wonder they grew apart.

While my mother was living in a flat with my brother and me at the back of the hotel in Bognor, Bill rented some land from the owner of his local pub, lived in a caravan and built himself some wooden stables for four horses. It seemed inevitable that the young girl Diana helping him would become his girlfriend. My brother remembers on one occasion when he was recovering from an illness, aged around four, our uncle took him over to Runcton for a weekend, forcing him on Bill and his new lover. Michael was put in the tack room to sleep, with a rough blanket thrown over him. Bill's new partner Diana gave him an orange, a rare and exotic fruit at the time. I was nearly two and according to my mother whenever I heard Bill's motor bike arrive in the forecourt of Bridport Hotel, I would exclaim 'Vrrm, Vrrm! Dada, Dada!'.

Diana had been a nurse during the war and came from a farming family near Chichester. She had grown up with her grandparents since her mother had left her father when she was two – just as my father had left my mother for her. Her father Bob Field had been a private trainer and was now a 'nagsman', keeping hunters and making sure they were ready for their owners. He was employed by Cyril Marshall to teach Bill how to train racehorses, as Bill had no experience in this. Diana met Bill while accompanying her father to the stables. She was twenty two at the time, considerably younger than Bill, but keen on horses, having ridden in local point-to-point races. She was an ideal partner for Bill to begin his life as a jockey-trainer out of a caravan.

She eventually become his wife and mother of three boys Tom, Dick and Harry and a daughter Sarah, and helped him build up his successful career. With her, he was able to concentrate on the real love of his life: horses.

With his pre-war experience racing in Australia and South Africa, he became an amateur jockey and soon began riding winners, including one at Fontwell near Chichester in 1948 on the day his mother died.

My mother can remember how he often fell off horses in races. She had a photo of him on horseback from this period looking very raffish, with unruly hair and no helmet, dressed in thick corduroy trousers, a hacking jacket with its collar turned up and a thick tie.

He was undoubtedly a brave man. When a horse went berserk

at Fontwell and attacked a woman, Bill was the only one to try to restrain it. He managed to get the horse away but was badly savaged himself in the process. His stomach was lacerated and he had a large bite in his thigh close to the groin for his pains. His thumb was nearly cut off and from that day it was at a 45 degree angle. He spent four days in hospital recovering. His wound was so bad that blood even dripped through his mattress. My mother kept an article in the *Bognor Post* about the event.

When he bought his first horse, he had no money in the bank but persuaded the comedians Bud Flanagan and Chesney Allen of the Crazy Gang – my mother had taken my brother and me to see the comedians and song writers in London – to foot the bill. Flanagan co-wrote 'Underneath the Arches' when sleeping rough in London. The horse called 'Qui Va La' won in September 1946, with Bill in the saddle as an amateur rider, at excellent betting odds. I had just been born. Chesney Allen went on to become his best owner and closest friend for 36 years; Bill called him his 'fairy godfather.'

Three years later he turned professional but his best seasonal score was only five wins in 1949/50. As a trainer it was a different story, and the first of his many winners was 'Danger Light' at Windsor in February 1951.

My mother was right when she said that she could not have kept up with Bill. Their early lives had been so different that it is difficult to see what they had in common, apart from two children. They only met because pilots would have parties at the Bridport Hotel and his mother played in the same bridge club as my grandmother. Bill had grown up on a farm with a fun-loving mother and somewhat stiff father. He had run away to sea at an early age and roughed it in different parts of the Empire. My mother had had a completely sheltered life in Bognor, only once being sent away for a short time to boarding school in Surrey because of her asthma. She was totally dominated by her mother. When she married Bill, she had lived as a resident in the family hotel, served by the staff and unable even to cook. She did not even like horses whereas for Bill they were the great love of his life.

5

THE WORRIED MAN

When my mother was twelve, her parents had moved to Bognor from East Finchley, London, where my great grandmother's parents had retired. My grandmother and her husband had enough money to build a hotel by the sea. It was mainly for my grandfather's sanity. He had been apprenticed as a painter and letterer to the coach building firm set up by his father Hugh Payne, born in 1846. He had come up from a small village in Dorset to Holloway in London and become a self-made man. He was a hard and quick-tempered task master and with the arrival of the motor car his trade was doomed. He treated my grandfather, the second of seven children, so badly that he had a 'breakdown' at the age of nineteen – a mysterious complaint for me which had momentous overtones. It explained why he didn't go into the army during the First World War. His brothers did and two were killed in the trenches.

Before I went to primary school we moved from the hotel to the new, spacious sunny house with a large garden a few houses up the road called 'Chideock'. His mother had married a Payne in her first marriage and then, by extraordinary coincidence, a second Payne who had no direct link with the family of the first.

As a grandfather – we always called him Pop – he was mild, gentle and helpful. He was completely dominated by his wife and to escape her rule he would retreat in old age to sit by the coal fire in the front lounge in winter or to his large garden shed and lean-to greenhouse in the summer. I was told that during the war he would entertain the pilots billeted at the Bridport Hotel (and their girlfriends) with jokes and antics.

Behind the bar, my grandfather would pretend to go down some stairs to the cellar when in fact the floor was level and solid. He particularly liked to imitate the Scottish music hall comedian and singer Harry Lauder, author of 'Roamin' in the Gloamin' and 'Keep Right on to the End of the Road.' We had a curling 'Harry Lauder' stick under the stairs which had been one of his props. But with his carefully pomaded hair parted in the middle my grandfather

My grandfather Alfred (Pop) and me dancing

looked more like Fred Astaire, especially when he set forth to a local masonic function in evening dress with my grandmother in furs. Even after retiring, he was always very dapper, usually wearing a jacket and tie.

There is a photograph of him dancing with me on the lawn when I was about three, wearing black and white shoes.

Spending so much time in the garden in the summer, his face went nut brown. He was a great potterer and bodger in his long brown shopkeeper's coat and flat linen cap and his shed was full of old paint and garden pots, nails, sacks and tools. The backs of his brown hands, with their thick veins and dark liver spots, were often bruised and scabbed. He had bantam chickens next to the coal bunker and in his garage-sized shed he built a large cage for pigeons. He would spend hours talking to them and stroking them, but it did not prevent him from ringing their necks and plucking them for dinner.

He loved his garden and in the front of the house there was a lawn behind a low wall and then a bright bed of dark red and golden yellow roses and colourful gladioli. In summer, he would often have a bud in the lapel of his light linen coat. Down the path from the wooden gate to the entrance to the house there was a line of sweet-smelling wallflowers whose heady scent grew stronger in the afternoon sun reflected from a low partition wall. When I first heard my mother describe her friend who was not invited to dance as a 'wall flower', it seemed to me a compliment.

In the back garden two lawns were divided by a winding flower bed. At the end was the large vegetable patch, with the shed and greenhouse on one side and a large Beauty of Bath apple tree. Some apples ended up in my grandmother's pies, but most were left to rot. I ate hundreds of the small, soft, pithy apples with red stripes, trying to fill up a permanent cave of hunger in my belly.

Looking down the garden from the greenhouse, there was a large pond with a low rock garden around its edges which Pop dug and lined with concrete. He put some weed in it, a lily and some ornamental gold fish. It flourished with myriads of tiny creatures swimming around it in the summer.

One day, my grandfather took my brother and me fishing in a dyke next to the mud flats of Pagham Harbour. We caught some roach, which he put in a net in the water because he did not like to kill them. 'You should always put your hand in the water before holding them,' he warned, 'Otherwise it will feel like a red-hot poker.' A few roach were put into the pond where they soon bred. When Pop knocked the shallow end of the pond, they would come up with the goldfish to be fed.

When I was about eight, I was sword playing with my cousin Lindsay and forced her back towards the pond. When I homed in, she suddenly toppled backwards into the pond, causing a massive tidal wave and surfaces covered in weed and lilies. I was horrified at what I had done, but got her to tell our parents that it was an accident.

When my grandfather became ill with attacks of nerves and prostate cancer the pond was neglected, the fish not fed, and the weeds took over the rockery. Then one winter thick ice cracked the cement and all the water drained out leaving a thick, foul-smelling mat of wriggling creatures and weed roots. The only fish we saved was a huge, fat 'Shubunkin' with large, drooping fins and red, white and brown colours. It was put into a bucket under the outside tap; it was so large it could hardly turn around. And there it remained for a couple of years, its bucket occasionally filled up from the tap when we noticed it was half full and gave it the odd piece of bread. How it survived in its awful captivity is beyond me. We were sad one day to see it lying on its side and buried it in the garden but soon forgot about it.

A big event of the year was Guy Fawkes' night. Pop was the master of ceremonies, the priest of the fire ritual. He would build a large bonfire on the poor ground between the car garage and the pond. He would put seats in the emptied garage and candles around it for the spectators which usually consisted of our immediate family – my brother and me, our mother and grandmother. The Guy Fawkes, made from trousers and shirts and pullovers stuffed with crumpled paper with a grotesque mask with a curling moustache, was placed on a high stick above old bean poles and garden waste. We did not know who he was – history, politics and religion did not enter our household in an organised way – but we knew he represented evil and was best burnt on a cold, damp, dark night of early winter. Only later did I learn that Fawkes was one of the few men to enter parliament with honest intentions.

When Pop lit the fire with paraffin, the reflected light in the candle-lit garage created a warm world of mystery and excitement. He lit Roman candles which the women of the house reacted with

Our house at Chideock, 10 Stocker Road, Bognor Regis. My brother Michael and I slept in the sunny right-hand bedroom.

prolonged 'AAAhs!' and exclamations of 'How pretty!' But my brother and I loved the bangers – which we threw at each other in the damp darkness of the garden beyond the fire – and the rockets which whished up to the stars and which left swirling, acrid smoke in their milk-bottle launching pads. I once let off a jumping jack close to my mother in the confines of the garage, and was suddenly horrified that it ended up under her skirt. The end of the show was marked by the Catherine wheels which Pop nailed to the side of the garage, spinning great whirls of sparks and light until there was a slow glow which finally stopped like a dying creature. Going reluctantly to bed meant abandoning the mystery of the deep wilderness of the garden at night, the warm glow of the candle-lit garage, the roaring fire and the cascading lights in the sparkling night sky.

Bognor Boy

I would often come home in the winter on the bus from primary school, having walked the last few hundred yards in the driving rain sweeping in from the sea, and find Pop slumped in the gathering gloom. He would poke the fire into a blaze and make me some 'French toast', cooked on one side with a fork and melted with butter sprinkled with sugar on the other. It tasted deliciously of sugar and coal smoke, crisp and soggy by turns. Or he would clear the coal and roast some chestnuts on the embers in a brass toaster with a Dutch scene of a couple in clogs in front of a windmill on its lid. It would turn the flames green and turquoise.

Although my grandfather rarely spoke when I knew him, he had been an astute business man on a small scale. He may or may not have played the black market but he certainly came out of the war wealthier than when he went in. Pilots from nearby Tangmere aerodrome, including some Poles, were billeted at my grandparents' hotel. They made sure that there was no shortage of food and drink, especially of rationed products.

In Stocker Road where we lived, the second road in from the seafront, he owned the Bridport Hotel and St Helen's Hotel as well as Chideock where we grew up. He also developed and bought properties in Chichester selling them at a profit on the property market.

There was also a mysterious and secretive side to him. In the sunless dining room at the back of the house which was only used

My grandfather Alfred (Pop) and grandmother Nellie (Nanna)
at a 'Ladies Night' held by the Freemasons of Bognor

at Christmas, there was a locked door in a heavy wooden dresser. I was told that I should never open it so naturally I wanted to. One day when everyone was out of the house when I was about eight, I found the key and opened the secret chamber. It contained a strange apron covered with an opened divider on top of an unturned triangle. I opened up one of the big black books and saw symbols of pyramids, columns, a protractor, and a piercing eye under a triangle. I heard someone at the door. I quickly put everything back and turned the key and went up to my room, conscious that I had discovered a great secret and violated the Holy of Holies of my grandfather. I never opened the cupboard again and felt the eye continue to follow me. Only later did I realise that he had been initiated into a secret society and the symbols I had seen were from secret books of Freemasonry.

My grandfather was a Freemason and the Freemasons of Bognor Regis were the more prosperous shopkeepers, hoteliers, magistrates, estate agents, solicitors, accountants and police officers – in other words, those who ran the town. It was for men only; women were only allowed on special 'Ladies' Nights', when my grandmother and mother, dressed up to the nines, attended their dinners and listened to their dreary speeches.

He never discussed his freemasonry with me before he died. When I asked my mother what freemasonry was she said that its members helped each other and were meant to help other people. Its high moral ideals of brotherly love and truth had degenerated in Bognor where the local politicians and businessmen had wrapped up the town for themselves. On the other hand, I found out later that Bognor was the European headquarters of Rosicrucianism, so there must have been some serious spiritual seekers in the seaside town.

The sect and the rituals and the brotherhood of freemasonry must have given my grandfather a structure and support but it did not seem to help him with his own inner transformation. He was not an outwardly religious man and never attended church. He did not manage to carve the rough block of himself into something whole for he continued to worry.

The house was perfectly maintained yet one day he said to me:

'Look, Peter, look, can you see those cracks appearing in the ceiling.'

There were none there, at least to my eyes.

Not long after he was taken off to hospital in Chichester where he received something mysteriously called 'electric treatment' – high voltage shocks to knock out his worries. It worked only for a while.

He had always been a very mild man, similar in temperament to my mother. 'He's soft like me', she used to say. When he developed the first signs of prostate cancer, he went more and more into himself and would often fall asleep in his armchair. When I was thirteen the first friend I invited home from boarding school was the son of an army major, a serious and quiet boy. We were sitting around the fire after supper watching a Western on the small black and white television with my mother, grandmother and Pop when there was a sudden and terrible smell. And then I saw at the bottom of my grandfather's trousers a liquid dripping on the carpet. I was horrified and acutely embarrassed by it. Without explanation, my grandmother ushered us out of the lounge and to our cold bedroom upstairs. We were abruptly wrenched out of a warm atmosphere riding across the plains with *The Cisco Kid* to a mysterious world of dark forces which brought illness and death.

I didn't say anything to my friend about what had happened and he didn't either. I felt so ashamed and was sure that he would never want to come back to my home again. Next morning, Pop was not to be seen; he was in bed ill. No other explanation was given. I later learnt that he had become incontinent due to prostate cancer. He died soon after; I never saw him in hospital. When he came to be buried, I was told by my uncle to stay with the manager of Bridport Hotel because he thought that I was not old enough to go to a funeral. I was thirteen at the time. His ashes were apparently put under a rose tree somewhere in a cemetery near Haywards Heath. Since he had showered his grandsons with affection, it was sad for me that I never had the opportunity to say goodbye properly to him.

6

HIDDEN SECRETS

My grandmother was the mainstay and matriarch of the family. She was born in Holloway in London in 1888 as Nellie Louise although my brother and I always called her Nanna. She was the first of ten children. Her down-trodden mother was Louisa Cullen and her domineering father was appropriately called Henry Bull. It was only later that I learnt from her youngest sister that she had a twin who was born red all over with eczema and died before the day was out. As the oldest child, she had to help her mother look after the youngest ones. Her mother was not only regularly pregnant but had to look after her husband as well as a large family.

Her father was a self-made man during the Victorian era. He was a coal merchant with 20 trucks and 40 dray horses to look after and every day had to organise the men who went out to deliver coal on their rounds. It was the main form of heating at the time and the bane of maids and mothers who had to get the fires burning and tend them throughout the day.

George Bull was indeed a brutish man. He would return home with hobnailed boots covered in coal dust and horse droppings and demand his wife to kneel down before him with the words: 'Woman, take off my boots.'

He would sit at the head of the table and eat butter while his wife and children had to eat margarine. They would sit and eat during the meal in total silence and could only have seconds when the head of the family asked them. Whenever a horse passed the house, which was often as it was the principal means of transport, she would have to go out with a shovel to collect the droppings for the garden. One of my grandmother's happier memories, however, was riding through the cobbled streets on a cart decorated with ribbons for the Lord Mayor's show.

As the oldest girl in the family, she grew up very competent and strong. She married my grandfather Alfred Allen Payne in her early 20s. One of her brothers George Bull became the last Tory mayor of Islington and apparently drank himself to death at 68. We had a drawing of him in his chain and all his regalia on the drinks' cabinet at home. Nanna aspired to join the middle classes and the property deals carried out with my grandfather certainly enabled this.

According to her youngest sister Louise, she kept several skeletons tightly in her cupboard. Her maternal grandfather Charlie Cullen had been one of 22 children who lived in a two-roomed longhouse in Wicklow, Ireland. He was turfed out at the age of 12 to travel for work in Dublin. When he was 16 he took the ferry to Holyhead in North Wales and then travelled to London. He became a lodger of a Welsh woman who had come to London to look unsuccessfully for her husband who had onced owned a pub in Wales. Charlie then eloped with his landlady's daughter, who was two years older than him, marrying her soon afterwards. He worked as a carpenter and was once away for seven years working in a castle. He had five children, including Louisa Cullen (my great grandmother) and lived to a grand old age, dying at 96.

Another skeleton in my grandmother's cupboard was that her paternal grandfather Ishmael Bull had been a farmer in Crewkerne in Dorset and had married the illegitimate daughter of 'Lord Lovell Rolls.' Lord Rolls apparently had her raised by the local innkeepers who sent her to a good boarding school and visited her in the holidays. She met Ishmael Bull when she was 18 in the pub of her foster parents. They married soon after and moved to Charmouth in West Dorset where they had five children, including Nellie's father Henry Bull. The family then moved back to Crewkerne but when Ishmael died at 47, his wife moved to Marlborough Road in Holloway, London. Here the family lived in two rooms and were very poor.

Henry Bull left school at nine and apparently met Louisa Cullen in a pub in Holloway. He eventually had 10 children – five sons and five daughters. He prospered as a coal merchant and died a wealthy man. But it would never do for my grandmother to tell us boys that she had illegitimacy, albeit of a lord, as well as Irish blood in the family. I would never have known if it had not been for her sister Louise who told me the story of her real ancestry before she died.

It was my grandmother who decided to follow her retired parents from London to Bognor and set up a hotel with her husband. They had built the Bridport Hotel in Stocker Road in the fashionable West End. To this day the house opposite called 'Crewkerne' after the town in Dorset bears the insignia 'A. & N. P. 1929.' It shows a nice equality in my grandparents' undertaking

Bridport Hotel

and the date of their arrival from London. They soon had built
the new hotel called 'Bridport' after the town in Dorset where my
grandfather's forefathers had been farmers and rope makers.

She was determined to have her initial on the plaque. She
advised her husband on how to run the Bridport Hotel while
he did the accounts. She was the chief cook in the kitchen and
arranged all the other staff of the hotel. She was also a keen bridge
player and had her own club at the hotel.

My grandparents moved briefly out of the hotel to a smart, mock
Tudor house with a big garden and orchard in Tudor Close, on the
edge of the nearby seaside village of Middleton. Being so close to the
fields and woods, I liked it there when we visited. I was fascinated by
a big wooden trunk with brass knobs in the hallway and a turquoise
doorknob made from cut glass which – like a prism – reflected the
rainbow of the sun in all directions. But they complained that it was
too quiet there and move backed into Bognor.

They built the house 'Chideock' just down from Bridport Hotel
and opposite their property St Helen's Hotel. My mother and we
two boys also moved down to the new house from our small flat at
the back of the Bridport. We grew up there. When we were young
and Nanna was retired she still had her 'Bridgites' around; we
waited impatiently until they had gone so that we could scoff down
the dainty triangular sandwiches and cakes which were served on
three-tiered stands lined with doilies.

Bognor Boy

I remember my grandmother as a plump woman with glasses who made her own clothes on her own Singer sewing machine and enjoyed crochet, embroidery and knitting in the evening. Unlike my mother she was an excellent cook and every day made a classic English meal of meat and two veg plus a pudding. I thought that her steamed puddings like spotted dick as well as her apple and rhubarb pies were brilliant. But the best was her 'Queen's Pudding' which consisted of mashed up bread soaked in milk topped by jam and meringue. In the evening in Chideock, it was my mother's turn to cook for us which meant usually a meal of baked beans, squashed sardines or tomatoes on toast. Having experienced two wars, my grandmother stuffed the larder with tins which she said were for a 'Third World War.' Fortunately the tins were never used and eventually went rusty.

She was not very good with animals. In a dark corner of the breakfast room at Chideock the yellow canary was badly neglected. Its nails grew long, so long that it had difficulty holding on to its perch. Its cage was so small that it could not stretch its wings and never saw the light of the sun. One day it was found dead at the bottom of the cage; it was not replaced.

We also had a huge ginger tom cat called, not surprisingly, 'Ginger'. He often eyed the canary when it was alive. Ginger had a torn ear and scratched nose and hardly ever came into the kitchen. Whenever I tried to stroke him he lashed out with his paws. He scratched the face of my cousin so badly one day that we were told never to pick Ginger up again.

My grandmother liked her evening 'Gin and It' (Italian red vermouth) but I only saw her drunk once when she encouraged me to throw her beloved cut glasses into the grate like a Russian aristocrat. She always appeared cheerful and jolly; she even called her drink 'Gin and Giggles' which it certainly was.

I loved my Nanna and she was very good to Michael and me. But as I grew up I realised she had dominated my mother and tried to make her into a little 'madam', sending her to private school and making her take elocution and piano lessons when she was young. My mother always lived at home, even when she was briefly married to my father. She was unable to escape fully from the shadow of the ample bosom of her own mother with her colourful but secret background.

Hidden Secrets

When I was about eight my grandmother sent me to Penge in the southern suburbs of London to stay with a middle-aged couple who used to come down to the hotel for their annual summer holiday. They had no children and could not cope with my brother and me together so they would invite us up on separate occasions. In our 'museum' Michael even had a ticket of the last tram in 1953 in London collected during his stay there. I travelled up on my own in the guard's van of the steam train and was met at Victoria station by my 'Uncle Fred.'

He worked somewhere in the city and departed every morning in his regular uniform of bowler hat, raincoat, rolled umbrella and well-used leather briefcase. His wife was called 'Auntie Pip' and always had her long, plaited grey hair tied in an elaborate bun around her head. They were not my real uncle and aunt but I liked them very much. They lived on the ground floor in a large semi-detached house in a broad avenue lined with mature chestnut trees. They rented out the next floor to a young man. I loved the smell of Auntie Pip's home-made bread; when she served it with lashings of butter and thick cuts of ham my mouth watered. She was also very adept at making junket sprinkled with nutmeg which I enjoyed very much along with her blackberry and apple pie.

At mealtimes the elderly couple went through the same ritual. He would say, pursing his lips and wiping them with a large white starched napkin:

'That was delicious. Thank you very much, dear.'

She would say: 'Why not have some more? There's plenty of it.'

He would reply: 'No, dear, that was perfect. I've had more than enough, thank you.'

He pushed his empty plate away from him.

Then she would say: 'Go on Fred, have a little bit more.'

It was only, on the third asking, would he reply:

'Oh all right dear – if you insist. But only a little bit, mind you...'
And he would tuck in as if he hadn't eaten at all.

There was a boy of about my own age next door who would come over and ask me to go out and play. His knees were scuffed and one of his socks was invariably down.

'Don't go very far', my aunt would say. 'Stay around the house.'

He led me up to all sorts of tricks, though I was a willing accomplice. We made catapults together but soon got tired of aiming at an old tin. He tried to shoot some coloured birds but I was pleased that he had no success. Next day we made some bows and took some sticks to make arrows which supported Uncle Fred's dahlias. It turned out that his dahlias were his pride and joy. I got a great row from my normally passive 'uncle' when he found out.

The greatest escapade we had was when my new friend showed me, one day, the way across the busy road at the end of the avenue. We scrambled through a broken wooden fence into a great park beyond. There we crouched through the undergrowth and trees with our bows and arrows, pretending to be real 'Red Indians.' Suddenly we came upon a large lake; I looked up only to see a huge dinosaur bearing down upon me. Gore dripped from its huge teeth and I was certain that it moved towards me. I stood back terrified. It was only after a few minutes that I realised that it was stationary. It was a terrific shock and I quickly said that I wanted to go home. I later learned that we had broken into Crystal Palace.

I slept at night in the front guestroom which had a high ceiling and thick curtains. My aunt made me kneel down in front of my single bed every night before I went to sleep and say the 'Lord's Prayer' after her. It felt strange since I had never been asked to do so before in our non-religious family. On the marble mantel piece above the disused fire stood a loudly ticking clock covered with a glass dome. I was fascinated by its brass moving parts.

I sometimes went upstairs to the young man who rented the flat above my 'uncle and aunt.' I always found his room, with its semi-closed curtains at the rear of the house, gloomy and slightly menacing. But he taught me how to play Canasta with two packs of cards and we would sip smoky Lapsang Suchong tea in delicate China cups. It was new to me and felt very exotic and grown up.

7
THE WOULD-BE ACCOUNTANT

My uncle Allen, the older brother of my mother, took over Bridport Hotel when we moved into Chideock. He was tall, thin and had been head boy at Chichester High School. He had been offered a place at Oxford but decided to become a chartered accountancy clerk in Bognor and stay with his parents instead. He expressed some sympathy for the Mosleyites, fascist followers of Oswald Mosley who strutted up and down in black uniforms along the promenade in Bognor.

During the war, he had tried to fly but had been sick, so joined the Pay Corps. The closest he ever got to university was in the RAF Pay Corps at Jesus College where he once gave some money to the actor Richard Attenborough, whom he said was a cheeky young air man. He spent some time in India delivering despatches; he used to rave about the beauty of 'Eurasian' girls who he claimed threw themselves at the English 'Tommies.'

Uncle Al (Allen) as a young man

Bognor Boy

Having failed his accountancy exams after the war – he said he couldn't concentrate any more – he drifted into managing hotels and pubs. He set himself up as the 'authority figure' in the family, bullying his own father and giving us boys a hard time. Although aggressively conservative in politics and having expressed sympathy for Mosley, he was no racist. He introduced us to the exotic world of curries and took us on camping holidays in France, Spain and Portugal.

His very name conjures up for me a tall, shouting figure who had thin straight red hair (auburn, my mother called it) who went red in the face whenever he got angry – which was often. When I was about five, for some reason I ended up walking with him on a sunny day in Hotham Park in the east end of Bognor, far from home. It was like being in a hostile foreign land. There were dark trees at the entrance and then the wide path went past a terrace of tall buildings on the left. Their shutters were closed; no one went in or out of the buildings which were in the shade. As we passed my uncle pointed at an entrance in the rusty iron railings which led down a winding stone steps to the cellars. He lent over me from a great height and said:

'If you're a naughty boy and don't do what you're told, you'll be sent down there and witches will boil you in a large tub! No one will ever know what will have become of you.'

I longed to get out his clutches and into the warm sun again and as far away as possible. The next time I walked with my mother in Hotham Park I refused to go past the buildings. I wasn't sure whether I had been naughty but I was certain that I didn't want the witches to get hold of me.

When I first heard about Hell where bad people would be punished I came to associate it with the steps going down to the cellars of those buildings, to a hot and dark place where horrible people did horrible things to you. The threat in the long run didn't make me into a good boy but made me reject the whole idea of Hell and of punishment as a means of reforming character.

It was my uncle who carved the Christmas turkey at the top of the heavy wooden table in the back dining room of Chideock. Whereas our grandfather was a small man, his son was over six foot, with a slight stoop. He felt Christmas was a waste of time; he used to sit by the fire with his long legs stretched out, only occasionally opening parcels which invariably contained socks, handkerchiefs and ties. He said they were all he wanted.

My mother Vera, Pop and Auntie Barbie

We feared his sudden anger. It was probably due to the frustration of being an intelligent man who did not have the staying power to see his studies through. He usually took the easy option. His first wife left him during the war and soon after he married Barbie, a secretary who had come to stay in the hotel with her family.

Auntie Barbie was blond, curvaceous, warm and fun. She painted her toenails bright red and often wore low neck lines. She always smelt good and would often talk about the parties they had in the war. She had a soft spot for our absent father whom she said was always good fun to be with. At the same she hated what she called 'conshies'– conscientious objectors – and said they should have been given white feathers for their cowardice. She could never understand why the British people voted out Churchill after the war after 'all that he had done for them.' She had one child Lindsay. Barbie slept in a separate bed because, she said, Uncle Al had smelly feet.

Uncle Al was not all bad however and he liked animals. When I was about seven my uncle suddenly announced in the autumn that my brother and I would go up to London in his wide Zephyr car (which had seats like sofas) to get a dog from the Battersea Dogs Home. It was a great outing because I had only gone up to London a couple times to stay in Penge and to see the Crazy Gang at the Victoria Palace on a day trip with my mother.

The streets around the dogs' home were mean and empty with litter blowing in the cold wind. The home itself stank of urine and dog shit. Dogs of all sizes and colours barked and jumped up against the wire of the cages trying to get out. Some lay asleep on the concrete floors amongst all the pandemonium. In the end, we chose a small, black and white mongrel with a rough coat and one floppy ear. It growled in the cage on the long journey back to Bognor before it fell asleep. On arrival, it bolted down its food in a second and then curled up on an old blanket in a dark corner of the kitchen.

I loved the dog which we called 'Skipper.' I would take it on a lead down to the beach to throw sticks for it into the sea. But it would sometimes refuse to come back and ran off along the beach. The trouble was it had been a stray and liked the excitement of street life in London and now in Bognor there were open spaces and the long promenade where other dogs congregated. But I still loved him even if we saw him less and less. He would often return after three days looking dishevelled and guilty, gobble up his food and drop into his corner. Once refreshed, he was then looking for an opening in the house to run off again.

One day, I was playing with my lead soldiers at the top of our house when I heard a terrible noise outside. Looking out the window, I could see that there was a massive fight between Skipper and a huge white Bull terrier in the middle of the road. It was owned by the chef in the Bridport Hotel and had small pink eyes and a thin upright tail. Passers-by were now converging on the fighting dogs. I ran down stairs to see the Bull terrier had seized Skipper around the throat and despite his twists and turns held on tight. I wanted to pull him off but a neighbour shouted to me to get out of the way. One neighbour then came out of her house with a broom and began to hit the Bull terrier on the back; it only enraged him all the more and he began to shake Skipper from side to side. At that point, Skipper freed himself from his jaws and ran screaming down the street. I ran after him, calling him back. Soon he disappeared but I saw drops of blood on the pavement.

I looked everywhere for him along the beach, shouting his name, but never saw him again. I cried and cried and cried until there were no more tears. Some weeks later, I heard that a dog answering the description of Skipper had been found dead on the beach under the pier. He had a deep wound to his neck. I learned that once a Bull terrier has clamped its jaws shut, they cannot be opened and the only effective way to stop dogs fighting is to throw a bucket of cold water on them. Skipper was the first creature that I loved and lost. Nothing happened to the Bull terrier which killed my dog.

8
BESIDE THE SEASIDE

My brother and I spent all our free time on the beach which was only one road away from our house Chideock in Stocker Road. It was our wide open playground where we roamed and played to our hearts' content. It meant freedom, adventure and mystery. We were never prevented from going down there and came back home only when we were hungry. We just had to be careful crossing the road.

When we were very young our Pop and Nanna had the first hut in the long row at the top of the shingle beach – where the willow trees began. In the summer, when the tide was in and it was a quiet, sunny day, the sea was a bright blue with small waves lapping on the pebbles. When the tide was beginning to go out, many families sat on the beach with their children until they, at last, could go onto the famed 'golden sands' of Bognor.

My brother Michael, my mother and me

Bognor Boy

There was a large rusty storm outlet on the beach. It always seemed to have some water coming out of it which fanned out across the sands. My brother and I would spend hours building dams across its streams and watching them fill up with water until they overflowed. We also built elaborate castles and tried to block the incoming tide with high walls. We were of course always defeated but learnt of how water could never be contained and how it could wear away the hardest rock.

At low tide large rocks emerged far out at sea, including what the local fishermen called 'King's Rock', which had been the original shoreline until it was breached by storms hundreds of years before. Along the foreshore in the West End of Bognor, from Aldwick to Pagham there were also rich beds of a mixture of London Clay and sand containing fish fossils, particularly teeth, which could be discovered at low tide

When I first heard the story of King Canute who asked his courtiers to place his throne on the beach facing the incoming tide in nearby Bosham, I felt immediately that it was not to show his incomparable power in holding back the waves but to demonstrate that there was something more powerful than him – the sea and the land, Nature as whole. It was something I had simply learnt from building castles and dams on the beach. You can't hold back water, however much you try.

It always seemed sunny in summer in my childhood; Bognor after all was meant to be the sunniest place in Britain. Some have said that this later contributed to my generally cheerful and positive character, my so-called 'sunny' nature. But it also meant, especially early in the season, that we would return home with terrible red sunburn on our backs and arms and legs – red like a cooked lobster. It was only with the application of some cooling calamine lotion by my mother that I was able to fall asleep. But she never told us to cover our backs or wear any cream. We just got burnt brown as the season rolled on. We quickly learned to swim by ourselves – wearing itchy, droopy, home-made woollen swimming trunks!

In the summer the seaside resort was full of holiday-makers; one of my earliest memories was finding my way amongst all the knees of their shorts and skirts along the promenade. The old and tired would nod off in their deckchairs; the young with their buckets and spades invaded the beach while their parents rested on their rugs and towels, with an occasional dip in the cold water.

Beside the Seaside

In the winter, I would listen to the waves crashing on the shore through the leaded windows of our front room. The shingle moved along the beach despite the wooden breakwaters or 'groynes' as we called them. The promenade was often covered in pebbles thrown up by the sea and my brother and I would dare each other to run under the crashing waves without getting wet. They inevitably got us in the end and we would go back home cold and dripping and laughing.

The music hall song I would hear in the variety shows in the Esplanade Theatre expressed my feelings about growing up in Bognor:

Oh! I do like to be beside the seaside,
I do like to be beside the sea!
I do like to stroll along the Prom, Prom, Prom!

But one day at dusk walking home alone beyond the pier, a rough-looking boy told me to move out of his way along the railings on the promenade. He was bigger than me but I did not want to give way; I simply said 'No.' He then gave me an almighty hit in the face and I reeled over clutching my nose as blood poured out of it. He quickly disappeared in the dark. I assumed that he had hit me with a knuckle duster. I was more wary of meeting another 'rough boy' alone in the future.

When not at school, we were left largely to our own devices. In our mother's dark room on the top third floor – which I shared with her for a while – my brother and I spent hours playing 'soldiers' on the floor, with small painted figures made from lead. There was a set of 'American Injuns', with their red-brown bodies and colourful headdresses, and I often chose them against the soldiers. Perhaps I was already unconsciously supporting the 'underdog', particularly as I was the younger of two brothers.

We also had a 'museum' in a large cupboard. We could climb into its dark interior and illuminate it with a candle. We collected curious and strange objects for the 'museum', including the jaw bone of a sheep, different coloured sands in a glass container taken from Alum beach on the Isle of Wight, a domed cylinder containing a miniature winter scene of a cottage in fluid which if shaken created falling snow, a dark Victorian penny with a seated Britannia holding a shield and trident on one side, colourful stamps from all over the world, and the last tram ticket in London.

Bognor Boy

Our preferred place for swimming was at 'Number One Beach.' It was reached by turning left out of our house, going past the Bridport Hotel, crossing over to the tennis courts and then turning right. The beach was between two breakwaters and next to the one used by the Yacht Club. There were attractive girls with tanned legs there and jolly men in blazers and cravats. When they came in after a race at high tide, they would have to jump out in the deep water to stop their dinghies from crashing onto the shingle. But for some reason we never joined in and we soon got our own rowing boat instead.

We would go swimming from April to the end of September; the water always seemed warm although we came out shivering in the hot sun. We found the best time to swim was at high tide when the sea had come across the warm sands.

One summer, when I was about eight, we made a raft in the back shed at home. We used some old oil drums and there was a wooden platform held together by some string. We managed to

Me and Michael

get it down to 'Number One Beach' just as the sky darkened with an oncoming storm and flashes of lightning ran across the horizon on the sea. It had just passed high tide and the tide was going out. My brother and I didn't think about the elements but wanted to try out our new raft. So we got our cousin Lindsay, a year younger than I was, to clamber on the home-made raft and pushed it out to sea through the rough waves. To our horror, and even more to hers, the raft started to drift out to sea. We didn't know what to do. We were saved from our predicament by a man wearing trunks. He dived into the sea and slowly pushed the raft back to the beach. We made our cousin promise not to tell Uncle Al or anybody at home.

I loved the sea and the beach and all of the creatures that lived in and from it. From the shrimps and crabs in the pools at the end of the breakwaters at low tide to the reeling and squawking seabirds overhead in the sky. When I was about nine my brother, two a half years older, won £10 from a National Bond which our mother had given him. With it he bought an old rowing boat which was about nine feet long, clinker built with overlapping planks, painted with innumerable coats of old white paint. I bought a pair of oars for the boat from my savings. Later I bought an outboard motor which never really worked so we went back to oars, which I preferred.

The boat was called 'Zena' and eventually became for us what the sledge 'Rosebud' was for Citizen Kane in the Orson Welles film. It had a plaque on the transom saying that it had been at Dunkirk when the remnants of the British Army were evacuated. It had been part of a flotilla of pleasure boats helping the Navy in the early summer of 1940. It meant that we were linked directly through the boat to the Second World War.

Fishing soon became part of our life. I had before fished with my brother off Bognor Pier, usually in the spring and autumn. I had nightmares of having to crawl on hands and knees in rough weather along the wooden boards without the protecting balustrades. I would then be slowly pushed by the wind into the dark raging sea below.

On one wet day a different sort of nightmare became true. My brother cast his tackle far out to sea when a hook caught into his little finger right to the bone. The wound was dark red, with blood and the guts of the lugworm bait oozing out. The old man in the tackle shop arranged for an ambulance to take him to hospital; he came home looking very white with a big bandage around his finger.

We spent our days fishing in our boat. Fish were plentiful and we fished for them in many different ways. We learned how to dig with a fork in the sand for lugworms and the fewer but faster rag worms at low tide. We laid a trot line down which consisted of two bricks and a long nylon line stretched out between them, with hooks at the end of a short line placed at regular distances from each other. We then baited the hooks with lugworms, juice squeezing out of their bodies as we fed them onto the cold metal hooks. We would lower the trot line in the sea, with floats and a flag attached to each end. Sometimes from the boat but more often than not we laid it out on the sand when the sea was out and collected the catch after one high tide. We always caught some fish, mainly flatfish like plaice with brown skins and red spots, but also some grey silver sole, and occasionally a skate which had a face on its underside which looked nearly human. Some fish which had been caught for many hours had the hooks half-digested in their stomachs.

I did not think the method particularly cruel at the time since it seemed quite natural. But I mainly liked to catch the fish from the boat at anchor using an old wooden reel of my grandfather's, watching the brightly coloured float bob up and down on the waves only to be suddenly taken underwater by a fish. Then the line would tug and the rod would bend and the world disappeared and you would have to play the fish at the end of the line before bringing it on board. I would then – as my grandfather had taught me – hit it on the back of its head with a metal 'rollock' to try and put it 'out of its misery'.

The best fighters were the bream which were fine to eat but had little flesh. Bass were rare – they were not only good fighters but also good to eat. Brightly coloured wrasse with thick lips full of teeth, which lived near the rocks, put up a good fight but we threw them back or used them as bait because they were too bony to eat. The worst fighters were the whiting which had soft mouths and soon gave up the struggle. When shoals of mackerel came up the Channel in the summer they were so plentiful that you would merely have to put in a few feathers on the hooks on a trace in the water and pull up a couple of wriggling fish. The biggest fish we ever caught was a five pound bass. It nearly reached from my chest to my feet.

Holiday-makers would often stop us as we walked home and asked to buy the fresh fish. We earned enough money this way to buy our tackle and repaint the boat in our grandfather's shed in the winter.

Beside the Seaside

I didn't particularly like fish to eat but our grandmother did. Her favourite meal was fish, chips and peas followed by vanilla ice cream. Her face lit up when we arrived at the back door with what was left of our catch, her apron and hands covered in flour. When she told us that there was a poisonous part of the crab, pointing out a dark area in the middle of the upturned shell, we went off her crab sandwiches.

We enjoyed trolling for shrimps along the sea shore with our wide nets around a wooden hoop on the end of a broom handle. But when I saw them jump out of a boiling saucepan of water on to the Raeburn hob, they never tasted so good again. The lobsters we caught took so much time to die in the boiling water – as my grandmother held them down with the lid of the saucepan – that I never fancied them afterwards.

We would often sing an old song taught to us by our grandfather as we launched our boat through the crashing waves on the shingle:

Heave ho, on we go,
Over the briny ocean,
There's lots of fun for everyone
When the boat's in motion,
Lovers bold, young and old,
Their fairy tales to tell,
While listening to the music
Of the Clacton Belle.

We would also sing it as the boat rose and dipped in the swell, substituting 'Zena' for 'Clacton.'

I loved it out at sea when the warm rain or drizzle would descend on us and there was a slight swell. A hush fell all around, except for the sound of the oars in the rollocks and the water swishing by the hull. We were cut off from the rest of the world but it felt secure and cosy in the old boat alone with my brother. We didn't have a compass but always tried to keep our bearings before the land disappeared. Somehow we always managed to row back to the shore although not always where we had intended.

We kept our boat on the shingle close to the inshore fishermen's boats at the West End of Bognor. They had large clinker boats with Seagull outboard engines and rowed them with long oars crossed over. When they were not working out at sea they would sit quietly in front of their tarred huts, smoking and mending their nets or making lobster pots from the withies cut from the willows grown by their ancestors behind them along the promenade. Our clinker boat was heavy and they often helped us pull it up the shingle with their gnarled hands when the tide was out. They never questioned the fact that boys aged about nine and eleven were allowed to go out to sea on their own in their boat. They clearly kept an eye on us.

If the wind was blowing hard and the waves crashed on the beach, they would never say directly 'Don't go out today' but would carry on quietly mending their nets and smoking their pipes and observe obliquely in their broad Sussex drawl:

'It's a bit rough today. I don't think I'll go out.'

And if they didn't, we never would.

But one day – to my dismay – my brother turned down his boots when he was about fifteen and began to strut along the promenade. He was looking out for the 'birds', girls who came down to Bognor for a weekend or holiday with their parents. And then he started to go out with the daughter of a local fisherman by the pier. I knew that our boating and fishing days were over. It was the end of an era. I couldn't understand at that stage why he should have given up something so wonderful for something which seemed to me so unimportant and so strange. The pull of the tides had given way to the rising tug of sexual desire – for the time being at least…

I loved the sea, building sand castles, swimming and boating. I always wondered what was beyond the horizon far out to sea. I knew that France was in front of us but the Channel linked up with all the seas of the world. The experience of the sea as a young lad in Bognor almost certainly made me a traveller later in life.

I gradually learned growing up that my home town lay in a wide bay on a curving, shifting shingle beach which stretched east from Selsey Bill. It had once been further out to sea and the dark, kelp-wracked rocks of the old seashore appeared at low tide. They remained deeply mysterious to me, the haunt of crabs, conger eels, bony wrasse and dogfish. Between them and the shore were light grey sands, often called 'golden' to attract the holiday makers who used to come down to fill the hotels and the beaches. The constantly shifting pebbles – made from rounded flint – just below the promenade were held in check by wooden groynes which pushed out into the sea at high tide.

Beside the Seaside

For most of its life, Bognor had been a small fishing hamlet where the lads supplemented their catch by smuggling in cheap booze over the Channel from France. In the eighteenth century however a person called Richard Hotham, a former East India Company man and 'Mad Hatter' (a provider of hats and no doubt to some degree mad), saw its potential as a seaside resort. He bought up land and built elegant terrace houses and a large mansion for himself. By Georgian times, it had become a fashionable spa – Stein Road still had some of the original buildings. Hotham Park, open to all in the east end, was in the grounds of the founder's grand mansion, long disappeared. Bognor however never achieved the status of Brighton at the other end of Sussex.

Soon after the French Revolution a quiet painter and poet came down from London to live in a small thatched cottage – still standing – in Felpham at the east end of Bognor (now close to the barbed wire fence of Butlin's Holiday Camp). His name was William Blake. While staying there he saw angels playing in the waves breaking on the sands and composed some of his most lyrical poems, including the famous anthem Jerusalem. He found it a sweet place for study because he felt it was 'more spiritual' than London. But his peace was disturbed by a drunken soldier whom he pushed out of his little garden, allegedly saying: 'Damn the king! The soldiers are all slaves.' For which he was sent to the assizes in nearby Chichester for treason, a hanging offence at the time, but was cleared by a jury of Sussex yeomen. Blake, rattled, returned to London.

Bognor continued to be a quiet, staid seaside resort for the 'well-to-do' for most of the nineteenth century. It was given its title Regis – 'Of the King' – in 1929 because whenever King George V fell ill his doctors sent him down to Bognor to recuperate and benefit from the 'ozone' – the fresh sea air. The royal residence was at the west end of Bognor near where we lived. A dark leafy lane, which we called 'Lover's Lane', snaked along its high wall.

Being sent to Bognor with its dreary, tree-surrounded mansion and all-too-fresh sea air came to feel like banishment for old George. He preferred the fogs and vapours of London. It was no doubt on his mind when he died in 1936. Two schools of historians, so it is said, dispute his final words. Some say, they were 'How goes the Empire?', while others declare that he said with his last sigh: 'Bugger Bognor!' The phrase became a music-hall joke and Bognor never recovered from the description.

It had become popular with middle-class families to take their young children to the Bognor Sands – a clientele which my grandparents catered for in their two hotels. Working-class people – my grandmother's term, not mine – also came down from London by the train for day trips, weekend or annual holidays, staying in the many B & B's and guest houses near the seafront.

Being born in 1946 in Bognor meant I grew up after the war in a town which was still flourishing, full of fun and energy. In the summer, the sun always seemed to shine, which is not surprising since it vied with Bournemouth for the longest hours of sunshine in Britain. You could not get much further south than Bognor on the Channel. In the summer, crowds swirled up and down the promenade and families filled the shingle beaches at high tide.

The Scotman of 9 January 1958, when I was twelve, quoted a letter from London which said: 'Bognor, renowned for its air, sunshine, sands and background in the Sussex Downs, is one of the few popular resorts near London which has wisely retained its overgrown village character. It has no need to pretend to be a seaside London, though it can and does absorb the crowds.'

One of my unknown near contemporaries was Cynthia Payne, who was later acquitted of running a brothel in London but had parties in which elderly men dressed up in lingerie and were spanked by young women for their Luncheon Vouchers. The film *Wish You Were Here*, in which a young unmarried girl becomes pregnant, was largely based on her experiences in Bognor and conjures up well the town by the sea as I knew it.

But as soon as autumn was over the atmosphere changed. People disappeared. The town went quiet. The town and the beach became our own again. For the rest of the year, hardly anybody could be seen on the wind-swept and shingle-strewn promenade. Apart from the odd shuffling old man or middle-aged woman walking her dog, we – my brother and I and the waves crashing on the shingle – had it all for ourselves.

9

HEALTH AND EFFICIENCY

We had no books in the house yet my grandmother and mother believed in 'EDUCATION.' My grandmother was largely self-educated and my mother had very little education because of her severe asthma, yet they thought that their 'two boys' should be 'well-educated.' They regularly corrected my speech, saying for instance that I must pronounce the 'T' in 'water' and in 'butter' unlike their fellow Londoners. My grandmother in particular was insistent that we should say 'I used not to' rather than 'I did not use to.' Both had middle-class aspirations. My mother had even been sent to elocution and music lessons as a child and had awards to prove it.

I was first sent at the age of five to a private school at the end of Victoria Drive run by a Miss Paston. It was in a large house set in spacious grounds. We had the third of a pint of milk issued by the government at elevenses, in a dark cellar which smelt badly of old sour milk. Miss Paston, who seemed to take most of the lessons, was a strict disciplinarian if not a sadist. If you did anything wrong – and it wasn't always clear what was 'wrong' – she would take you to a dark narrow room at the side of the house and beat you with a bamboo cane on the hand. The room had long strands of raffia tied on a hook on the back of the door. She would also often use a ruler to beat us in class if we were slightly out of order. She seemed to enjoy beating her little charges. I soon began to resent her unnecessary discipline and authority.

I used to travel there by bus. My mother was invariably late in the mornings and with a coat over her nightdress would rush us through Wilmot's Garage to the bus stop in Aldwick Road, often eating burnt toast with too much butter and marmalade on the way. Occasionally, we had time to eat some lumpy porridge at home.

When I was about seven I walked the mile or so along Victoria Drive to school which seemed a vast distance away. I also learned

Writing as a primary school pupil

to ride a red bicycle and which had a basket in the front. One day, I was so intent on watching some tadpoles wriggling in a jar in the basket, that I crashed into a stationary car and went flying over the handlebars. The jar was broken, the tadpoles were lost in the gutter and I received a nasty lump and bruise on the forehead. For the first time I felt that reality had suddenly imploded. It was a huge shock.

When I was eight I was sent to a private 'prep' school called 'Etonhurst.' Its very name was meant to convey a sense of 'class' to aspiring parents although I was naturally unaware of this at the time. It too was based in a large house but only a few roads away from us. As a prep school, it was intended to prepare young boys for the common entrance exam at the age of 13 as a stepping-stone to public school. Some boys though took the 11+ exam to enter a grammar school. It was here that I began to learn some Latin. My mother would test me for my Latin verbs, having already instilled in me my 'time tables'. I was often sent to the dark, wood-panelled study of the old headmaster. He would readily beat me on my bottom with a cane on the recommendation of a master for disturbing his class.

It was while attending the school that I became aware of SEX. When I was very young, before I was five, I shared a room with my mother on the third floor of Chideock under the sloping roof. She woke me up inadvertently one night coming into the room from the cinema to which she went every week with a friend. I opened a sleepy eye to see her completely naked. It was a sudden flash of something not to be seen. I quickly turned over and pretended to be asleep. I felt I had penetrated into some terrible secret. Thereafter I knew what a naked woman looked like, but I would have preferred that it had not been my mother's body.

I didn't think about sex, or at least consciously, until I was about eight years old when my brother pointed out a young neighbour of about twelve getting undressed in her room in the house next door. But I was first introduced to the mechanics of sex on the beach when I was at Etonhurst. I was walking, aged about nine, along the deserted promenade on a cold, windy day with an older boy.

"Do you know how they do it?', he asked me

'What do you mean, do it?'

'Have sex, you know, make babies. The birds and the bees.'

The very idea made my cold cheeks go redder.

'Not exactly. How then?'

'Well, it's like those dogs we saw the other day. Your willy goes hard and you push it in the girl's fanny, you know. Then they become pregnant and have a baby.'

I was fascinated and repulsed roughly in equal measure. I had seen my cousin's fanny but I couldn't imagine getting mine into it. It didn't even go hard.

'Are you sure?', I said.

'You bet. They do it in the shelters at night. I've gone along with a torch and seen them do it, with his going in and out of hers. They hate it when I turn the torch on. You ought to come with me one night.'

I never did. I was too shocked by the idea.

'Hmm… Birds and Bees, so that's what they called it', I said to myself.

About the same time, my cousin Geoffrey who lived at Crewkerne and went to the same prep school came across some *Health & Efficiency* magazines in an old, cobwebby shed which we opened in an overgrown garden behind the Bridport Hotel. They were billed on the front cover as the world's leading 'naturist' journal established in 1900. The site of the bare-breasted women in sporting poses, playing tennis or diving into a lake, was very exciting and we eagerly flicked through the dusty and faded magazines. It promoted nudism in the open-air. But I knew it was strictly forbidden. We had broken into someone else's property and discovered a terrible secret. We were moreover 'Trespassing' and could, as the signs said, be 'Prosecuted.' I thought of the dire consequences of the policeman's hand on my shoulder and of being shut up for an indeterminate period behind bars.

'We must leave these here and never tell anyone', I said to my cousin.

'We can take a couple, no one would notice', he replied.

'No. We must leave them all here', I insisted. 'We could get into real trouble. If anyone found out, we would be prosecuted for breaking in and taking someone's property…'

We heard a noise at the far end of the long garden and dropped the magazines and ran, without closing the door of the shed. Back on the safe ground of the hotel, I made my cousin promise that he would never tell anyone what we had done or found.

A few weeks later, we were in a classroom at Etonhurst during a maths lessons. I was at the front of the class and my cousin at the back. There were giggles in the back row and the master, a tall man with thinning dark hair, a pallid face and long fingernails, marched to the back of the class and grabbed something which my cousin was trying to put it into his desk. He held it up – it was the *Health & Efficiency* magazine! The rest of us were saved by the school bell.

I was worried about what was going to happen to my cousin but relieved that I wasn't involved. Or at least, I thought so. In the middle of the next history lesson, I was called down to the headmaster's study. It was a large sunny room with dark wooden panels and a long desk. The old Headmaster always wore his gown over a tweed jacket with leather patches. His study smelt of sweat, pipe tobacco and dust. My cousin was red-faced and looking down at his feet, simpering. I noticed that one of his shoelaces was undone.

The offending magazine was on the desk. All those jolly bare-breasted ladies having fun in the open air were now in the crabby and balding headmaster's clutches. He pulled is academic gown around him like armour and lifted the offending magazine up and said:

'Did you or did you not go with this boy to take this magazine?'

'No, sir.'

'He tells me that you found it together.'

'That's true but I didn't take it, honestly I didn't, sir!'

Health and Efficiency

'That's enough, Marshall. I don't believe you. I'm now going to teach you a lesson you won't forget. Let me tell you that you don't trespass on other people's land and take their private property. I shall have to be cruel to be kind. You will eventually thank me for this. Now bend over, Marshall!'

I had been hit before but never for so hard and for so long. I counted ten swipes with the thin cane.

As I got up, my bottom stinging unbearably, tears burst into my eyes but I repressed them with all my might. The headmaster had a large vein thumping on the side of his hairy neck and his face was bright red.

We left together. I couldn't believe what my cousin had done. I was more indignant at his betrayal – snitching on me – than with the punishment which I felt was in some way deserved. Not only had he broken his promise not to return to the shed, but he had broken the most important rule of our school days – however great the injustice, however severe the bullying, it was the golden rule, the supreme moral principle, that you never sneaked on your fellows. It was some time before we became friends again and went out together on our escapades.

But worse was to follow. I had never felt at ease with the maths teacher. He seemed particularly friendly to me but I felt he was always creepy. Once he called me to his desk in the classroom while the other boys had their heads down doing calculations – or rather trying to do them. As I stood there in my shorts, he put his soft hand on my leg and slowly worked it upwards. I hated the feeling and quickly stood away. I made sure that I never got into his reach again. He still tried it on with other boys.

School and home had always been kept rigidly apart and that suited me perfectly. Imagine my horror when I came home one day from the beach, to find the maths teacher with my mother in the front room. Sitting on the sofa, she was trying to look concerned. Obviously something very serious had happened.

The master went over the whole magazine affair with my mother, using the word 'pornography' which I didn't understand and the phrase 'breaking into private property' which I did. My mother listened gravely, and politely offered him more tea and biscuits. I kept quiet, my head down.

When he asked me what I had to say, I simply replied 'Sorry, sir.' At last, he got up, put on his heavy raincoat and left. What a relief!

'Don't worry, dear', she said, afterwards, laughing. 'Boys will be boys. But you shouldn't really go poking about in other people's sheds!'

And that was that – except that by making such a mountain out of a molehill the master could have ensured that I would forever unconsciously associate sex with guilt and punishment. He could also have defined me as anti-social criminal for life. Fortunately, my mother's cheerful response dispelled the clouds and the incident mainly confirmed my dislike of hypocrisy. I still enjoyed a copy of *Health & Efficiency* when I came across one. But it wasn't in the shed in the next-door garden, for soon after it was firmly locked with a new padlock. I only hope the owner's wife never found out.

My mother took 'her boys' on 'outings' regularly along the promenade. The first was to the Esplanade Theatre where my mother – as an amateur chorus girl – had once high kicked in fishnet stockings. As a young lad I did not enjoy particularly the 'variety shows' which usually consisted of an entertainment made up of a variety of acts including musical performances, comedy sketches, magicians, acrobats, jugglers, ventriloquists with dolls, incomprehensible jokes, popular songs and slapstick humour. I enjoyed the mystique of the theatre though, with its draped lights and warmth and bustle. Once outside, I loved to hear the noise of the sea crashing on the shingle.

However, the outing which I most enjoyed was going with my brother and mother (dressed in a pretty frock) along the promenade to the pier in high season. On the way she would buy a cornet at Macari's, an 'ice-cream parlour' run by an Italian family. On the pier we would go into the Entertainments Arcade where she would change some money and give each of us many large pennies to use as we pleased on the machines. Our excitement held no bounds as we tried to extract a trinket from a gaudy pile behind glass with a miniature crane, bet on mechanical horse races, or to multiply our pennies in machines depicting Hollywood film stars like Ava Gardner, Jane Russell and Gary Grant. When I was tall enough to reach it, 'What the Butler Saw' was a revelation, although it eventually dimmed with the jerky repetition of a man looking through a key hole at a women undressing only to reveal her high laced boots, frilly underwear and tight, wasp-like corsets.

What I found most intriguing, however, was seeing at the end of the pier a chained man in swimming trunks put in a sack with a large padlock. He was then immersed into a tank. Bubbles came out of the sack which he pushed in all directions. Then after what seemed an age the man emerged triumphant, swam to the surface gulping in the air to tumultuous applause, including mine. He looked very red in the face. Perhaps it hadn't worked out as he had expected.

A third outing, which only lasted a couple of years, was a trip on the train to the Victoria Palace where we saw a matinee performance by the Crazy Gang. My mother laughed out loud at the antics of the comedians, which included Bud Flannigan and Chesney Allen, but I did not find them very funny. I was probably too young for their wartime humour. Even so, I loved the journey there, watching the steam and smoke coming out of the locomotive, hearing the whistle of the guard as he waved his green flag, and the rhythm and noise of the train as it sped over the tracks.

10
TRAVELS WITH
MY UNCLE

One good thing about my Uncle Al was that he would take Michael and me on holidays. He always called us 'Boys' and I suspected he was disappointed to have only one daughter Lindsay. He regularly invited us to his home. I was first introduced to North Wales visiting his hotel at Llandudno Junction next to the railway track and the old white suspension bridge which crossed the estuary and led to Conwy Castle.

When I was about eight, I went up to his hotel one Christmas with my brother, mother and Nanna in my Pop's new Rover car. My mother had poured a pan of boiling oil over her leg and it was still in a bandage up to her knee which she had to keep straight. My brother and I squeezed with her in the back of the car which was full of Christmas presents and luggage. It was not very comfortable and the journey was very long and very cold.

Coming down a steep hill at dusk it began to snow, with thick flakes swept away by the overworked windscreen wipers and settling on the road in front. My grandfather, who suffered from nerves, became worried and his anxiety soon spread to the back of the car.

'We will be soon stuck in the snow and what shall we do then?' Pop said.

As usual, my Nanna imperiously dismissed his fears and told him to 'Drive On.'

Fortunately, we arrived in Shrewsbury before the road had become impassable and put up at an old Coaching Inn. The only room available for us had a sunken four-poster bed in a dingy back room with dark, heavy beams. Since my brother, two and half years older, regularly fought with me, my mother separated us with a feather bolster in the middle of the bed. I fell asleep in the damp sheets thinking of the snowflakes falling over the hushed landscape of the lit-up hedge rows and dark snow-strewn fields beyond.

Next day the sun came out, the roads had been cleared and the snow was beginning to melt. We pressed on to my uncle's hotel in Llandudno Junction. We were welcomed warmly as usual by my Aunt Barbie while my cousin Lindsay, a year younger than I, did not know how to react to the sudden irruption of her first cousins.

My uncle was serving drinks. He had an African grey parrot in the public bar which used to say 'Good Boy' over and over again. It also had 'Barbie' in its repertoire and in addition the local customers had taught it some Welsh. Although he was irredeemably English the locals liked my uncle because his beer was good and he allowed a 'lock in' after time was called. Even the local constable used to knock at the back door for a pint or two while doing his rounds. I only later found out that they had taught the parrot to say:

'Twll din bob sais!' ('All Englishmen are arseholes!').

My uncle told me that in the autumn when there was little moon some of his customers used to row out in the estuary at night in order to catch the salmon which were going up the river Conwy to spawn. They regularly brought him a salmon, coming in for a few pints before they went to bed. But their method even then seemed cruel and unfair. They would pull behind their boats a small raft of big hooks strapped underneath to foul catch the salmon in the back as they rose. They wanted to get one over the local English Bailiff as much as catch fish.

My uncle and aunt had a boxer puppy which they called Sparky. My brother and I used to play with him for hours in a long corridor at the top of the hotel. One of us would hold him at one end of the corridor while the other would be at the opposite end. He would be released and then, bounding along the corridor and up a few stairs, he would pounce on the boy lying crouched on the floor with his arms around his head. His sharp teeth would bite into my ears; he would slobber over my hair; and I loved it and laughed.

One evening I had a bath off the corridor which was deserted. I got into the deep, old tub in shallow tepid water for the hot water had soon run out. I then realised that for some reason I had locked myself in without any clothes. The water became colder and colder – even colder at Christmas without any central heating. I shouted and shouted but no one heard me. What was I to do? I was shivering and unable to open the door. The cold water was slightly warmer than outside so I got back in the bath but could not stop my shivers which grew worse. Eventually my mother came to find me, having long forgotten me whilst having a drink or two in the warm bar below. I had almost died of hypothermia upstairs.

My mother later told me that one evening she had been drinking with Barbie well after time and had set off with a group (under the full moon) to climb nearby Snowdon – at 3000 feet the largest mountain in Wales and England. It was about 30 miles away. Stumbling as they walked, they soon became very cold and did not get very far. It must have been very beautiful up the mountain under the moon with this merry party, the better for drink, stumbling on the path amongst the silvery rocks.

On a rare day off, Barbie took Michael and me around Conwy Castle – crossing the white suspension bridge opposite the hotel. It was a grey Castle with large towers, not dissimilar to the ones I used to build on Bognor sands. It was built in the 13th century by Edward I to hold down the Welsh. After a walk on the ramparts from which we could see the estuary and the land stretch out before us, she showed us 'the smallest house in Great Britain' on the quay just outside the castle. Set in a terrace, it consisted of only one room. It was indeed very small, more fit for a bent old lady, I thought at the time, than the local fisherman who lived there with his family and who couldn't even stand up in his own home.

My greatest experience however was when my uncle arranged with a regular in his public bar – a steam train driver for British Rail – to take me on board his steam train foot plate. It was unbelievably exciting for an eight-year-old boy to walk along the track to the station at Llandudno Junction where the huge, grinning man with his face smeared in grease and soot picked me up and put me into his cab. It was full of strange instruments. His even blacker assistant shovelled coal into the fiery red furnace. After the whistle of the smart guard on the platform and much shaking of his green flag, we moved off slowly after a long hoot which expelled steam. The great metal wheels soon picked up speed. Our destination was Holyhead, the main ferry port to Dun Laoghaire near Dublin in the Republic of Ireland.

It seems that the driver was famous for going round the long bend of the track opposite my uncle's hotel at great speed. He leaned out of the cab to wave at my family as we sped past in a welter of smoke and steam. He was reputed to have the record for the fastest time on the North Wales railway track. He told me to sit quietly on a metal seat on one side near the instruments. The countryside of a patchwork of green fields and hedges rushed by.

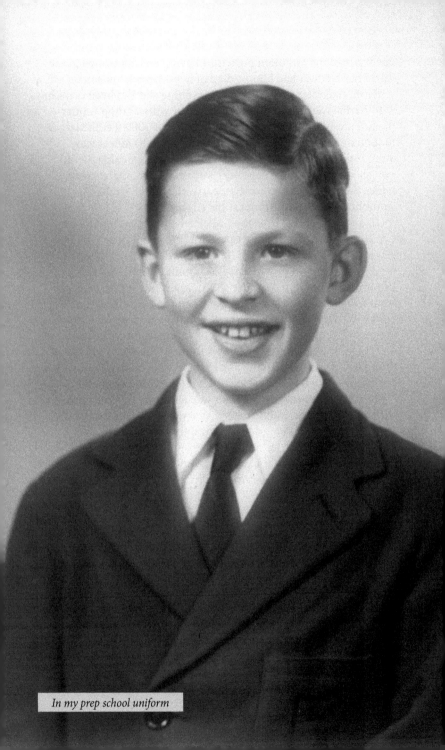

In my prep school uniform

The metal plates below me twisted and turned as the assistant shovelled in more coal. I wanted to go even faster. By the time we reached Holyhead and turned round it was already dark, and the coal-smeared men tending the huge red furnace seemed like figures out of hell. But I was in very heaven until a speck of coal from the fire lodged itself in my eye. Water poured out of it and my rubbing only made it worse.

By the time we had reached the junction, my eye was extremely painful and virtually closed. The driver then gave me a lift back to the hotel on his powerful shoulders. It was pitch black by now and I could see little in the dark night and I almost fell asleep, lulled by the regular crunch of his boots on the stones at the side of the track, and by his strong smell of leather, coal and sweat. We eventually arrived at the pub where he downed a couple of pints in quick succession in the brightly lit bar, 'to lay the dust' as he put it.

My uncle was clearly worried by my swollen and closed eye. I went into the kitchen with my aunt and he returned with a short, fat doctor with balding hair who had been drinking in the lounge bar. His bad breath smelt of drink.

In a strong Welsh accent, he said 'Now what have we got here – a speck of coal dust in the boy's eye. I know exactly what to do! '

He asked my uncle for some HP sauce and a matchstick. He then rolled up my top eyelid with the matchstick and poured in some of the dark, hot sauce into my eye. It hurt terribly and my eye ran profusely. He then pulled out a dirty handkerchief from his pocket and wetting a rolled corner in his mouth, he lunged at my eye until he got out the piece of coal.

'There it is', he said, holding his handkerchief up to the light. 'I think I deserve another whisky for that!'

I was sent to bed with a painful eye and that night and many nights afterwards I dreamed of driving a steam train fast on a long bend in the dark, the chimney belching smoke and the red furnace roaring. The distant noise of the trains shunting in the junction was strangely reassuring; if I woke up in the middle of the night, I listened to it in my warm bed and soon fell asleep.

Since my brother and I made so much noise together, particularly as we were both so competitive, my Auntie Barbie and Uncle Al decided to take only one of us on holiday every other year. When I was very young – about nine years old – they took me together with my grandparents and cousin Lindy on an old longboat on the canals. It poured with rain most of the time but I loved it, especially the hedges and trees and fields passing slowly by. I would jump off the longboat on to the towpath in order to open the gates of the locks. I was even able, with great effort, to raise the heavy sluices with a large 'key' like a heavy bent metal rod. The locks going up a hill were a particular challenge and delight.

It was permanently damp on board but I did not mind. The only heating we had was a paraffin stove which only increased the condensation inside the boat. I once went on board after a lock to see my grandfather sitting over the stove trying to dry Nanna's voluminous corsets. It was that bad.

We went up the Oxford Canal and after many locks eventually went through the long, dark Harewell Tunnel on the Trent and Mersey Canal. The canal men used to lie on their backs and moved their barge forward by pushing against the roofs with their heavy hobnail boots. Their horses – which normally towed them – would then be taken over the hill to meet them at the other end of the tunnel.

My uncle frightened me by saying that the disused neighbouring canal was haunted by the ghost of a murdered woman whose head was chopped off and her body dumped in the cold, dark waters of the canal. I was pleased to come out into the bright sun and see once again the green hedgerows and fields around me in the soft rain.

We then made our way up the Coventry Canal where our engine conked out in the city. Since he did not want to jump into the filthy water of the canal which had come to a dead-end, my uncle paid for a young man to go over the side. He came up with a long piece of barbed wire which had wrapped itself around the propeller. At least I was able to take shelter from the cold, driving rain in the new Coventry Cathedral which was attached to the old bombed-out mediaeval cathedral.

As always, my uncle got one of his 'boys' to do his dirty work. I never saw him walk in the grey streets of the 'industrial North' unless he was forced to. So one rainy Sunday morning he drew a rough map on a piece of paper and sent me to the town in order to buy his daily packet of fags. It was wet and misty but I managed to find my way to the local newsagent early in the morning. Using the map on the piece of paper to come back to the canal was not so easy and I soon got lost. I thought they might leave me behind and I began to sob. A middle-aged man with a flat cap and long raincoat saw me and came over to ask:

'What's the trouble, young fella?' he said in a strange but friendly accent. 'I've got a boy about your age.'

I showed him the map and told him I was looking for our boat on the canal. He laughed and said:

'You've been reading the map the same way to get from the canal to the newsagents. To get back you need to go in the opposite direction! Don't worry, I'll show you the way.'

And he took a back way through the empty, wet streets to the canal. It was a huge relief to see our boat again. I had learnt a lesson the hard way in elementary map reading.

My Uncle Al also took me on camping trips down through France, and introduced me to the delights of French cooking in roadside Les Routiers (I loved the *petit pois* and *pommes frites*). I had my first yoghurt in a glass pot and loved it. He spoke good French and encouraged my first attempts at the language.

His love of cars, caravans and boats all came together when he took me once with his wife Barbie, his daughter Lindy and a chubby friend of hers called Maureen all the way through France pulling a caravan cum boat to the Mediterranean. He sat in the front of an old Land Rover with Barbie and I sat with the other two girls on deckchairs on the metal floor in the back. It was not only extremely uncomfortable when we went over bumps and potholes but was also extremely dangerous when we swerved side to side around corners.

I could see up the legs of the girls who were a year younger than I was. I was intrigued by their flashing thighs and white knickers as we bumped around on our deckchairs in the back of the Land Rover. As I was so young, my sexuality had only been partially awakened. Lindy was after all my first cousin and I treated her like a younger sister.

I found my aunt more attractive, with her blonde hair, her slightly plump body, her low necklines showing the top of her breasts, brightly painted red toe nails, and soft caressing touch. On one occasion I had an overpowering desire to hold her hand and kiss her. 'But she's my aunt, for God's sake', I thought, 'how could I!?'

We eventually arrived in Sète and went to the shore of a salty lagoon called the Etang de Thau. Along its shores it had pink flamingos (which I had never seen before) and it was full of oyster and mussels beds with old nets sticking up on poles. We launched the boat/caravan on the murky, salty water and poodled around, driven by an old Seagull outboard attached to the stern.

I liked the spa town of Balaruc-les-Bains by the Mediterranean where we did our shopping; I would break off and eat the end of the morning's baguette which was said to bring luck. The holiday was not a great success – my uncle and aunt were not getting on very well. While my uncle and I liked the idea of using the amphibian, the girls, surveying the featureless wasteland, insisted that we spent the rest of the holiday on dry land in camping sites with facilities. We cut our stay short and much to my dismay came home after a week or so. I was greatly disappointed. It was not long afterwards that my uncle sold the 'boat' having previously kept it on the river Arun near Amberley in West Sussex.

The greatest journey that my brother and I undertook with our uncle, however, was when we sped through France and Spain to Portugal in his Ford Zephyr. I was eleven years old and my brother was thirteen. We crossed into France by ferry from Newhaven to Dieppe and then drove down to the Spanish border as quickly as possible. My uncle hated stopping and even when we wanted to have a pee he carried on for some time before letting us out of the car. Lunch was a quick stop and consisted invariably of a delicious fresh baguette and a *Vache qui Rit* triangular portion of cheese (my brain went dizzy at the idea of infinity when it was pointed out that the cow on the round packet had earrings of the same packet). We also had a large warm tomato each, and, if we were lucky, a fresh, juicy peach.

One day I saw a lorry back up on the bank of a river and then the driver pulled a lever to slide thousands of ripe peaches into the swirling water. I was horrified and couldn't believe it.

'It's the market', my uncle explained. 'There have been too many peaches this year and the market is swamped. The cost of transporting them is greater than what the farmers would get in the market. The farmers dump the peaches to make the prices go up.'

'Why can't they just ask people to come and help themselves? Why spoil them after all that effort in growing them.'

'It's capitalism', he said, as if that explained all.

If that were capitalism, I felt that there must be something seriously wrong with it. The more I learned about my uncle's version of economics, the more unfair and absurd it appeared. Why couldn't those beautiful, ripe, golden, juicy peaches be given to the needy and poor. There were plenty of them.

We put up our old, musty ex-Army waxed canvas tent in a campsite at dusk. In the tent, my uncle slept in a large canvas bed with wooden frames which towered over us. We would have to sleep on the hard ground. At night, he would often under the light of a torch put on coloured glasses – 3D glasses he called them – and get out a French girlie magazine.

Whenever we arrived at a campsite I would first look around me, often with a wooden peg in my hand. It was good to breathe in fresh air, away from the hot car on the noisy and dusty road. But my uncle would say impatiently, going red in the face:

'What do you think you're doing?'

'Taking it all in…'

'Well, stop daydreaming, boy, and get on with putting up the tent!'

The phrase seemed to irritate him deeply, for whenever I stopped to look at the view, he would say: 'I suppose you're taking it all in again!'

The day we crossed into Spain, my uncle even refused to stop for lunch.

'We're behind time', he said.

'What time? We're meant to be on holiday!' my brother said.

'We're behind our average. By now I should have covered at least another 100 miles.'

By brother and I were by now gasping from thirst. The only thing we had in the wide car was a melon which he had bought at the roadside the day before. But we had no knife to open it; the knives were in the boot and my uncle was not going to stop to let us get one. We were reduced to trying to open it with a collar stiffener but since the melon was ripe we managed to cut into its sweet and succulent flesh. It was paradise.

The dictator Franco was still in charge in the late fifties in Spain and I couldn't believe the differences between the rich and the poor. On the baking, yellow central plains we could see emaciated donkeys pulling stones over scattered wheat and peasants throwing the crushed grain in the air to separate it from the chaff. Some people were still living in caves.

Rather than visit the painting collections of the Prado in Madrid, my uncle took us to the royal palace of El Escorial to see the vast memorial Franco had built to the fascists in the 'Valley of the Fallen' to commemorate their victory in the Spanish Civil War. There were long terraces leading up to the entrance of the building which was built in the side of a mountain and crowned with a huge cross. It was full of garish religious icons and smelt sickly of incense. He didn't feel it necessary to mention the tyrannical origins of Franco's dictatorship. He just seemed to be impressed by the sumptuousness of the monument. For me, it felt dead and I was pleased to come out in the hot sun and fresh air.

We had our own experience of grandeur when we swopped the stony ground of the tent for a posada State hotel in an ancient castle although. The experience was rather marred, however, by my uncle saying repeatedly how cheap it was.

One night we camped in a wild and remote spot amongst scattered trees on the banks of the higher reaches of the river Tagus. The splash of a nearby waterfall combined with the dry ticking of the cicadas. At dusk the midges began to bite. We made a fire from the bone dry wood and cooked a meal. The stars began to stud the clear sky. As my uncle lit up a cigarette, a broken twig in the distance suggested that some creature was nearby. He picked up a torch and shone it in the direction of the noise. By a thorny bush, I could just make out the silhouette of a man. He slowly walked towards us. I could see my uncle looking worried.

'Act normal', he whispered. 'I'll try and make him go away.'

The colour had drained out of my uncle's face. What did 'act normal' really mean? I just kept my head down and looked at the fire.

The man had a thin, sunburnt, lined face. He had straggly hair, stubble on his chin and looked a bit menacing. His clothes were worn and dirty. He squatted by the fire and warmed his gnarled hands against the flames. The distant murmur of the waterfall became a roar.

My uncle was visibly shaken by his sudden appearance. With a gesture the newcomer asked for a cigarette from my uncle. He offered him a beer and a cigarette which he took. He remained silent, looking intensely at the flames. I noticed a bead of sweat appear on my uncle's brow. When the uninvited guest had finished after what seemed an age, he made a sign for another cigarette. My uncle got up and went into the tent; while he was gone the man winked at us. He came back with two packets of cigarettes and gave them to him and then made a sign that it was time for us to go to bed. Our visitor got the message, said something in a rough accent, gave a gesture of thanks and disappeared into the dark as silently as he had come.

'Phew', my uncle said, visibly shaken. 'That was a lucky escape. No one knows we're here. The guacho could have knifed me and pushed my body over the waterfall and taken everything. I don't know what would have happened to you boys! He might come back tonight so let's go to bed now and wake me up if you hear any unusual noise…'

'Who did you think he was?' I asked.

'I don't know. Probably a shepherd.'

I thought of him stealthily coming back and slitting my uncle's throat; I had no idea what he might do to my brother and me afterwards. But listening out for strange noises I soon fell asleep to the distant rumble of the waterfall.

When suddenly I woke up the sun was out, the tent was very hot and my uncle was snoring on his camp bed. I got out of the tent to see the dead embers of the fire and beyond the swirling green river a glorious red sun was coming over the horizon. We were safe.

I realised afterwards that our unexpected night visitor was probably lonely and had been simply attracted by our fire. No doubt he would have shared his rough bread, goats' cheese, onions and tomatoes if we had been lost in the bush.

My uncle sped on to Lisbon, with all of us sitting on the front seat of his Zephyr. He talked about the 'birds and bees' to my elder brother – my uncle was obsessed with sex but probably because he did not get enough of it. He said that I was too young to understand, but I listened intently and knew enough about the subject to half understand what he said and to feel strangely excited by it all.

In Lisbon we met up with my aunt and cousin, who had come by boat from England. We booked into a guest house in Cascais by the main road overlooking the sea. The owner was a middle-aged, fussy English woman and the food was horrible. It mainly consisted of boiled potatoes and octopus which I had never tasted before and which seemed like chewing rubber. We couldn't even go on the beach. We had to content ourselves with days out in the car. Only Black Horse Square in the centre of Lisbon seemed interesting because there were lots of pigeons which came to you as you sat on a bench.

One evening, my aunt went to see an old friend whom she had met when he was a boarder in a school in Sussex. She dragged along my uncle. Her childhood friend had apparently inherited a large estate from his father and made a famous wine from the grapes. My aunt said that they had had an elaborate meal on the veranda of his house and afterwards listened to some Fado music, the traditional Portuguese music. He had especially hired for the occasion one of the most famous guitarists and singers. My aunt found the whole evening enchanting but my uncle gave his grumpy verdict the next morning:

'It was boring, really dreary. I don't know why they go on about such music! If that's the best Portuguese music you can hear, it's not for me. It sounded like a box of jangled nerves!'

I could see why my aunt was fed up with him.

11
BOARDING SCHOOL

I went to a boarding grammar school in Steyning, West Sussex, following my brother. My uncle thought it was not good for me to be at home with two women, my mother and grandmother, and an ailing grandfather.

'You need male influence', he said, 'when growing up.'

Why this was the case, I could never understand. I had enough of male influence with my brother, grandfather and him around me but in matters of finance and education his views always prevailed in our family. My grandmother doted on her only son. No one dared to oppose him. Being a dayboy (as he had been at the nearby Chichester High School for Boys, only six miles away) would have been fine for me. It would have meant that I would have had local friends and not suffered the organised cruelty of a traditional boarding school.

So having just squeezed past the necessary exam and having an interview with the headmaster, I was sent to Steyning Grammar School about an hour's ride in the car away. The headmaster, a severe-looking bald man with thick horn-rimmed glasses, asked me sternly:

'Where is the Weald, boy?'

'I'm sorry Sir but I come from Bognor Regis. We don't have a Weald over there', I replied, thinking that I had blown it.

He explained that the Weald was the flat land to the North beyond the chalk Downs. In fact the word comes from the Old English word for 'Forest' with a later version meaning 'Wild' since much of the area had been covered by trees. Despite my ignorance, he still let me in, probably because I had an older brother at the school.

I arrived having just passed my 12th birthday in 1958. When I left for the first time in my grandfather's large Vauxhall car and said goodbye to my mother it could have been going to the other side of the moon. At least my brother Michael was with me. I managed to hold back my tears until I was under my blankets in my new dormitory – with about eight other boys – in the old part of the ancient school.

My knowledge of boarding school was not inclined to make me like it. My brother told me that he had been 'bog-washed' for no apparent reason. That is to say, he was turned upside down, his head put in a toilet and the chain pulled. A diminutive fellow of 11, one of his dormitory captains had tried to rape him.

In the meantime my grandmother found at home that one of the pullovers she had made for my brother was ripped. He refused to say who had done it, following the code of not sneaking on a fellow pupil whatever the provocation. She told the matron, a kind, good-looking Swedish woman whose fiancé had been killed in the War. It was eventually established that older boys had ripped his pullover.

No wonder Michael once ran away from home one rainy autumn night to avoid going back to school. Although I was only nine I went off into the wild night to look for him, first in the shelters on the promenade and then along the empty, windswept street a block away. I eventually found him huddling and sobbing amongst some leaves at the entrance of a jeweller's shop.

'Everyone is worried about you. Pop is really upset.' I managed to persuade him to come home. He eventually decided to go off to the dreaded school.

But he became friendly with some stronger boys of his year who defended him from attack and he grew stronger himself. When I went to school I hardly saw him because of the rigid differences between the years but at least he was there if I needed him. Not surprisingly, he was called Marshall I and I was called Marshall II in the daily roll calls.

The school was set in Steyning, a picturesque village nestling in the rolling hills of the chalk Downs in West Sussex. It was about five miles or twenty minutes north of Shoreham-by-Sea by the steam train which still operated along the branch line to Horsham. On market days, the farmers would come in with their animals, Sussex burr, flat caps, old sports jackets, leather gaiters and hobnail boots.

Its High Street had several tea rooms with dark oak beams which we were allowed to visit if we had enough money or if we were taken there by our parents on a rare visit. There was also a family grocer's under a tall clock tower in the middle of the High Street. In the tiny tuck shop opposite the Old School in Church Road the boys would trick an old lady (sweet in more ways than one) by sending her into the back of the shop while helping

Steyning Grammar School, old entrance

themselves in the front. I instinctively felt that this was wrong and never did it myself.

The Grammar School itself was endowed in 1614, two years before Shakespeare's death, by a man called William Holland. Holland was born in Steyning and had three times been elected Mayor of Chichester. It had at that time less than 50 pupils and one master. In the eighteenth and early nineteenth century the school declined to such an extent that there was barely one pupil per year. The school was revived in the nineteenth century and taken over by the County Council in 1912 but remained, to my permanent consternation, a single sex school.

Its main entrance was through a large ornate arch in the narrow Church Street, up stones steps worn by generations of reluctant feet. It should have read over its heavy doors: 'Abandon Hope all ye that enter here.' Life at boarding school proved to be nasty, brutish and long for the most part. Up the steps was a landing which led into large rooms with huge oak beams, a tower and a second floor. It was called 'Brotherhood House.' The main room where the boarders met for the daily roll call, to make sure none had absconded, as well as evening prayers, was called 'Big School.' It had great dark beams and on the whitewashed walls were wooden plaques with the names of those pupils who had died in the First and Second World Wars.

Traditions had hardly changed over the centuries and it was run very much on the lines of a minor nineteenth-century public school. The boarders tended to be the children of armed service families, broken families (as in my case) or of parents who just didn't want their children at home. One came in a Rolls Royce but most in the new cars of the professional middle classes.

The school had about 100 boarders who made up members of Holland House and about 300 dayboys, many from the surrounding villages and towns. The boarders called them 'day bugs.' The school was devoted to producing 'good characters', that is to say, those who are willing to do what they are told and then tell others what to do. It was not an ideal training ground for those who wanted to think and act independently like myself. On the other hand, it was perfect for preparing the sons of the middle classes to be servants and rulers and administrators of the empire. The fact that the sun was setting fast on the British Empire at the time seemed to have entirely bypassed the boarding school in Steyning.

The first-year boarders would stay in the old part of 'Brotherhood House' for the first year. Each year you were moved to a different house which was scattered in a large area which had once contained family houses and gardens. You moved from 'Upper' or 'Long Dorm' in the Old School to Coombe Court, then to 'Mid Dorm' and finally to Wykeham House.

In my first year I followed my brother and was sent to 'Upper Dorm.' Down some wooden steps there was 'Long Dorm' where most of the first-year pupils stayed and who, when they could, sent a raiding party to attack us above them.

There were about half a dozen of us in a narrow room at the top of the house with leaded windows. We slept in narrow beds, with horse hair mattresses which sank in the middle, which were divided from each other only by a small cupboard. The dormitory captain's bed was near the entrance. I made friends with Charles Linford, the son of an officer in the Army who was stationed abroad. I also had a sparring relationship with a boy called Richard Stone ('Stoner') whose parents were artists in nearby Shoreham. We were about equal strength and periodically had serious fights together. On one occasion we slogged at each other for a couple of hours on the sports field. We retired exhausted but not before I had bloodied his lip and he had given me such a blow on the nose that he probably broke it. As I grew up it became noticeably bent; I used to joke that as it turned to the right, I moved to the left.

I was spared the delights of being bog-washed, but the dormitory captain would beat me with the metal spikes of his running shoes or whip me with metal-tipped football laces. One evening, with the help of the dormitory captain from 'Long Dorm' below, they forced me to climb – without my trouser bottoms of my pyjamas on – to one of the old oak beams. They then tied my ankles around it with a piece of rope and pulled me along, with the splintered, iron-hard wood cutting into my thighs. Why they did this I do not know, but it was probably for the fun of it. It was akin to torture.

The school with its unchecked brutality was undoubtedly a training ground for those who might engage in physical, mental and emotional torture later on in life. No wonder those who had gone to British boarding schools could command their men to shoot protesting crowds in Africa and India without batting an eyelid. They had been well-trained to witness, if not enjoy, the infliction of suffering on others.

At the same time, we had 'midnight feasts' of tins of fruit and evaporated milk but the delight of breaking the rules after 'lights-out' was more delicious than eating syrupy fruit cocktail. We climbed a ladder, for instance, which led up to the leaded window which was the fire exit onto the roof. We could easily have fallen to our deaths from the steep slate roof but I enjoyed the surreptitious pleasure of breaking the school rules. Nor did we refrain from having pillow fights when the captain wasn't around; or from chatting after 'lights out' until he came to bed in the corner near the heavy curtain which served as a door.

It was necessary to form uneasy alliances in order to ensure survival in this world of war of all against all. You normally kept with the group you started off with in the first year, especially as you tended to stay with them in different dormitories. In 'Upper Dorm' we stood together against the ring leader and his lieutenants of the larger 'Long Dorm' group below. Some pupils outside the main groups were left alone, while others were bullied mercilessly. The physically tough were generally left alone; the thicker ones were manipulated by the would-be leaders. Since I was of average build, I survived partly by fighting and partly through a way with words. My brother Michael used to say that we had 'the gift of the gab', which helped us to persuade others at school and which may partly explain why we both became writers later on.

I felt continually hungry at boarding school. At the village grocer's in the High Street, the thin owner (in a brown coat) and his wife (with thick arms and ample bosom) would sell me broken biscuits from a tin barrel, slabs of dates, and tins of Fussell's condensed milk. I also reluctantly filled up in the canteen on some revolting slices of bread called 'slogs' by the boys. These were large slabs of bread with a thick layer of whitish margarine covered in wet tea towels to stop them becoming too stale.

We could help ourselves to dark brown stewed tea in a large metal urn with a tap. It was said that it contained the chemical bromide to lessen our sex drive. The loose tea was put in a stocking to soak in the hot water. It was rumoured that this stocking was a cast-off of the old wrinkled cleaner who was cruelly called 'The Wart' and who suffered from varicose veins and had black hairs growing on her chin.

The best food I remember was a cheese, potato and onion bake served on Saturday night before the weekly cartoon and film. After the freedom of the afternoon walks on the Downs these were the highlights of the week. I never found the *Tom & Jerry* cartoons particularly funny. Perhaps the constant violence of the cartoon mirrored the life I was leading at boarding school too closely. But I appreciated the way the mouse sometimes got the better of the cat through guile and cunning.

The noise of the whirring projector and the flickering numbers counting down to the crow of the cock or the roar of the lion which announced the beginning of the main feature film were delightfully anticipatory. When it was interrupted by a change of reel or a sudden break in the film which needed a repair, it was a brutal shock to come back into the airless room with all the other boys shuffling and whispering in the gloom. But as soon as it was on again, we were off on another sleigh ride of the imagination and escapism from the daily grind of school. For suspense and intrigue, I particularly enjoyed the black-and-white *The Thirty Nine Steps* which took the hero fighting against German spies from London to a remote part of Scotland. *The Third Man* too was wonderfully atmospheric, following the lonely anti-hero through the dark, wet streets of Vienna.

I very much enjoyed *High Society*, a film in Technicolor about a popular jazz musician who tries to win back the affections of his ex-wife (Grace Kelly). Although about rich Americans, I liked it mainly because of the appearance of Louis Armstrong and his band. I also enjoyed *The Benny Goodman Story*, which showed the life of the great clarinetist who once put together a jazz quartet featuring my heroes Gene Krupa on drums, Teddy Wilson on piano and Lionel Hampton on vibes.

Jazz became one of my passions, perhaps because its expressive improvisation mirrored by own love of freedom in an oppressive school and partly because I unconsciously identified with the down-trodden black Americans who were its main players. It is much easier to appreciate the state of freedom – to make your own choices, for good or bad – when you do not have it and feel controlled and enslaved.

12
AGAINST THE GRAIN

Discipline and obedience at boarding school were enforced by systematic and organised violence. The headmaster could beat you, the prefects could beat you and the dormitory captains could also beat you. Having been beaten themselves, they saw nothing wrong with beating those weaker and younger than themselves. In short, everyone beat each other. The most important value inculcated was unquestioning obedience. The boys when they arrived were not inherently cruel or aggressive but the system encouraged these aspects to the extreme. And it was condoned by those in power.

If you ever queried anything or questioned authority, however tentatively, the immediate reply was:

'Marshall, do you want to be beaten for insubordination as well?'

The word 'insubordination' permanently rang in my ears. Insubordination was clearly one of my original sins.

If anyone complained about the widespread bullying, they were also beaten for having broken the first moral code among the boys that they don't sneak on each other. No doubt it was considered part of 'character' building. But what type of character? We may have been taught a degree of tough independence but it was at the expense of all-round emotional development. If you broke a school rule or did not obey someone in authority, you were beaten. The boarders were allowed to do virtually what they liked to each other.

In my second year, aged 13, we went to Coombe Court, a partly condemned building with a large garden which sloped away. Once we had to chase a donkey owned by the housemaster which had escaped and was ruining the carefully tended beds of the vegetable garden below. Half the house was condemned as dangerous and reportedly inhabited by ghosts, but we still climbed over the wooden barrier on the back stairs and explored the rooms empty except for mice droppings and cobwebs and splintered floor boards. We managed to sneak in without getting caught.

There was no heating in the dormitories except small cast iron electric heaters which hardly took off the chill. In winter, ice formed on the inside of the windows. You washed in cold water in basins in a room on the ground floor. You took all your clothes off in one go and jumped into bed in your pyjamas. In the morning, you could slip on vest, shirt, pullover and tie all in one piece.

The bullying continued. Soon after my arrival in Coombe Court some older boys grabbed me and blackened my balls with shoe polish and squeezed toothpaste on to the end of my penis – it was excruciating. I suppose it was some sort of initiation rite which all new boys had to undergo.

I was once locked by older boys in a trunk and left for what seemed half an hour. It was terrible in the dark, feeling so confined and unable to get out. It was a wonder that I did not develop a sense of claustrophobia for life. The experience no doubt fostered my love of open spaces and long views – something you could experience walking on the Downs.

The system of 'fagging' which had developed in British boarding schools operated in the second year. The only difference was that you called your 'fag' – the younger boy who was your servant – your 'slave.' In my case, my 'slave' was my cousin Christopher Fry in the year below. Christopher's home was a flat at Crewkerne, built by my grandparents in Bognor. He got off lightly and I only asked him to do things to keep up appearances. I sent him on a few errands to get some sweets or to clean my shoes, but soon I did not bother him. It was easier to do things for myself and the system seemed absurd and unjust like so many other things at school.

Most of our spare time in Coombe Court was spent in a bare room on the ground floor (which had a table for ping pong) or the cellars (where there were showers next to an ancient coke-fired boiler, a boot room, and an adjoining tuck box room). The tuck box, which you could lock, was the only personal space which was not invaded by others. It was considered a particularly heinous crime to break into one – apart from this and grassing on your mates, just about every other action was acceptable! My light brown wooden tuck box, which my mother bought for me in Brighton, had its corners protected by metal. It had a special smell, partly because it was kept in a damp cellar and partly because of the cake and mince pies which I brought from home and which I kept until the mildew formed on them. Their presence in my tuck box was more important than their taste, even though I felt constantly hungry between meals while at school.

I also loved the warm, homely smell of my socks knitted by my grandmother or mother before they were sent to the laundry. They were my last direct link with home.

My tuck box contained all my most precious possessions, especially the ones I did not want the other boys to take from me: weekly letters from home (which contained a sixpenny coin which I immediately spent on sweets), a penknife, a sheath knife, compass, bits of string, a broken watch, and as I grew older, contraband tie and trousers and shoes which I used when I escaped out of bounds.

After school we would often sit on our tuck boxes – again the only personal space – and eat sweets and occasionally scrap. It was in this damp, dark cellar, illuminated only by one grimy window, that one of the worst incidents of my school days took place. I looked on in disbelief, unable to stop it. To pass the time before the evening meal the leader of the 'Main Dorm' gang, and his henchmen, decided to pick on a thin boy who was constantly trying to ingratiate himself with them.

'Smart. Come here.'

The startled boy reluctantly got up from his tuck box. They pulled over a long, metal rubbish bin. I could see the dust mites dancing in a shaft of light.

'Get in there!' he said.

He stood up to his knees in the narrow bin on his own in the middle of the room surrounded by the seated boys. I could see some faces looking worried, others eager for some sport.

The ringleader then said:

'We've decided to put you on trial here today. What is your crime? For being a snotty-nosed, miserable little worm, that's what. What do you say in your defence?'

'That's not fair. I've done nothing wrong. Let me out of here…'

'You stay there until you confess.'

'Confess what? I'm innocent. I've done nothing wrong.'

'Yes, you have. You're a worm. Now say "I'm a worm" or I'll hit you.'

He went towards him with a stick.

The thirteen-year-old boy looked terrified. He began to cry.

'Stop crying, you snivelling cretin. Now say, "I'm a miserable worm".'

'All right, if that's what you want, I'm a worm.'

'A miserable worm.'

'A miserable worm. Are you happy now? Can I get out of here?', he sobbed.

'Not yet. We've got to decide on your punishment. What do you think boys? What does he deserve for being such a miserable worm?'

'Run around the house, naked', said one.

'Have his balls blackened', said another.

'Give him a hot and cold shower', said a third.

The last punishment was agreed upon. The boy was hauled out of the rubbish bin, forced to strip and made to run through a boiling shower and then a freezing cold one.

The room was full of steam. Most of the 'Long Dorm' gang were laughing, following their leader who urged Smart on with a stick. The thin lad was crying, his body bright red with the scolding. At last, the bell rang for dinner. The tormentors all ran off to eat, leaving the boy to get dressed as fast as possible without drying himself properly so that he would not be punished again for being late at dinner. He was simply guilty for being alive, for breathing the same air as everyone else.

On another occasion I had a close shave in Coombe Court. Peter Dawson (the son of an RAF officer and a young, attractive mother) joined in the third year and soon became a firm friend. We were in the lower dormitory – which opened out to the garden – with my friend Charles Linford as well as Peter Norman from Worthing who had also became a close friend. Peter Boulton-Lea, who played the piano and, unlike me, took a keen interest in the church, was also present.

Peter Dawson remembers that my brother and a friend of his rushed into our dormitory through the open French windows which gave onto wooden steps leading up from the garden. He then asked me to hide an air pistol. He had shot at a member of the public for some reason. Against my better judgement, I apparently decided to put it on my bed at the foot under my travel rug.

A few minutes after my brother and his friend had disappeared, Scragg – the feared headmaster – suddenly arrived himself through the French windows from the garden. Dawson told me that he appeared 'with a big smile on his face and uncharacteristically engaged us all in a friendly pre-lights out chat'. To our horror and dismay he sat down on the rug at the end of my bed.

'Hoping, desperately, that our blood-drained faces didn't give

Outside our dormitory in Coombe Court. I am standing on the front right, holding the railing, while Peter Dawson is on the front left, sitting on the steps

us away', he told me later, 'we tried to maintain a conversation (ironically, about the Second World War) for five minutes which seemed more like five hours'.

But he then suddenly got up and went out of the door. We all breathed a sigh of relief.

'It could possibly have been this episode which led to some people saying he was at times an insensitive arse!', my friend commented.

It was certainly typical of my brother to get me in serious trouble.

The fiery and much-feared headmaster John Scragg had been educated at Manchester Grammar School and went to Brasenose College in Oxford afterwards where he did a degree in Politics, Philosophy and Economics. He later did an Oxford diploma in anthropology and spent some time teaching in Accra on the Gold Coast (present-day Ghana) in West Africa. He did some ethnographical research upcountry and even contributed to the third 1950 edition of Philip Benton Brown's *Common Errors in Gold Coast English: Their Cause and Correction*, published by Macmillan. He certainly liked Correction, correcting our speech as well as our behaviour. And he remained an imperialist and colonialist as long as I knew him.

He caught malaria in West Africa which occasionally broke out when he was headmaster at our school. As a result, he retreated to his bed and handed over the responsibility for the school to his deputy. In general, he appeared to me an irritable, angry and frustrated man.

In the Second World War, he remained teaching although he did join the local Wiston Patrol of Auxiliaries – one of the units set up in case of a German invasion. He enjoyed fishing and would spend much of his time trying to land a fly on a saucer at the end of his immaculate lawn. He even beat me once for crossing the corner of his lawn, a corner about the size a folded table cloth, close to his study.

His way of relaxing was to go fly fishing on the well-stocked lake at Wiston House. There is a photograph of him holding up a pathetically small trout by its lake.

Most pupils I knew felt he was both intimidating and harsh as a headmaster. They kept clear of him as much as they could. He taught a version of muscular Christianity at every opportunity.

If he and the preachers were right, to hellfire I was surely bent. It certainly seemed a more exciting place than the heaven to which he and his upstanding cronies would go. The poets Milton and Blake would at least keep me company; I preferred their heretical Christianity to his sadistic version. By beating me for trivial things and encouraging the prefects and the dormitory captains to beat the boys under his absolute rule, he taught me a lifetime hatred of cruelty, violence and oppression.

For all the thousands of hours of homily (in assembly and after prayers) that I was obliged to listen to him, only one of his endless observations hit home:

'Boys, you'll find that in your life you'll make hundreds of acquaintances, but you are unlikely to make more than two or three real friends.'

I was shocked at the idea at the time – perhaps that was why I remembered it – for I felt I had lots of friends. But it was true that not many people developed life-long friends whom they could call upon in the most difficult situations. Fair-weather friends come by the dozen, true friends are rare.

Scragg insisted on prayers and hymns twice a day for the boarders – in the morning at general assembly and in the evening after 'prep' (we didn't call it homework for we had no home to go to) in Big School. On a Sunday morning we had to form a crocodile queue, two by two, and walk down the hill towards the Anglican (C.of E.) church dedicated to St Andrew and St Cuthman – located on the way to the railway station and cattle market. The thin, grey-haired vicar would drone on incomprehensibly; his pulpit was even hidden by a pillar. Yet it was a fine Norman Church, with light shining through its upper clear windows on the stone arches whose columns were capped by heads of people worn away by time. Its tower was square. Above all, it had brightly coloured stain-glass windows and an exterior wall of dressed flint which had been found in the local chalk of the Downs.

Some pupils, including my brother, wiled away the time during the interminable Sunday services by carving their names on the wooden pews. I used to look at the motes in the air in the rays of the sun which streamed down from the fine windows and daydream away without listening to the vicar or readings from the Bible.

In the evenings, we had another service, this time with the hymns accompanied by one of the pupils who often hit bum notes on the piano. And although I was 'stone deaf' (as I had been told in my primary school) and had to stand behind the big boys in the choir, I still liked to bellow out the hymns – probably because it was a release of the energy suppressed during the interminable services and assemblies with their meaningless pep-talks.

I was taught Christianity of the worst muscular kind. The lay preachers on a Sunday evening were even worse than the vicar in the morning, threatening divine punishment if we strayed from the straight and narrow. They talked about heaven and hell as if they were real places. The headmaster never seemed to tire of giving out the numbers from *Hymns Ancient and Modern*. He would beat you mercilessly and at the same time urge you to become a 'Christian Soldier.' When the Bishop of Chichester confirmed me into the Anglican Church by laying a soft, fat hand on my head in his cathedral it was the final straw.

The sermons at the church, coupled with the hypocritical Christianity of the headmaster and the lay preachers on Sunday evening, was enough to put me off that type of religion for life. It was a long time before I met a Christian who was not a hypocrite or worse.

How could they teach 'love your neighbour' and at the same time beat you for some minor transgression? Why was the church, which taught 'turning the other cheek', full of the tattered and faded flags of the Armed Forces? Why was the roll call of dead pupils in two World Wars – engraved on a plaque below the school device of an upstanding lion – so conspicuous and important? Why must I promise on my 'honour' to do 'my duty' to God and the Queen? Where was the love and forgiveness which the Sermon on the Mount taught?

I did not therefore imbibe the type of hypocritical Christian ethics which the headmaster and the preachers did their best to teach me but I did have a sense of justice and equality which I inherited from my mother at an earlier stage. I had a sense of fair play which I was taught on the football pitch and in cross-country running and I never knowingly cheated, either my fellow pupils, elderly shop owners, or in an exam.

13

THE DOWNS

I loved the South Downs which surrounded Steyning. The chalk hills with their dips and ridges went on for miles. On their tops, I deeply appreciated the play of light and shape, the sense of openness and uplift. But my gaze invariably turned to the blue and grey sea of the Channel below the green slopes. The inland view across the patchwork of fields and hedgerows and the occasional copses of the Weald showed the hand of generations of farmers who had carefully worked the land. But the sea was untameable, constantly changing but always itself – I associated this with freedom.

The Downs gave me a love of long views and a dislike of being hedged in. The countryside outside the school was our playground, our escape, our release. There you were not only exposed to the permanent forms of the natural world and the changing seasons, with summer sun and winter rains and winds, but could escape the constant surveillance and bullying at school.

Yet we could not walk wherever we liked for there were definite boundaries or 'bounds' as they were called. They were invisible yet every boarder knew where they were. They roughly formed a circle, with the diameter across about three miles from the school, from Chanctonbury Ring on a scarp in the Downs in the west to Upper Beeding beyond the oozy river Adur in the east. Woe betide anyone caught 'out of bounds'! If you were caught beyond this invisible boundary, defined by roads, woods, fields and paths, you could be severely beaten.

The walks every afternoon after school and at weekends were the most enjoyable experiences of my boarding school days. Oh what freedom to leave the confines of the school and the constant surveillance of the masters and prefects! Oh what bliss to explore the dark, secretive woods or to clamber up the grassy slopes of the ridges of the Downs where I would find wide-open spaces, soaring skies and views down to the sea! To stride or run along the white paths or cut across the springy grass was like flying into the air. In the summer the bright light brought a shimmering haze along the chalky and flinty tracks; in the winter the grass turned brown and the few trees were gaunt and angular, hurled and tossed by the bitter sea wind blowing up from the south west. I have since always associated nature and the countryside with relaxation and ease as well as life-enhancing energy. I've ever after felt more at home in the countryside, even at night, than in the city with its bright lights and hectic life.

I often went with my friends Charles Lynford and Peter Dawson. Later on Pete Norman would join me. I was fortunate in never having the embarrassment and awkwardness of not being able to find a friend to go out with like some other boys.

Watercourses and dens had an irresistible pull, the former to play in and the latter to be oneself in without the pressure of school. It was a great feeling to be hidden and in a small group of friends. We made camps in trees and found cosy dens in copses where we ate broken biscuits, sucked on tins of condensed milk and chomped through red apples.

The quickest way to reach the Downs was straight up a narrow track to the upper 'Horseshoe' which consisted of a curving hill of open grassland shaped like a horse's hoof around a deep hollow full of trees. Beyond the Horseshoe you reached the spine of the South Downs which led to Chanctonbury Ring to the west. The latter – which was visible from miles around – consisted of a great circle of beech trees growing on a spur. I was told that it was planted by a boy who walked to school from Storrington in the seventeenth century and planted trees to amuse himself. However, the Goring family of Wiston House below claim that one of their young members planted the circle of beech in 1760.

On the eastern side of the Horseshoe was a chalk cliff famous for its fossils, and we would chip away and find large sea snails or skeletons of fish. It was odd to think that this part of the high Downs had once been under the sea.

I found that the chalk broke away easily so decided, hidden from view by brambles, long grass, bushes and saplings, to burrow into the chalk to make a den above an old quarry. Every afternoon, a couple of friends and I went up there on our walk and began to tunnel a passage which we could crawl through for about a couple of yards. We then started to cut out a chamber, discarding the waste rather like badgers at their set. In the meantime, we started to stock our den with camping plates and cutlery. We put candles on rough shelves. It really felt like home, a hidden and secret place away from the prying eyes of boys and masters.

I liked the idea of playing as if we were living in the Stone Age. We whittled spears with our sheath knives and fashioned bows and used chipped flints for arrow heads. We even set snares by bending down a sapling, tying the end with a loop of brass wire (we had shifted to the Bronze Age) and weighing it down with a stone. If a rabbit got caught its struggling would release the stone and make the sapling swing up and break its neck. It did several times, but when we found a rabbit had been caught by its back paw and was half eaten by another animal we stopped setting traps. We didn't know what to do with the rabbits anyway.

All went well until one afternoon as I sat in the cave, there was a crack, a few pieces of chalk began to fall from the ceiling, and then a mighty whoosh as the passage collapsed. I was entombed inside! I felt I would have a slow, lingering death. I was too hidden away for my shouts to be heard by a passer-by on the track.

After the initial shock, I realised that in fact I was not in complete darkness and there was a chink of light just at the beginning of the collapsed passageway. I could breathe and there might be a way out. Trying to keep calm, I managed to open the chink into an orange size and then it fell in – enough for me to scramble out. I was covered in chalk dust but managed to shake and brush most of it off before going back to school without evoking too much suspicion. That was the last time we tried to burrow into chalk, or any other material. I was lucky to have escaped with my life; but it was the end of my tunnelling days.

One of my favourite walks was up Mouse Lane on the west side of the High Street of Steyning which had large banks and was covered over in tree branches. When it rained in winter and the trees were bare a stream ran down one side of the lane. We used to throw in small sticks or broken twigs high up the lane and raced each other to see which one reached the bottom first. They swirled, bobbed, dashed and often got stuck. In the summer the stream would be reduced to a trickle.

Creepers, as thick as a little finger, curled around the trees. We would cut the old ones off with a sheath knife, strip the peeling bark and smoke the inner core. It produced an acrid smoke, made us cough and soon went out, but when we couldn't afford any cigarettes they were all we could inhale while pretending to be older than our years.

They were no substitute however for the packet of five Woodbines which you could buy (along with a bottle of orange-coloured Tizer lemonade) at a flint-covered corner shop at the beginning of Mouse Lane. Opposite was a medieval timber-framed building which had once been a parish Workhouse for the poor and unemployed; I hoped I would never end up in the modern equivalent.

At the top of the Mouse Lane on the left among dense foliage was a large crystal clear pond fed by a chalk spring. Light shone through the leaves to dapple the still water. Inside we saw skimmers which darted across its surface, water boatmen rowing underwater, large diving beetles with a tiny bubble of air on their backs, water snails, little shrimps, small black wriggling leeches, newts which remained motionless and then suddenly darted forward with a twist of their long tails. In the spring countless tadpoles would wriggle around or stay still on the sides. Mating dragon flies and damson flies, red, green and blue, hovered and – in summer – dipped their long bodies to lay eggs on weed just below the surface. If I dipped a jam jar in the water, it came out full of twitching daphnia. The whole pond throbbed with life, only disturbed by a few boys, badgers and deer which came down to drink. It was a very tranquil spot and I often returned alone there.

If you walked along the track at the top of the lane you would eventually come to Wiston House which had been mentioned in the Domesday Book and which had an old 16th-century building. It had high, barbed wire fences and was rumoured to be used by the M15 for interrogations and for debriefing spies. We did not go near the buildings but often visited the lake, which was hidden by trees and overgrown bushes. It had an old boathouse and punt.

On one occasion, we borrowed the punt but felt very exposed in the middle of the lake. We had just put it back when who should appear but our headmaster John Scragg. He was clearly in a good humour and told us to clear off and not come back there again. We were clearly saved by the prospect of trout fishing.

After Wiston House, the track from Mouse Lane eventually led up a sunken chalk steep path through beech trees to the fabled Chanctonbury Ring on the sweeping and bare grass of the high Downs. There in the summer you could see countless little blue butterflies – chalk hill blues – and lie in the long grass and hear the song of the linnets and the larks sing and hover high in the sky. A gentle breeze would come from the Channel and fill the air with the smell of sea and grass.

Whatever the Wiston family said, Chanctonbury Ring itself was already very ancient, having been a circular prehistoric earthwork, a late Bronze Age hilltop enclosure with the remains of two Romano-Celtic temples. Given its strategic position, you could see why it had been so important and impressive.

Some boarders were distinctly unpleasant to the dwellers in the woods by Mouse Lane. An old agricultural worker lived in a small cottage there. He was bowed with years of hard work and smelt of urine. Although he periodically shaved he had a great tuft of hair growing out of his grimy shirt and a dirty neck. The boys taunted him with the name of the 'Wild Man of Borneo' to his face but made sure they kept their distance. He just shuffled off, shaking his head.

I also came across some older boys taunting a young lad, either from the secondary modern school or a farmer's boy. He had a dark complexion. Three older boys had cornered him in a dilapidated barn which had part of its roof fallen in. They chanted mercilessly 'Half Caste!', 'Half Caste!' He was simpering, huddled in a dark corner of the barn like a trapped deer. He had his arms around his head, trying not to hear.

Being outnumbered, I was unable to do anything, apart from saying:

'Leave him alone. He hasn't done anything wrong. You can see he's crying.'

They ignored me. I felt helpless. The boys were baying at him like a pack of hounds at their cornered prey, simply because he had a slightly darker skin and he wasn't one of them. Only when a farmer appeared did they scarper. I was appalled. The incident left me with a lifetime hatred of racism and cruelty. For a long time after the taunts of the boys echoed in my head. We were brought up to think that the British Empire was wonderful; I soon realised that it wasn't. Not surprisingly, there were no African or Asian people in our school.

To the east of Steyning was a small village called Bramber. It had a ruined Norman castle with raised earthworks. There wasn't much left of it, except a tall flint wall. But you could wander around it at will and on Sunday afternoons, when we had nothing better to do, we would lie in the sun on its grassy mound and listen to the 'Pick of the Pops' on the radio. But as a budding jazz enthusiast, I couldn't understand my friends' interest in what had gone down or up or what was the new entry that week. I also did not like its inane catch tune, 'Countdown' and being called a 'pop-picker.' Still what else can you do on a lazy summer afternoon when you have no money left or girls in sight and your friends do not want to get up to any escapades?

Further east of Bramber was the River Adur. The latter was a muddy, oozing river in a wide alluvial plain which came out at the sea by Shoreham. We occasionally went fishing in the river under a bridge but only caught eels. They often swallowed the hook and even when you cut off their heads their slimy bodies still wriggled. We didn't know what to do with them so just threw them back in the muddy water. The wide river plain was drained by dykes and in winter we had to break their ice and plunge through their filthy mud on cross-country runs. In the spring, we caught sticklebacks and tadpoles under the duck weed in jam jars only to throw them back.

At Bramber there was also a Victorian museum. It was stuffed full of animals and birds as well as 'sports of nature' and curiosities collected and arranged by a man called Walter Potter, the son of a local innkeeper. It had displays of stag's heads caught by the hunting fraternity and trophies brought back from India. It was a taxidermist's and bottler's delight, with grotesque embryos and stuffed specimens of two-headed lambs, four-legged chickens and a kitten with three legs sticking out of its back. There was even a human embryo in a bottle preserved in brown formalin. The collector must have picked up most of his specimens from the farms around.

A central piece was a huge tableau depicting the death and burial of cock robin in the popular song. It was full of beautiful but slowly rotting birds, including a rook and barn owl. You could see rats in a pub, mice playing dominoes, squirrels fencing, and rabbits sitting behind their desks at school. There was even a cabinet of little fairies in a woodland scene.

Some of my friends liked to spend a large penny to see it, but I found the place gloomy and depressing. It was a museum which reflected the Victorian fascination with taxidermy but it left me with a permanent distaste of stuffing animals and exhibiting freaks of nature.

Rather than visit the grotesque museum of the dead and the decaying, I preferred to get my fingers greasy with hot buttered toast in the nearby tea rooms. I liked to see birds flying in the sky and the rabbits run across the fields, not stuffed behind glass in boxes.

14
OUT OF BOUNDS

The great escape from school, apart from the rambling on the Downs, was the Scouts. I had already gone through the Cubs in Bognor at St Wilfred's church hall. As part of the ritual, I used to – with the other little boys in shorts – squat on my legs with fingers outstretched in two Victory signs and chant 'Dib, dib, dib, dob, dob, dob' and then jump and tell our very pretty young cub leader 'Akela, we'll do our best' – and with her soft, cool hands and winning smile we certainly meant it. Her name (meaning the 'Big Wolf') was taken from Rudyard Kipling's *The Jungle Book*. At the church hall, I learnt to distinguish between different knots and trees; I had badges on my khaki shirt to prove it. I did 'Bob-a-Job Week' in Bognor, calling on houses to ask them for some work for the movement. Whereas my aunt asked me to brush the yard which was quickly done, another old woman asked me to weed her flowerbeds for hours in a sunless part of her big garden. With a little help from my grandmother, I even won second prize in a sponge-making cake competition and learned how to knit a scarf. I began to whittle wood with a penknife and could make a fire with a wigwam of kindling sticks.

According to an old document, I first moved up from the Cubs and joined the Scouts in September 1957 at St John's Church in London Road in Bognor, having just turned eleven.

I learned with my brother what it was like to sleep on the hard earth, first on our garden lawn and then on a slope on the Downs above Fair-Mile Bottom near Fontwell. Our first tent was made from a Second World War parachute. See-through and pea-green, it was light enough to carry but whenever it rained a thin spray filtered through and soon soaked our feather-stuffed sleeping bags. But however uncomfortable it was, I found camping to be great fun. It was wonderful to have your own dwelling for a while and have control over your life away from the eyes of 'grown ups.'

My first introduction to the Scouts proper was a summer camping holiday on the Isle of Wight (organised by the Scoutmaster 'Flab' Wright) with my older brother and other boys all older than I was. I tagged along even though it was a year before I went to Steyning. I just wanted to be one of the older boys.

It was near Alum Bay and the Needles; I took back as a souvenir a small glass with different layers of the coloured sand. We slept on straw amongst the bales in a barn; I remember the wide open doors letting in the sunshine, dark corners of the tall barn and the smell of the straw and dust.

One day while running across a couple of fields of grass to the chalk cliff, I went headlong into an unseen electrified wire. The shock on my bare thighs, which literally seemed like a bolt out of the blue, sent me sprawling. There was suddenly a complete change of reality and I didn't know momentarily where I was. Lying on my back, I saw the great white clouds piled high in the blue sky. Despite the pain, I got up and hobbled down to the beach, scrambled down the cliff and dived into the cooling, cleansing sea.

I carried on the Scouts as soon as I went to boarding school. I continued to learn how to recognise different trees – oak, ash, beech, silver birch, sycamore, elder and alder – as well as how to tie knots – reef, bowline, clove-hitch, sheep shank, sheet bend, slip-knot, figure-of-eight, eye-splice, round turn and two half hitches. Being a young lad, I was intrigued by the 'hangman's noose' and often made one. I was also soon able to dig a latrine and cook 'twists' with a green stick over a fire (consisting of flour mixed with water and sugar) and pitch a tent. 'Flab' later made me a patrol leader of the Lions.

On the face of it, the Scouts encouraged some of the worst values of British imperialism. Founded by the arch-imperialist Robert Baden-Powell after the Boer War, it was based on muscular Christianity, demanded obedience and trusted you 'on your Honour' to 'do your Duty to God and the Queen.' Its motto was 'Be Prepared.' As the great founder once said, 'a Scout is never taken by surprise; he knows exactly what to do when anything unexpected happens.' Yet scouting enabled us to get away from school, get out into the country, to go 'out of bounds', become dirty and messy and have a good time.

I undoubtedly enjoyed the 'war games' organised by the Scouts. A flag was placed on a hill on each side of the Horseshoe and the aim was for each team to seize the one on the opposite hill. It was indeed war and probably intended to encourage the basest instincts of fighting in the boys and to feel that the seizure of the flag of the opposite side – whether it be German Nazis or Kenyan

Mau Mau as the enemy – was exciting and challenging. We would have to seize a member of the opposite side and hold him up for three seconds, chanting 'British Bulldog 123' and then he was out. I generally survived to the end because I used stealth, hiding behind the trunks of trees, to advance and was a fast runner if I happened to be discovered. We did not have army cadets and did not learn how to shoot a rifle but the Scouts was the nearest thing.

When I was about thirteen years old, I went with my brother on a camping and cycling trip from Bognor to Ringwood in the New Forest. It was a gruelling slog up and down the hills on heavy bikes with horizontal handle bars. We went with our first cousin Geoffrey of *Health & Efficiency* fame. Unfortunately, he had asthma like my mother and would wheeze up the hills. We often had to wait on a brow for him to catch us up. Our destination was a distant aunt living in the New Forest but when we got close enough for a telephone call she told us that we could not come – no spongy lawn for a bed, no hot bath for our sweaty and dirty bodies, no change from baked beans and egg.

One particular night we hardly slept. We pitched our tent under the full moon in an old wood down the end of a dark lane. That was bad enough, but we had gone to see a film called *The Fall of the House of Usher* in a deserted village flea pit with broken seats. It was an adult film so how we got into the empty cinema remains a mystery. We mainly went because we wanted to dry out and warm up.

What happened in the film will always stay with me. There was a long driveway lined with trees leading up to a mansion in a wild wood. It was owned by the Usher family who had a long history of evil and cruelty in the family. A young man is the final heir of a decrepit and creaking house and asks a friend to visit him. One night his sister falls into a deathlike sleep, and thinking that she is dead, they bury her in the family crypt. But she wakes up and in a wild frenzy breaks free. When she confronts her brother she falls dead at his feet. The evil house in the dark wood then slowly begins to collapse around them. When the dim lights went on in the broken cinema, it felt like being in the House of Usher!

I had never seen such a terrifying film in all my tender years. When we left the cinema we had to walk down a similar lane with the branches of the trees moving to and fro like arms in the whistling wind. The moon appeared and disappeared behind dark clouds. In the wet, dark and wild wood, owls screeched. We ran the last few hundred yards and quickly got into our sleeping bags in our flimsy parachute tent. The images of the film tormented me and I could not fall asleep. When I did, I dreamed that the mad woman, woken from the dead, was coming down the tree-lined avenue to get me…

We were allowed to go on camping trips with a friend at weekends at boarding school from about the age of thirteen. We would take with us a packed lunch which consisted of a lump of cheese, a couple of slogs (large slices of bread covered in marge), a boiled egg, a tomato and an apple, all neatly wrapped up in grease-proof paper. With a bottle of lemonade (preferably Tizer), it was the perfect lunch for a hike. Sausages and baked beans usually made up the evening meal.

We would get our equipment from the Scout hut – tents, sleeping bags (fortunately with clean inner bag given the natural tendency of young boys to enjoy their fantasies in the warmth), billy cans and a collapsible spade. The latter was for digging a trench to serve as a latrine, but we usually went behind a hedge or under a bush. We made sure we took a box of matches – a fire with sticks of wood was essential at night under the stars. As long as we kept to certain 'bounds' or boundaries, we could go where we wanted. We had to say where we were going though and to write up a report on our return.

Camping out in the woods and grasslands of the Downs around Steyning undoubtedly deepened my love of nature and writing the reports for the Scouts encouraged the close observation of its creatures and plants and my growing interest in natural history.

For inspiration in writing up the imaginary log we would look into old reports gathering dust in the Scout Room; it was just as well we were never interrogated by suspicious masters. As a patrol leader and therefore potential officer material, I would have been really in for it. But it encouraged me to use my imagination and become a writer as much as the countless English lessons at school.

Chanctonbury Ring was a favourite place to camp after I had joined the Scouts. One Saturday afternoon in the summer term my friend Pete Norman and I, then aged fourteen, trekked up Mouse Lane (not forgetting to buy some Woodbines at the corner shop) and past Wiston, the old country house and estate. We then clambered up the deep chalk track – through the steep wood of huge beech trees – to the Ring which was in open country on a spur of the South Downs. I did not fancy camping in the circle because it felt strange for some reason – there was almost an unseen presence – although we could see the remains of a human fire in the middle. So we decided to pitch our tent on the northern side by the beech wood which descended sharply down the escarpment to the Weald. We made a small fire and had our meal and smoked a cigarette but soon felt exhausted after our long trek with our camping gear on our backs. We fell asleep soon after dark but were suddenly woken up in the middle of the night to hear drumming and chanting.

I opened the tent and couldn't believe what I saw: a large fire was roaring in the middle of Chanctonbury Ring, sending sparks flying into the air. Dark shapes were gyrating around it. We crept closer on our hands and knees and were amazed to see under the full moon that the figures were naked women, their breasts bobbing up and down to the rhythm. I could make out the dark bushes of their pubic hair. I had never seen anything like it. I was overwhelmed by contradictory feelings – it was all deeply exciting, enticing and repelling at the same time.

I suddenly thought that we had come across a coven of witches who were performing some dark satanic rituals. I had read somewhere that witches often engaged in human sacrifice, especially of boys. I did not want to become one of them.

'We ought to go', I whispered urgently to my friend who was as enthralled as I. 'If they find us, they could sacrifice us on the fire and no one would know what had happened to us!'

'You're right. Let's go before they see us! We could be roasted like a pig!'

We moved slowly away, squirming on our bellies and elbows as if we were 'Red Indians.' When we thought we were out of sight we got up and ran with all our might, jumping over a wire fence and then tumbling down among the cool, damp leaves of the great, dark, welcoming wood. We stayed there huddled together leaning against a tree trunk, nodding occasionally off, until the first streaks of dawn lit up the branches of the huge beeches. When we emerged the revellers had already gone and their fire was reduced to a few spirals of smoke. At the site, we found some empty bottles and a necklace with a figurine of a horned goat.

Large quantities of pigs' teeth and bones had been found in one of the ruined Romano-Celtic temples within Chanctonbury Ring. They were probably ritual offerings. A small bronze statue of a wild boar, symbol of strength and fertility, had also been discovered nearby at Wiston. The revellers we had seen were probably engaged in some ancient fertility rite on the night of the full moon. I also learned that local folklore claimed that you could experience strange things about the place which gave rise to all sorts of chilling stories. One was about raising the Devil by walking round the Ring seven times on a dark night. If he offers you a bowl of milk, soup or porridge and you accept it, he will steal your soul. Ghosts and fairies abound.

We got back to school the next afternoon, dirty, exhausted and shaken by what we had seen. Needless to say, when we wrote down our Scout report, we mentioned the kestrels hovering over the Downs, the blue chalk butterflies and the deer in the wood, but not the coven of intoxicated and intoxicating 'witches' dancing around the fire.

Given my love of the Downs and roaming in nature, I joined the Natural History Society in my second year. It had a room in the attic of Coombe Court which was full of specimens gathered by generations of boys who had explored the surrounding Downs on their walks. It was overseen by the prefect 'Beetle' Barker at the time.

Our interest in 'natural history' was encouraged; we became good at observing nature and natural organisms and learning their names. We often carried around Stag beetles in match boxes, shiny black bugs with large pincers, and tried to make them fight each other. In the season, we collected May bugs, large sticky creatures which flew erratically and often crashed landed.

One memorable evening 'Beetle' Barker took a few boys from the Natural History Society to go badger-watching. We walked out of the village along the Storrington Road until we pulled off left. We then continued a little way down a track to a large badger set which he knew. It was dusk in the autumn. We positioned ourselves downwind of the set so that the badgers would not smell us and were told to keep quiet. We waited and waited until it was almost dark, listening to the noises of the wood around us and the screeching of owls in the distance. We started to become restless, kept as quiet as we could, but still there were no badgers. After a long wait, they at last appeared from their holes, snuffled about, and started digging up earthworms. Owls screeched to each other. A moon rose in the starry sky through the branches of an overhanging tree. We then trudged back to the school.

It had been a magical evening under the eerie white glow of the moon and it was great to miss 'prep' for once. But we were never allowed out again. The only thing I saw of badgers after that were their sets and the occasional jawbone or whitened skull. I never forgot though that you have to position yourself downwind of a set in order to see them.

White mice were my favourite pets at this time. We were allowed to keep some in a wooden box which we had made in the Natural History Society room in the attic of Coombe Court. I had a white mouse which I called Marie-Antoinette. I carried it around in the pocket of my herring-bone jacket or let it crawl around my body inside my shirt. It was very tame. My friend got a couple more and we fed them on thick, greasy 'slogs' of bread stolen from the canteen.

Marie-Antoinette escaped from her cage but then suddenly turned up a week later. She grew fatter and fatter until I found that one morning she had given birth to about six brownish mice. She must have mated with one of the wild mice which scuttled under the floor boards of our dormitory. They grew fast and started to tear around the cage. They were much faster than the dozy white mice. When I tried to pick them up, they would bite me with their sharp teeth. In the end, we released them in the condemned part of Coombe Court to fend for themselves. They were a slightly lighter colour than the wild mice but just as crazy. I will never know whether their new genes helped or hindered them in their struggle to survive and reproduce.

Our interest in the mice began to wane and it became a chore to clear out their cage and feed them. My friend and I decided to take turns each week to look after them. Then on one occasion when it was my time I glanced at the cage through the glass to see a terrible carnage had taken place. Two of the mice were dead and half-eaten, their white fur splattered with flecks of blood and their gnawed rib bones sticking out. The only survivor was Marie-Antoinette, making mockery of her historic fate. She too had blood on her white coat and small wounds.

My friend had forgotten to feed them and being starved they had eaten each other. There must have been a terrible fight. I was horrified by the spectacle and the idea of cannibalism deeply shocked me. I decided there and then I would have to kill Marie-Antoinette and throw away the cage. I took her cage out to the back off Coombe Court and then picked up a large brick. As she came out of the cage, I smashed her against another stone. She was a pulpy mass of flesh and bone and I could see that she was pregnant again. Feeling disgusted by what she had done and by what I had done, I buried her in the rough ground down by the disused air-raid shelter. I then put the urine and blood-soaked cage in a bin. That was the end of my mice-keeping days. But it left a nasty after-taste and I never forgot what I had done and seen.

However, my most memorable contribution to the Natural History Society Room in Coombe Court nearly destroyed it. On the western side of the Horseshoe round the chalk Downs there was a rifle range used by the army. It was definitely 'out of bounds.' When the red flag was up we made sure we did not crawl through the wire and undergrowth. When it wasn't, we made forays into the range, and could see the damage done to the saplings: it could have been our flesh which was torn. We were looking for live bullets and sometimes we found them amongst the used cartridges.

Our greatest find was an old canister which we took back and placed with the other trophies – sheep jaw bones, owl pellets, chalk fossils – in the Natural History room. When a prefect found it there, he reported it to the housemaster and then all hell was let loose. The fire alarm went off and the whole house had to be evacuated. The police and the bomb disposal squad were called out. We all stood at a distance in the lane, expecting the condemned Coombe Court finally to explode in a great and wonderful explosion. As it was, the offending article was taken away in a small box.

It turned out that it was a live grenade from the Second World War which had been slowly rotting in its bed of leaves in the wood on the edge of the firing range. My friend and I expected the heavens to fall in on us and, at least, that we would undergo a good beating. But in the event the housemaster simply reprimanded us for bringing the found object back to the school. Perhaps the headmaster that day was away fishing on Wiston Lake.

15

MASTERS AND SUBJECTS

The masters, whom we always had to call 'Sir', were a mixed bag. Not all of them were bad – at least to me. Since being at boarding school meant that you were away from home for almost three-quarters of the year, they had an inordinate influence on your development from about the age of 11 to 18 (if you entered the sixth form). Whereas they were the masters, we were definitely the subjects.

I heard the wonderful adventures of Raffles, the Gentleman Burglar, from the art master John Alabone who was in his late twenties (and also coached the under 14s at football). He would get us to paint an episode of our choice after hearing a story, thereby encouraging our imagination as well as our painting skills. Raffles was a great cricketer. The gentleman and his side-kick Bunny would burgle the rich and aristocratic to maintain their extravagant life-style as well as for the adventure and excitement of it all. But as a 'gentleman', there were certain things Raffles would not do. At a dinner party, for instance, he would steal from the guests but never from the host. I particularly liked the fact he was a master of disguises, a deft hand with false beards and a wizard with regional accents. The art master and Raffles were the first to fire my imagination for stories.

Alabone also read from the short stories of Guy de Maupassant which I have always liked ever since, especially the story where an old peasant helps out a wet nurse suffering from too much milk in her swollen breasts in a hot railway carriage.

If Alabone, who painted delicate landscapes out of school, ever caught you making too much of a row in class, he would twist your ear painfully, or even worse, kick you in the backside through soft canvas seats. It was excruciating. He would also throw the wooden duster from the blackboard roughly in the vicinity of any boy who talked behind his back. But the pupils still liked him.

On one occasion, Alabone who lived in Shoreham-by-Sea, saw

a friend and me hitching out of bounds and stopped his car. We thought we were undone. Yet the hard taskmaster gave us a lift and said he wouldn't report us but asked us to be more careful again: 'You could get into real trouble with the headmaster'. We didn't have to be told. Perhaps it was a mutual admiration for Raffles which had worked for us here. I was more inclined to listen to someone who tried to persuade us with reasonable arguments than those who enforced their rule through the cane. I later did 'A' level Art with him, and enjoyed the paper dealing with the history of art, particularly the Post Impressionists, as well as drawing and painting from nature.

My growing radicalism was encouraged by Arthur Lee who taught us history in a room on the right of the ground floor of the condemned part of Coombe Court. He was a handsome man with straight black and white hair who had gone to Oxbridge and been in the Second World War. He always held our attention and never had any trouble with discipline. Although clearly middle-class himself, he had considerably sympathy for the poor and oppressed.

The class came alive when he used to go off the tiresome curriculum:

'Now boys, I'll get you all through your 'O' levels if you do a reasonable amount of work', he would say, 'but let's talk about something else for a while. I'll tell you about something in history which I think you should know.'

Then he would launch into a discussion close to his heart about the French Revolution and the Russian Revolution. He would tell us about the iniquities of the *ancient régime* in France and the great principles of 'Liberty, Equality and Fraternity' which the revolutionaries adopted. Living under the tyranny of boarding school where you were constantly surveyed and beaten, these principles seemed much more attractive to me than obedience to God and Queen. On other occasions he would describe the state of serfdom under the czars in Russia and how the peasants and workers had a revolution and tried to create a new society where all would be free and equal and could realise their potential. Sometimes he would say how the last war had been fought for democracy and freedom although those principles weren't extended to those living in the British Empire who fought on our side against Hitler.

I would listen spell-bound to these exciting new ideas and felt let down when the school bell rang. It was heady stuff and certainly predisposed me to becoming a socialist later in life despite being surrounded by conservatives at school and at home.

Teachers could be demanding. One fierce English teacher, Peter Coltman, who lived with his family in a cottage down Mouse Lane, initially destroyed poetry for me by analysing it too much. When I came across Wordsworth's words 'we murder to dissect' I knew exactly what he meant. During Coltman's lessons the sun shone outside the lattice windows of the old school in Church Street and beckoned me to leave my schoolbooks behind and enjoy the freedom of the Downs outside. But simply by his enthusiasm for writers he encouraged a lasting appreciation of literature.

I began to like novels and poetry because they showed how other people lived, how you could live, and how you could express your feelings. I was taught that it's not good to show emotions at school. That would be a chink in your armour, a weakness mercilessly exploited by the other boys. The atmosphere was so competitive and cruel, the masters in general so authoritarian, that if one of them was kind and friendly to you it came as a great surprise.

This was the downfall of one English master who was prematurely balding on his large dome head. Because he tried to please, the boys would not listen to him in class and he was constantly trying to keep order. He had very large feet and not surprisingly the boys nicknamed him 'Boots.'

They would taunt him behind his back with the words 'Boots! Boots! Boots!' The final straw came one afternoon in a schoolroom above the physics lab in the new block when some boys of my class put a pair of large football boots on his table. When he came in to give his lesson, he saw the boots and slumped behind his desk and put his large head in his large hands.

'Why do you do this to me? Why do you do this to me?', he murmured.

And then he sobbed. It was terrible to see a grown-up cry, let alone a master. They were meant to be so strong. I thought it incredibly embarrassing. Eventually he recovered and carried on with the lesson. The boys knew they had gone too far this time. After that day, they were easier with him but he left the school with his highly polished boots not long afterwards.

We were obliged to do four or six hours of sport each week, with different activities counting for an hour or half an hour. The nickname 'Shocker' suited the gym master Bob Webster. He was a tough customer, not to be thwarted, no doubt because he had been a PE instructor in the army. He always wore a black track suit. He would hang any boy who caused trouble from the wooden beams around the gym until he dropped. He also made us run stark naked through a freezing cold shower with water shooting out from each side of a metal frame. But I learned with him how to climb ropes and jump over a wooden horse and do a work-out around the gym. It was difficult for the other boys to catch me on the wooden beams as I moved so fast like a monkey without touching the ground.

I represented my house – Holland House – in football and played on the right wing. I was quite fast. It was not a rugby school but Peter Dawson brought his rugby ball to school one term. We managed to find a master who had played it and knew the rules. We formed a couple of teams. Being quite small, I became the fly half at the side of the scrum. I loved the rough-and-tumble of the scrum and the game seemed a good excuse to fight other boys. But it was short-lived. One of a pair of hulking West Country brothers had his tongue almost completely bitten in half during the first game. Then after a couple more someone broke his arm or leg. The rate of injuries was too high and, unfortunately for me, it had to be stopped.

We also played hockey occasionally. I represented the school in a match against the girls at Worthing High school. With their muscular legs and flaying hockey sticks we were no match for their vicious play. We retreated back to Steyning with severe bruises on our shins where they had deliberately hacked us despite our pads. With misplaced chivalry, we avoided hitting their legs – they were girls after all and meant to be the 'weaker sex' – and tried to hit the ball instead. I don't think we played them again; certainly I didn't.

I did not play much cricket either in the summer and never represented my house or school. Having been hit in my face badly early on in my cricketing career by a fast-bowler, I was too wary of the hard, stitched leather ball when I batted. Perhaps also I didn't have a very good eye for the ball. I found fielding tedious as it seemed that the ball rarely came my way. It seemed to me that you had to hang around a lot and nothing much happened.

Instead, I was keen on athletics which took place in the summer term. Of all the houses the boarders inevitably won the athletic 'standards' since they were fit and hungry. I usually got at least eight standards at different sports, but I was particularly good at the longer running races, the 220 and 440 yards. Pole vaulting was my speciality; I loved the feeling of going up and twisting over the bar, flying for a split second, and then landing a long way down on the unforgiving earth.

However my sport par excellence was cross-country running and I enjoyed its loneliness and solitude as well as the release it offered for the pent-up emotions of living in such a closed and tyrannical community. The Upper Horseshoe was a regular cross-country run about three miles long, which meant a long slog up a steep lane, a welcome lung-filling respite around the rim of the ridge and an exhilarating, long-legged, arm-circling hurtle down a track back to school. 'Round the top' was considered an hour of sport, while 'round the bottom' – the Lower Horseshoe – counted as half an hour. A few of the boys would cut across the horseshoe at the bottom and have a fag in the wood and then catch up with you on other side. But I carried on, despite the pain. One of the few pleasures of boarding school was to lie afterwards in a large steaming hot bath in your own cubicle experiencing the after-glow of a gruelling run.

Every year, the whole school was obliged to take part in a cross-country run and we set off for a long run around the village and over the Downs at different stages according to our age. It was thought that the handicap would even the competition out. When I was about thirteen, I had the pleasure as well as the pain of keeping up with the front runners and in a final burst down the lane back at school overtook a boy to come third out of the whole school. The headmaster came up to me afterwards as I leant over gasping for breath and said:

'Marshall, what are you doing here? I didn't know you could run. Are you sure you didn't cheat?'

'No, sir. Honest, sir' I said but I thought, 'What a bastard! After all that effort and he doesn't even appreciate it! Bugger him!'

I captained the boarding house team for cross-country running on several occasions and my high point was to run in the West Sussex schools championship. I completed the course somewhere in the middle of the pack and was quite satisfied with my performance. I also ran against Lancing College near Shoreham, running across the wet fields adjoining the meandering river Adur and breaking the ice of the dykes to run through them.

I would always try to overtake others on the slopes in cross-country running. The steeper the slopes, the more successful I was. I not only enjoyed the loneliness of the long-distance runner but developed considerable will power – over myself rather than

others. It stood me in good stead afterwards. I always thought
I was average in body and mind but I excelled in some respects
because of my perseverance. For this, I thanked the 'cross-country
spirit', as my brother and I called it, especially when the going got
rough and you had to push yourself on.

It was the French master Derek Drew who encouraged my
growing interest with jazz. In one of the front rooms after school
in the condemned part of Coombe Court my friend Peter Norman
and I discovered the joys of jazz. Listening to the scratchy vinyl
records on an old record player with a pick-up needle – usually
an EP – we would pretend to be musicians, blowing a horn or
drumming wildly, and jumping and leaping up and down like
maniacs on the faster numbers. We listened over and over again
to the Paris-based clarinetist Mezz Mezrow and saxophonist
Sidney Bechet. I also began to like the early jazz musicians such as
the cornetist Bix Beiderbecke, the blues singer Bessie Smith, the
trombonist Kid Ory and his New Orleans style, and of course the
early Louis Armstrong before he became too schmaltzy.

I soon graduated however to the bebop music of Charlie Parker,
Dizzy Gillespie, Charlie Mingus and Art Blakey. I then liked
the cool sound of the Modern Jazz Quartet with Milt Jackson
and Miles Davis. I particularly liked Thelonious Monk and John
Coltrane. I thought liking cool modern jazz made me cool and
modern. It was simply a 'cool' thing to do to 'dig it.' So-called 'free
jazz' seemed to reflect my wish to be free in a world of excessive
discipline, punishment and hierarchy. My love of jazz was no
doubt a partial release for my pent-up emotions when growing up.

My brother and a friend from Storrington had founded a Jazz
Society the year before; my brother had even built himself a double
bass during his last term at school when he retook maths at 'O'
level. By the time I took over as 'President' at the age of fourteen
with Pete Norman as my right-hand man, we were supported by
about half-a-dozen other boys.

Derek Drew, a trad. jazz buff, came to all the meetings of the
Jazz Society after school. He would correct pieces of French
homework at the back in a corner, only adding the odd word of
encouragement to us. He played jazz piano and together with my
friends Pete Dawson (on drums) and Charles Linford (on trumpet)
and others formed an occasional group. The closest I got to playing
an instrument was trying to learn a banjo at home but didn't carry
on because I felt there was no real point at the time.

Masters and Subjects

In the Jazz Society, I would often give a talk and illustrate it with extracts from vinyl records. Talking about the life and work of jazz musicians undoubtedly gave me confidence to talk in public and honed some elementary research skills. Since most great jazz musicians were black Americans, my studies made me respect their abilities and feel indignant about the injustices they had to suffer. My love of jazz deepened by belief in equality and justice which had been first awakened by my mother's comments on the monarchy.

One afternoon, coming out with a friend from the disused bomb shelter near a Methodist Chapel at the bottom of Coombe Court reeking of cigarette smoke, I bumped into Drew. I couldn't stop myself from going bright red in the face. He must have known that we had been smoking – an expellable offence – but he just said hello and walked on. A common love of jazz had saved us from dire punishment; out of oppression sometimes comes forgiveness.

I liked another French teacher called Ted Purver who for a while was the housemaster of Coombe Court. He was a retiring man but kept a braying donkey in the grounds. Naturally with a name like Purver he was called unfairly 'Pervert.' I was later told that he once took two boys from my year for a week's cycling tour in Normandy during the holidays. They would agree on their destination for each day. Since he was slow and had an old-fashioned bicycle with a front basket they usually arrived before him. As the days went by he seemed increasingly agitated and started talking to himself. On the last day he threw his wallet containing his money and the ferry tickets on the table and told them to take it. The last they saw of him was from a deck of the ferry arguing with the immigration and custom officers on the land below. They returned to England without him and heard that he had disappeared from the school. Boys being boys, they did not follow this up. I had moved on and never heard what happened to him.

Bill 'Digger' Gardner was another housemaster of Coombe Court, a short muscular man with thinning hair, who was the Latin master and loved Morris dancing. I did not do Latin with him but he would take the boys on the steam train down to Shoreham where we would have to change for Hove swimming baths. I enjoyed the outing and the freedom of getting away from the boarding school. In the baths, he would love to fight with the boys and tried to push them under the water; he seemed to enjoy the feel of the naked bodies of the boys grappling with him.

The deputy headmaster was 'Buffer' Williams, who took

chemistry. At a later stage 'Ike' Williams, the biology teacher, took on the role. Neither left a lasting impression, but I did enjoy the chemistry lessons when Buffer dropped some potassium in water and it exploded. I liked the experiment of electrolysis, putting electricity through water and then capturing in a tube two parts of hydrogen to one part of oxygen. The use of the Bunsen burner was also fun. The wooden desktops with their sinks had an array of acids in front of them. When Buffer was not looking, we poured hydrogen chloride on to the wood which became pitted and gave off smoke.

I learned anatomy and how the body worked from 'Ike'. But sadly there was nothing about how you had intercourse, the 'birds and the bees' – the bit that I was most interested in at the time. The biology textbooks just showed drawings of naked men with drooping penises and balls and women with the internal paraphernalia of producing eggs but they were entirely sexless. They could have been slabs of meat.

In maths, the lessons were sometimes taken by the head of the boarding school 'Glub' Goodall – who was reputed to have a first in the subject at Cambridge. He certainly was lugubrious and I never heard him tell a joke. At least he let my brother off in Prep when he blew up one of my mother's Ginger cakes. It was so unrisen it was like fudge and he hollowed it out and stuffed it with gunpowder taken from fireworks. I was taught the mysteries of algebra and equations, while my mother had ensured early on my proficiency in 'mental arithmetic.'

As for the physics master, I cannot even remember his name. I did learn the basics of physics from him however: how the world was made up of different types of matter, how light could be split by a prism and, in particular, how a pair of scales weighed different things using different weights.

I managed to get 'O' levels in maths, biology, physics and chemistry with little effort which shows how good the teaching must have been at the boarding school. It left me with a developing interest in the empirical method and inductive reasoning as well as the history and philosophy of science. My science masters must have taught me how to observe and experiment and how to understand the natural world around me.

The soft-spoken, elderly woodwork teacher was a Mr Ivor Jones who had a lovely Welsh burr. He lived in large dark house with an overgrown garden on the way to Bramber. I enjoyed his lessons. He spent his days dressed in a brown coat in a dingy room amongst wood shavings and sawdust showing reluctant boys how to use a spoke shave, a jig saw and a plane; how to use a chisel at the right angle and how to make dove-tail joints; and how not to cut their thumbs off or stab another boy in the eye. He taught us how to tuck our thumb in whenever we sawed a piece of wood. Under his guidance, I made a stool with a twisted raffia seat and two beautiful book ends in the shape of squirrels with great curling tails. He taught respect for tools and materials and whenever I see a piece of wood, I hear his gentle Welsh voice saying over my shoulder:

'Oooh lad, the line belongs to the wood.'

After Coombe Court, the boys had to move to the flint-built house of 'Dormer' or Mid Dorm. It was next to the headmaster's feared study in which I had been beaten several times, and opposite his ancient house which gave on to the narrow Church Street. The housemaster's name was Sauvain and he took geography. He was well-built, short man with a round face. Like most of the Masters and all the dormitory captains he was ready with the cane. He had a red Morris 1100 car but since he was colour blind the boys would prefer to call it his 'lush green car', mimicking his north-country accent.

In the Sixth Form you graduated to white-washed Wykeham House, which had a lower room for the rarely used television. Wykeham backed on to a large lawn with a mulberry tree. If you were really hungry you ate some of its fruit but since they tasted so sour most fell and became squashed. Sometimes in summer we played croquet there, waiting for the nearby canteen to open so that we could have the evening meal.

After a term in Wykeham, I was surprised to be made a dormitory captain in Coombe Court. But I did not beat any of the boys and appealed to their better nature, asking them not to make a noise after lights out so they would not attract the housemaster.

I would try to reason with them when they made a row after lights-out.

'Look', I said, 'I don't mind you making a certain noise but keep it down so the housemaster doesn't hear you. If you co-operate with me, I'll co-operate with you. Now, I don't want to beat you as I don't think it makes any difference, so pipe down, got it?'

And it worked. I found then that persuasion was much better at changing people's behaviour than brute force; certainly the pupils kept their noise within acceptable bounds.

In sleepy Steyning nestling in the Down very rarely did political events or international relations directly enter our lives. I sometimes read the daily newspapers which were brought in. They were the *Daily Mail* and the *Daily Telegraph* which were middle-brow, had a right-wing bias to their articles and supported Tory politics. I rarely listened to the news. However, two important events occurred which made me worried… but only for a while.

The first was the building of the Wall in Berlin in August 1961 which separated the Soviet bloc from the West. I already knew about the 'Iron Curtain' (a term popularized by Winston Churchill) dividing Europe which descended in 1946, the year of my birth. But then I (as a dormitory captain) and a few other boys were invited by the house-master of Coombe Court into his living room at the top of the house under the roof. He told us to listen to the radio. A crackly voice described the building of a wall across Berlin and the airlift of essential goods to the western zone.

'This is a most important event which will affect all your lives', he said gravely. 'The Cold War is in earnest.'

The Cold War. It sounded very ominous; would it ever become 'hot'? And what would that mean? Would there be a Nuclear War? But little more was said and we soon forgot about it. It seemed we would not have to use after all the rusting tins which my grandmother had stashed in the larder at home for the 'Third World War' or open up the abandoned air-raid shelters at school which smelt of damp, piss and cigarette smoke.

The other momentous event was the Cuban Missile Crisis in October 1962 between the Soviet Union and America. I knew that there had been a revolution in Cuba led by Castro and Che Guevara in 1959 against a corrupt dictatorship, but I still mainly associated Cuba with the beautiful boxes of cigars my grandfather kept in a cupboard and lit up after Christmas lunch. When Kennedy (JFK) warned Cuba that the USA would use nuclear weapons if the missiles planted by the Russians on its soil were not removed, it seemed indeed as if the Cold War was about to become very hot. Since Britain was a close ally of the USA we would no doubt be frizzled to death like the populations of Hiroshima and Nagasaki. It was a very tense two weeks. In the end, Khrushchev backed off while Kennedy was apparently prepared to order his Air Force to drop nuclear bombs if the missiles were not removed. The fact that Kennedy, who seemed to be the darling of everybody, was prepared to go to nuclear war considerably lowered him in my estimation and no doubt the experience and knowledge contributed to my later opposition to all nuclear arms.

When Kennedy was shot in November 1963, I knew of it but it was not a 'lightbulb moment' for me and I have no idea where I was on that day and at that hour. But I knew about the Civil Rights Movement in America and hoped that black and white could one day walk together as equals.

Apart from the history master Lee and possibly the art master Alabone, all the masters who taught us were probably Tory in politics and conservative in attitude. On leaving the school I soon moved to the left, the ground probably prepared by Lee and my direct experience of the tyranny of the headmaster, prefects and dormitory captains, as well as the general oppression, cruelty, authority and hierarchy I had experienced at boarding school. It not only left me with a horror of corporal punishment but confirmed my love of freedom, equality and justice which have never dimmed.

16
GLORIOUS SEX

Sex raised its glorious head quite soon after going to boarding school. My mother had only ever talked about sex with me on one occasion. One day when, I was about eleven, we were walking up a wooded hill to a tent which Michael and I had erected on its slopes. She seemed a bit odd; I thought she may have had a drink. Suddenly out of the blue she said:

'Do you know about the birds and the bees?'

'Yes', I immediately said, putting my head down and walking ahead fast. She was the last person I wanted to talk to about 'S-E-X' – three small letters which had such terrifying resonance.

During this period, I was much more intent on boating than sex. After boarding school the summers in Bognor seemed an endless period of sunshine, when we could get up early and after breakfast run down to launch the boat and spend all day on the beach or out in the bay.

Then my whole world changed when my brother started going out with the daughter of a fisherman. It seemed a double betrayal. He had not only turned his back on the sea but was no longer my constant companion. Surely girls weren't worth that – not the ones I knew well, such as my cousin and her friend.

In such an all-male community as boarding school, it was not surprising that homosexuality was common, both among some of the masters and the boys. My brother, when he first arrived at the school, had been nearly raped by one dormitory captain. Michael even joked that if a master was kind to you something was wrong with him. I had another experience of a master who tried to put his soft hand up my shorts while ostensibly looking at some of my work. I moved away, as I had done with the maths teacher at my prep school.

In my second year, when I was in Coombe Court (the old building in its own grounds) I had my own early sexual experiences. One summer evening in a dormitory on the ground floor, one of the six boys after lights out suggested that we paired up to have a wank with each other. It didn't appeal to me but since two coupled up and I didn't want to be left out, I got into my bed with one of the boys. I didn't like it a bit so after a few moments I said I'm not doing it. My friend seemed equally relieved. Thereafter I had no sexual relations with other boys although this did not prevent me from being somewhat confused about my sexual identity in my early teens. I had a much more broad-minded attitude later and didn't mind whether a person was homosexual or not.

The only females at school were the cleaning ladies and the cooks, nearly all middle-aged, large and dumpy, hidden behind plain green uniforms. One could not, or rather dared not, imagine what was under them. But there was one girl with a curvaceous body, a friendly smile and an Irish accent – she was lovely. One of the perks – and there were many – of being in sick bay was that you could look up into her garret opposite. However, she always pulled the curtains.

Fortunately, curtains were not always pulled elsewhere. The headmaster's daughter would sometimes leave her curtains open when she undressed – whether by chance or design, I shall never know. But she always closed them when she got down to her bra and pants. Some of us in our third year in 'Dormer' would gather after lights out to see the magical apparition, hoping against hope that she would forget to close her curtains so that we could see her take off her bra to reveal her budding breasts in the glow of a side light next to her bed. The yearning was unbearable. But never satisfied.

It was rumoured that the Matron, who spoke with a slight Scandinavian accent, had lost her great love in the war and therefore had never married since. She had once been very attractive but was far too old for us young boys. A young 'nurse' however came at one time – she could not have been much more than sixteen, having left school and set out on a nursing career. All the boys were bowled over by her. She was short with a neat figure, red cheeks and a sweet smile. Usually, the matron had a surgery in the evening in the room of Old Dorm in the old building and was accompanied by a trainee nurse. They were both dressed in starched white uniforms, but while one was stern the other was all softness.

If I had a minor wound, I would hope that the young nurse and not Matron would dress it. One evening, the young nurse cleaned my scratched knee with such care I almost swooned with her gentle caress. Her heady perfume rose above the disinfectant. The glossy waves of her hair threatened to fall from under her nurse's cap. When she stood up and smiled, I wanted the moment to last forever. But she only stayed at the school for a short while, and was replaced by a stumpy, spotty, ugly and rough girl. Perhaps the Matron realised how her predecessor had been sending every boy mad with desire.

There were a few girls in the village, mainly from the local Secondary Modern School. We were not allowed to talk to them – ever. While they paraded down the High Street (even at fifteen) with bouffant hairdos, buffed-up skirts and high heels – remember, it was in the late 50s – we had to walk along in grey flannel trousers, grey shirts and school ties, grey herringbone blazers and black rounded Oxford shoes. Our caps, even when we graduated to long trousers, had to be on at all times out of school.

Yet we still managed to meet a few willing girls clandestinely. To kiss a girl meant not only breaking the school rules but deliciously tasting forbidden fruit. When I was in Coombe Court I used to go down and have a fag with a friend by the air raid shelter at the end of a lane by the 'Three Tuns' pub. We'd meet a couple of girls from the village. I fancied one them who was slim and had short dark hair but I never got anywhere. Years later when a friend in Brighton mentioned my name to her married neighbour, she said:

'Peter Marshall. The first boy I had a crush on was called Peter Marshall. He was one of the grammar-school boys in Steyning. But I was chubby at the time and he never looked at me; he was only interested in my friend. I often think of him.'

She was the daughter of the innkeeper of Chequers Hotel in the High Street, the best hotel in the village. If only I had realised her true feelings at that time!

Not long after I camped, as I had done several times, with the Scouts in the pine wood at the end of the Sports fields on the edge of the village. The Scout master used to leave us to our own devices and we made a fire and got in some cider, Forest Brown Ale and some Woodbine cigarettes. We must have made a racket. There was a council estate nearby and one evening a couple of girls came over. One was the legendary Karen Hook who was rumoured to have slept with the prefects and for a short time went out with my brother. She was blond, petite, forward and very sexy. She went off with one of the older boys but I managed to entice her friend into my two-man tent. She was a brunette, gangly and surly but still a girl. I told my friend to go for a long walk. He sat moodily poking a fire in the distance.

She was about two years older than I was and much more experienced. I had kissed a few girls before and had even touched their breasts – Oh what delight! – but hadn't got much further. In fact I wasn't sure what one should do. We kissed for a while and I was surprised when she boldly put her tongue into my mouth. I touched her breasts without any of the feigned reluctance I had experienced with other girls. I then proceeded to go 'down below'. Again, no problem, and I had the joy of feeling her moist 'fanny'.

But being a tyro in these matters, I didn't know what to do next. I had an erection but what to do with it? Should I try and push it in? At that stage I could feel her beginning to lose interest and becoming impatient with me. My mind too was beginning to interfere with my body.

Eventually, she pushed me off, saying 'You're useless!' and climbed out of the tent, adjusting her clothing as she went. She shouted over to her friend: 'Oye, Kar, I've 'ad enough. I'm off 'ome'

'What a lost opportunity! I could have lost my virginity!' was my first thought. 'Am I really that useless?' was my second. But I wasn't letting on. I went over to my friend by the fire and boasted how far I had gone.

'Wow', he said enviously. 'You jammy old bugger!'

When I saw the girl next in the High Street, I went red with embarrassment and tried to say hello, but she ignored me completely. I felt ridiculous; she looked so grown up with her lipstick and black mascara and frilly white blouse and colourful skirt while I was dressed in my old flannel trousers, herring-bone jacket, grey shirt and tie, and had my school cap on.

'What a prick I must look', I thought.

Despite the general prohibition at this boarding school of any relationships with the opposite sex, there was strangely an annual dance in the gymnasium for the older boys. When I was in the lower sixth I once invited the younger sister of one of my brother's friends from Storrington to the summer ball. She was taller than me but I could see that she was very keen on me as we danced the twist and I made a sorry attempt at ballroom dancing. We escaped the heat and I suggested we went on the flat roof of my old dormitory 'to cool off and see the stars.' It was bliss to kiss her, however inexperienced I was, and she even let me touch her small but delightful breasts. But that was that.

As there were few girls available in the village and massive competition among the boys, it was necessary to go looking further afield. My friend Pete Norman had a very attractive sister who went to the local art school in Worthing and wore black stockings under her short skirts. When I visited his semi-detached house with its steep stairs, she would flash her long legs as she climbed two steps at a time. He also knew some girls who went to the local High School. The three friends he knew were much more pleasant than those of the hockey team – soft, giggling and sexy.

With Pete Norman I would pretend to go camping for the weekend but then hide our camping gear in a bush, take off our Scout hats and uniforms with their short trousers and neck scarves in 'woggles', and put on 'civvies.' I would exchange my shapeless grey flannels for black drain-pipe trousers and my Oxford toe caps for Chelsea boots with a sharp chisel point. The school tie and grey shirt were replaced with a dashing high, polo-neck jumper. I felt I was very 'cool.'

We usually went to Worthing in order to meet the three girls he had met. I went out for a while with an attractive brunette with a bouffant wavy hairstyle. But I was not allowed to go very far with her beyond kissing, despite my longing for more.

To meet the girls, we would go 'out of bounds' – beyond the invisible boundaries defined by the headmaster and schoolmasters – and hitch a lift to Worthing via Shoreham. On one occasion we spotted the headmaster coming down at us in his big, black car; we just managed to jump into a ditch before he saw us. Unfortunately on another occasion my disguise attracted his attention when he saw me on the Worthing promenade. He was fuming when he recognised me.

'Go back to school immediately and wait for me outside my study.'

I knew I was in for it. I waited there until it was dark. At last the light went on and he called me in.

'Marshall', he said, his eyes bulging through his thick glasses. 'This is an expellable offense. If I ever catch you out of bounds again, you're out. Do I make myself clear, boy?'

'Yes, sir. Absolutely clear!'

'Good. Now bend over.'

He gave me six of the worst with all his might. It was so painful that I thought I was going to die. But I refused to give him the satisfaction of seeing me cry and I bit my lower lip and squeezed my eyes shut.

'Now get out. I don't want to see you in here again.'

That night, it was difficult to sit down in prep. I couldn't understand what made a grown man want to hit young boys who were only following their natures. I assumed that it was because he had been beaten as a boy and saw it as a law of nature so that when he grew up he encouraged his prefects and the dormitory captains to do likewise.

I thought my beating was the end of the Worthing affair. But it wasn't. To my utter surprise and horror, the next Monday morning after prayers at general assembly in the gym, the headmaster called me up on the stage and made me stand in front of the whole school – around a hundred boarders and three hundred day-bugs. He then tore into me.

'You see in front of you, a boy who has not only broken school rules, by going out of bounds, but has been seen parading up and down Worthing promenade without his school uniform on. Marshall was found wearing tight trousers. Disgusting. There is nothing worse than following fashion. To try to be dapper, like this boy, is deplorable. I will not tolerate it.'

I felt utterly humiliated in front of the whole school. I could see my friends smirking and nudging each other. I tried to look into the middle distance. The gym went all hazy and I thought I was going to faint. The words of the headmaster, uttered with the utmost contempt, felt like hammer blows to my head. At last he dismissed me and announced the hymn. Thank God for that. Religion was never far behind punishment.

Afterwards, I looked up the word 'dapper' in my Pocket Oxford Dictionary to see what terrible sin I had committed. It said: 'Neat and precise, especially in dress.' That was the last thing I wanted to be. Henceforth, I cultivated an air of raffish neglect. But I never lost my hatred of boundaries, especially imposed ones.

The greatest adventure I had with Pete Norman was soon after. Raffles would have been proud of us. It was the summer term and the sap had been rising within us and without. We had heard that there was going to be a barbecue on the beach in Worthing and that the three girls we had our eye on might be there. So after lights out we waited a long time until it was dark and then filled our beds with pillows and climbed down the gutter pipe from the second floor in Coombe Court. We walked up the alley to the small road which ran past the old school building. At the end was Scragg's house. A full moon was rising and although it helped us see where we were going it also made us feel very exposed.

We had decided to borrow the bikes of the headmaster's wife and daughter which we had once seen in the garage. As we walked stealthily towards it, we had not counted on the excruciating noise of the gravel crunching under foot. We heard a cough from a bedroom in the headmaster's house and froze. At that moment, the moon came out from behind a cloud and caught us in the act. But then it disappeared again and after a moment's silence we continued.

Another obstacle was the bolt on the garage doors which made a racket as I pulled it sideways. At last it gave way and we carried the bikes across the gravel. Our hearts stopped when we heard another cough coming from the open window of the headmaster's bedroom. What a relief to jump on the bikes and peddle like mad down towards the High Street. But here was another dangerous obstacle. The street was wide open and for all to see. We stopped and carefully looked either way. The street seemed deserted, except for a black and white cat. We made sure our lights were off and then dashed across the road up towards the Downs. We heard a shout in the distance – we prayed it was a late night reveller from a pub and wasn't the local bobby doing his rounds.

There was a long, steep road towards the Horseshoe which took all our puff but we eventually reached the top and rested. Under the moon in the starry sky we could see the Downs stretching down before us towards the shimmering sea. We sped down hill, shouting to each other in triumph. I hit one bend too fast, braked and flew off. I only grazed my knee but I also scratched and bent one of the metal mudguards of the bike. But nothing was going to stop us now.

By the time we reached the beach in Worthing, it was about half past eleven. The fire was going out, the food had been eaten and only a couple bottles of cider were left. Most of the people had gone home. But two of the girls were still there and a small group of us went for a midnight swim. Naked. Gloriously naked. The feeling of the cold water flowing across my limbs gave a wonderful sense of freedom. The girls undressed at a distance so we couldn't really see them in the dark. It was freezing cold, but we splashed and frolicked about. I tried to move closer to one of the girls, showing off my dives to the bottom, but she swam off to be with her friend. Being naked and swimming with boys was clearly the farthest they were prepared to go that night. When we came out, the girls quickly dressed and went home.

'Our mums will give us hell, if they find out', one of them said. The girl whom I had tried to impress gave me a quick kiss.

Norman and I and another day-bug friend stayed on and rebuilt the fire with drift wood. Bottle in hand, smoking Woodbines, joking and laughing around a roaring blaze, we gradually dozed off. I awoke with a start, cold and with a sinking feeling in my stomach. There were already orange streaks on the horizon. We had slept a couple of hours but now we had a long way to go. Pushing the bikes up the long, steep, narrow road past a Norman church, with its flint stones, on to the Downs was exhausting. By the time we reached the top, our faces were running with sweat. The dawn chorus was in its full delirium and the warming orange-red sun was climbing into the blue sky. It was going to be a beautiful summer's day. As we free-wheeled down into Steyning, we could see the first signs of the new day. The milkman was out on his rounds. A few cars appeared on the road, their owners driving to work in Shoreham or Brighton. The closer we got to the school, the more worrying it was.

It was broad daylight by the time we cycled over the High Street and up the narrow road in front of the old part of the school. We could hear voices coming from the headmaster's house. We knew if were caught now we would be expelled – for stealing bikes (borrowed I preferred to call it), smoking, drinking, going out with girls and staying out all night. If the headmaster didn't catch us then the dormitory captain would realise we were absent. But we had no alternative but to press on. It was now or never.

We marched up the gravel to the garage, replaced the bikes as best we could and then ran frantically along a back route to Coombe Court and clambered over the wooden board which blocked off the condemned part of the house. Thank God, when we crept through the back door into the dormitory the dormitory captain was having a pee half asleep and hadn't noticed the pillows in our beds. We tore into our school uniform (vest, shirt, tie and pullover all one for ease of dressing), splashed some cold water

Glorious Sex

over our faces and walked exhausted but triumphant over to the canteen for breakfast. No one was ever the wiser. And I still savoured the kiss which promised so much.

Some may remember their stay at school as the 'best years of their life', but not for me. I was pleased to leave them behind. My experiences at Steyning Grammar boarding school no doubt taught me independence and self-sufficiency but at a great loss to my all-round emotional development. It was not natural to live in an all-male community in which talking to girls was forbidden. Girls were never seen as friends but always as potential prey, mysterious creatures 'to get off' with. Unfortunately for me, soon after I left school it became a co-ed and I met several beautiful women in later life who had gone there. If only had I been a student then.

With two girls in Worthing

17

THE LAST
TERRIBLE YEARS

As with my prowess on the athletics field, I did reasonably well but not brilliantly at school exams. I always thought of myself as 'Mister Average', both in height – five foot eight and a half inches tall – and weight – nine and half stone. I felt the same in intellect; I tended to come in the top half of the class but rarely in the top ten. I enjoyed the outdoor life too much to be a 'swot' at school.

I took my 'O' levels without much preparation when I was still fifteen and got eight with reasonable grades in the arts and sciences. What should I do now? My brother had left school to go to a Navigation School at Warsach near Southampton and was about to go to sea with the P&O as a cadet officer but I did not want just to follow him.

My uncle was urging me to train in a 'profession'.

'If you become an accountant, you'll earn a lot of money and the world will be your oyster', my uncle would say. But I didn't know about 'oysters' and when I tried one I didn't like its cloying sliminess.

Apart from becoming an accountant – the last thing I wanted was to become like my uncle – all that seemed on offer was becoming a solicitor or an estate agent. Those jobs would involve being signed on as an 'articled clerk', my uncle explained, but the very words filled me with dread. The thought of living out my life in Bognor seemed like the kiss of death. The last thing I wanted to become was like the smug young men in sports jackets holding the handles of their knobbly beer glasses discussing their cars and mortgages in the Fox pub in Aldwick. I wanted to escape from the provincial stuffiness and cultural narrowness of Bognor as soon as possible.

Since I refused to become an articled clerk, it was decided that I should go back to Steyning as a boarder to do my 'A' levels. I drifted into Art, Geography and French. I liked Alabone the art master and I enjoyed painting nature scenes out of school. The works and lives of the Renaissance artists, such as Michelangelo and Da Vinci, and the Post-Impressionists Van Gogh, Gauguin and Cézanne were exciting and exotic like the black American jazz musicians I had read about and listened to for the Jazz Society. With geography, I thought I could get about and explore the contours of the hills and valleys and follow the courses of rivers and the currents of the sea. And for all his right-wing politics and narrow concern with money, my uncle had definitely instilled in me a love of French culture which appeared to me at once sensual, intellectual and daring.

Nevertheless, in the first year of sixth form I felt decidedly restless. I had outgrown school. I wanted to be away, not forced to wear a cap down the High Street and look like what I thought was a 'real berk'. I was made a dormitory captain in Coombe Court and felt even worse sleeping in the same dormitories as the younger boys.

My obsession with the other half of the species – girls – was if anything even greater.

Apart from my trips to France with my uncle, I had a two-week holiday on my own when I was about fifteen in Limoges (at the centre of the Massif Central mountains) which I reached by train via the Newhaven night ferry. The visit must have been arranged by the school.

I stayed in a small château of a man who owned a porcelain factory mainly producing traditional ware. He had two young daughters, one of whom was about my own age. I loved the *surprise-partie* they gave in the afternoon with their girlfriends although we were not allowed to drink alcohol. I rock 'n' rolled to Johnny Hallyday and twisted with the best of them under the bright lights of their drawing room. However, I was unable to get any further with the lovely girls. I had breakfast with them – a fresh piece of broken baguette with butter and delicious milky cocoa in a bowl – but went into town when they went to school.

I also went on holiday with my uncle and aunt to Benidorm in Spain in the summer. We parked our caravan very close to the beach. I started eyeing a tall, lithe girl who was very brown and in a pink bikini. I eventually plucked up the courage to talk to her and it turned out that she was German and called Claudia. My German was non-existent but she was learning English. We soon became intimate friends. I would meet her after our meal in the evening and snog endlessly with her on the sand close to the sea. She seemed as eager as I was to learn about loving. She allowed

Aged about 16

me to fondle her small breasts with her hard nipples but pulled my hand away if I went lower and tried to find what was behind the bottom of her pink bikini.

Her father was a squat, balding man – a vet from Stuttgart. My aunt had previously hated all Germans and was opposed with even great violence to any peace-loving 'conchies'. Yet surprisingly she got on very well with him. Perhaps this was because he expressed anti-Hitler and anti-Nazi views. But I was only interested in the brown, slender, nubile Claudia and we usually walked around hand-in-hand. She taught me a few German phrases which I have never forgotten: *Ich liebe dich* and *Du bist mein klein schatz* ('I love you' and 'you are my little treasure').

After two weeks we had to say goodbye. She promised me that she would write to me at my boarding school. Tears flowed down both our cheeks when we said *Auf Wiedersehen* and that night I cried in bed in the caravan. I remember my uncle's leg touching mine as he said to me:

'Don't worry. You'll see her soon. You'll find that there will be many other women in your life who will break your heart!'

He was right of course although I did not want to hear him at the time.

Claudia was my first real love. I replied to her letters in my first year in the sixth form at boarding school but they became more intermittent as we got on with our lives. I did not see her until she came over with her parents a year later in the summer. I was digging a trench during the holidays at the caravan park where my uncle and aunt had a mobile home. I looked up from my hard labour in the wet clay and saw her towering over me. I realised then that I did not love her anymore. She no doubt felt the same. It was a sad ending to our innocent love in a foreign land. I later learned that she had been killed in a car crash when she was twenty four although her child survived.

What was really on my mind were other girls, how to escape from school and what to do with my life. At one stage, I played with the idea of becoming a civil engineer, of building bridges and roads, but did I really want to spend my life around Britain on muddy sites? Being a pilot like my father appealed and I thought of applying to Cranwell College, but I wasn't doing the right 'A' levels in science for that.

During the Christmas holidays, I raised the burning issue of my future career with 'Uncle Jim' who managed the Bridport Hotel for my grandmother. He was a handsome, dashing man who had met his Scottish wife when he was in hospital and spent most of his time at the local golf club. I told him that I wanted to do something exciting, something which would get me out of Bognor.

'Then why don't you become a purser with the P&O company like I was?' he said. 'It's the best company and it's a great life for a young man. You'll be on a passenger ship, travelling around the world – to America, India and Australia. You'll have a great time. As an officer, you'll have the run of the ship and if you want there's a party every night. If you don't want to stay in Bognor and want something adventurous, why not try that?'

'Why did you give it up?'

'Ill-health. I had too good a time and got stomach ulcers! But that's another story…'

Ever since I was a young lad playing sandcastles or making dams on the beach I had wondered what was over the horizon of the Channel and far away. And my Pop had told me when I was very young that if I dug a hole deep enough in our garden I would eventually come out the other side in Australia or New Zealand.

For a couple of years my brother had been a cadet navigation officer in the same company and came back with enticing stories of 'Aussie birds', of monkeys taken on board as pets, of picking apples in Tasmania, and of visiting 'Cherry girls' in Hong Kong bars.

So I decided to apply for the job. I read on an information sheet from the P&O-Orient Management in London (P&O had recently merged with Orient Lines) that the company ran a service of passenger liners to Australia, India, the Far East and the west coast of North America. "The Purser deals with the ship's accounts and clerical business', it read 'and supervises the service to passengers, their berthing, feeding, comfort and entertainment. His work resembles that of a hotel manager ashore.' Apart from academic qualifications in which English and maths were essential, a Purser cadet could join at 16 to 18 years of age. He had to show signs of leadership and be of 'good manner and appearance.'

The actual work all sounded rather boring but at least it would get me out of boarding school and the stifling provinciality of Bognor and go around the world. I applied for the job and was invited up to the main office in Leadenhall Street for an interview. I was still 16 at the time and my 'Uncle Jim' advised me to remember the number of the bus I took to the office in case they asked me.

He also told me to make sure that I cleaned the back of my shoes. In fact I went by Underground but I did carefully polish my shoes which were usually badly scuffed.

The interview took place in front of half a dozen imposing men, some of them in uniform, in a dark, wood-panelled room. There were paintings of past presidents of the company and of ships on the walls. It seemed very daunting, sitting alone in front of them, but I was determined to get the job and spoke up and was polite as I could be, calling them all 'Sir' – something which I was used to at boarding school.

They asked me why I wanted to join the company. I told them about Uncle Jim's recommendation (omitting the reference to parties), my family background in hotels, and my wish to travel the world. Then one of them leaned forward and asked intently:

'We often have mixed crews. What do you think of black people?'

In those days crews from Goa in India worked on the boats as stewards and there were Chinese men working in the laundries. The only Indians I had come across were the waiters in the local curry restaurants which my Uncle Al used to take me to (having been responsible for the dispatches in India during the war he was keen on curries).

'I don't know any, Sir', I replied. 'There's none at our school. But I think we're all the same, whatever our colour or creed. We have the same blood in our veins.' I didn't mention my love of jazz or respect for the black musicians of the United States.

I seemed to satisfy my inquisitors – a few weeks later I got a letter of acceptance. I was to report to Head Office at the end of August.

Fabulous. It would mean that I would only have a term and half of my first year in the six form to go. Not surprisingly, I did little work. The masters left me alone, for they knew I was on my way out. Because of the boredom, I spent a lot of the time playing poker with the other boys and built a large collection of IOU notes from them. When termed ended, they all refused to pay me and since I was leaving I could do nothing about it. Appealing to their sense of fair play was not enough. But it didn't matter for at last I was leaving Steyning Grammar School for good. I was joyous when I packed my trunk and emptied my tuck box for the last time. All my friends were envious as I said goodbye. They would have to return to the grind for another year while I would be off meeting girls and sailing the world.

During the summer, I got a job as a part-time gardener in a big house at the end of Victoria Drive in Bognor. In previous years I had summer jobs picking peas (back-breaking work, especially carrying a bushel full in a wooden crate) and packing lettuces in cardboard boxes at the end of an assembly line (utterly boring). By contrast, the gardening was light and above all there were 'foreign girls' to meet.

The husband in the big house travelled to London every day to work as a photographer on *The Times*. His imperious wife had a few foreign girls who had come over to learn English and a bit about the 'British way of life.' They were my age. It couldn't have been better. I soon managed to kiss a beautiful but slightly plump Moroccan girl by the lily pond but she soon left for home. There was a willowy French girl called Françoise who was next, and although she allowed me to go further, our passionate French kissing was slightly marred by the unfamiliar smell of garlic and Camembert on her breath.

A friend of the family, a fit-looking young man with curly hair, had his eye on the owner's beautiful daughter. He was keen member of the Young Liberals and would take me and the foreign girls with him in an old van on outings. For rustic culture, we went to a pub called the 'Lantern Arms' down a lane in a beech wood on the South Downs north of Chichester. Pints of beer were drawn from barrels in the candle-lit farmhouse kitchen. Around 'Time', when the drinkers were expected to leave, the old grand-dad would appear with a false leg topped with a gaiter and would sing saucy folk songs in a broad Sussex dialect. For high culture, we went to the recently opened Chichester Festival Theatre, which had a round stage, to see Bernard Shaw's *Saint Joan*. The director of the new theatre was the well-known actor Lawrence Olivier.

While giving me a lift home, the Young Liberal had a serious accident and wrote off his white van. I ended up with a massive egg on my forehead where I hit the windscreen. I didn't really understand his Liberal politics, but I liked him and his cheery manner and his talk about having free choice and free speech.

I knew these summer flirtations would soon come to an end but I didn't mind because I would soon be off to sea. As I was preparing to go to London a letter arrived from the P&O-Orient

company. As I opened it, I assumed that it would give me more details of my training as a purser cadet. Then I read:

Dear Mr Marshall,

Since you have already completed one year of your 'A' levels course, we have come to the conclusion that it would be in the best interest of yourself and the Company if you stay on another year at your school to complete your studies. You can then join us at the end of August next year.

Yours faithfully, &c

I couldn't believe my eyes. My whole world fell in. To have to go back to Steyning after having said goodbye to everybody – I couldn't imagine anything more embarassing! My mother frantically rang up the headmaster but he said firmly that there was no longer a place for me in the boarding school. If I wanted to come back, it would have to be as a day boy. To become a 'day-bug' of all things – what an unbelievable indignity!

I now had the problem of travelling to school. I had to go by train from Bognor to Steyning which meant I had to change at Barnham Junction, catch the Brighton train, and then change again at Shoreham by Sea and take the old steam train which went to Horsham. It took about an hour and a half each way, three hours travelling a day if I were lucky.

The only respite was an intriguing diminutive girl dressed in a black coat and with black gloves who travelled from Bognor to Worthing where she was in the sixth form at the high school. I deliberately became friendly with her younger sister from whom I learned that she was the daughter of a film director and already had a boyfriend. Such was my luck.

When the weather improved in the spring I went occasionally on my clapped-out motorbike, wearing Second-World-War overalls, via Amberley and Storrington. I wore goggles and enjoyed travelling in the sunshine with the wind in my face and trees, hedgerows and fields all around me. I particularly liked the 'fair-mile bottom' between Fontwell and Ringwood along the valley between ancient yew and beech woods and the undulating stretch from Amberley by the River Arun to Storrington. The big problem was that my old BSA 125cc Bantam motorcycle, acquired for £10, kept breaking down.

Closing in on the village of Steyning filled me with dread. I not only had to go back to a school as an ignominious 'day-bug' but only went through the motions of studying in class. I was often simply not prepared. At home too it felt very strange. I used to hate it when my mother praised me in front of others: 'You're a good boy.'

One day I shouted at her: 'You think you know me but you don't. I have an evil side as well!'

I slammed the front door and went for a run along the beach. I often did this to let off steam, sometimes accompanied by my grandmother's young dachshund dog which dragged its long body over the seaweed-strewn breakwaters. All the travelling and being a 'day-bug' were shredding my nerves. I just wanted the time to pass as quickly as possible so I could go to London.

I escaped that long winter into French novels and symbolist poetry. Stendhal, Balzac and Verlaine were my favourites. The latter summed up my dominant mood which was one of listless melancholy: *Il pleure dans mon Coeur/ Comme il pleut sur la ville* ('My heart weeps just as the rain falling on the town').

One evening I was engrossed in the novel *Madame Bovary*. Like me, she was yearning for romantic adventures and attachments beyond her provincial life married to a doctor whose conversation was as *platte comme le trottoir* ('flat as the pavement'). I knew exactly what she felt.

It had grown dark and I was reading by the light of the coal fire in the front lounge, lying on my stomach and stretched out on the rug. Then suddenly a blinding light was switched on. It was my tall Uncle Al, his eyes bulging and red in the face.

'What do you think you're doing boy?' he shouted at me. 'Reading a novel instead of getting down to your homework! You're useless. You'll never come to anything in your life...'

I hated him then for his rough incursion. I could have said the same thing about him, having not passed his accountancy exams then taken over his mother's hotel as an easy option. I realised later on in my life that it had been a crucial experience in my teenage years; nothing less than an existential shock. I was determined to prove him wrong, whatever the cost.

Still it did not change the fundamental problems of travelling to school and having no real friends in Bognor where I lived.

Having not bothered for my first year in the sixth form because I

Bognor Boy

was ready to go to London, I found the second year of my A-levels as a 'day-bug' not at all inspiring. I was tired out both by the long travelling and, now, being an outsider at the school. I passed my Art exams mainly I think because of the Art History paper and the nature painting I did which showed the roots of an upturned tree on the imaginary slopes of the Downs.

In French I learned long lists of vocabulary but they remained like beads on a necklace, not run together to form coherent sentences.

I liked French literature – Balzac, Stendhal, Zola, Flaubert, Maupassant – but mainly as an escape from my terrible predicament. The books I read were translated into English; I did not bother much with the language. Understandably, I failed my French A-level and was given another O-level as a consolation prize.

For Geography, a third of the final mark was meant to be based on a case study of 'the effect of longshore drift along the beach off Bognor Regis.' Of itself this was an interesting subject and I wanted to see why the stones collected on the eastern side of the wooden groynes. But I never got round to the study – the theodolite which I was meant to measure the drift remained on its tripod in the dark corner in the cupboard under the stairs. I never learnt how to use the instrument and it leaned in the dark as an eternal question mark and occasional reproach. When it came to the final exam I chose a paper instead on the use and understanding of maps which I then knew little about. Not surprisingly, I gained yet another O-level rather than passing the A-level.

The headmaster, the Scout master, the vicar and the masters had all tried to instill in me with their dreary speeches obedience to God, the Queen, Country and above all to Authority in general. They singularly failed. The British Empire in the late fifties and early sixties was crumbling fast but in the Home Counties its old values were still inculcated into us on a daily basis. Throughout my school career, the stress was on duty, not pleasure; on obedience, not freedom. The idea of freedom was a very intoxicating idea to a boy at a boarding school with such rigid rules and conservative orthodoxy.

Years later my brother wrote to me: 'It never ceases to amaze me how much trauma I got from that school, and it is nearly 20 years ago; the feelings now are, as I remember them, the same as that I felt in Steyning, a sort of quiet melancholy.' I felt the same, as no doubt many other boys did.

On 14 of August 1963, just before my eighteenth birthday, I got a letter from my brother who was 'at sea', having just entered the Mediterranean. He called France my 'second home' and urged me not to 'try to be too avant garde!' I took that as a compliment although he didn't intend it to be. But he finished the letter: 'All the best Pete, God Bless, your loving brother Mike.'

Then what I had been waiting for eventually happened. At the beginning of September, ten days after my eighteenth birthday, I went to the P&O-Orient Company in London, the great mysterious, wicked and intriguing capital. I caught the train to Victoria – those trips to see the Crazy Gang and the stays with my grandmother's friends in Penge had been my only previous visits to London. I had no idea where I should stay that night but I had heard that Aussies made for West London. I caught the tube there and came out at Earls Court at dusk in a duffel coat carrying a small bag to the sound of many pigeons cooing who, like me, were trying to find a roost for the night.

18
NOT SO
SWINGING LONDON

I felt great but also anxious. Great because at last I had left my school and the stifling provincialism of Bognor and was now in one of the great capitals of the world.

The year 1964 was meant to be the beginning of 'Swinging London', a reaction against the post-war austerity which I had definitely felt in Bognor. I had been prepared for it by 'Bill Haley and his Comets'; I had seen his film *Rock around the Clock* in the Picturedrome in Bognor with girls screaming and many dancing in the aisles. I had learned how to dance the 'Rock & Roll', the 'Twist' and the 'Shake' to the music of 'The Beatles', 'The Rolling Stones', 'The Kinks' and others.

There was a new-found freedom in the air, with money in people's pockets and a cultural revolution taking place in which the young challenged the old fuddy-duddy 'Establishment' and the class-ridden society which was still prevalent. There was even a revolution in fashion, with girls wearing 'miniskirts', high boots, and brightly coloured clothes – anything against the old, grey, middle-class, up-tight and conformist Britain. The 'pill' had been recently developed and many girls felt liberated, able to have sex whenever they wanted without worrying about becoming pregnant. Bob Dylan's 'the times they are a changin'' seemed to sum up the new atmosphere of innovation and freedom.

I really wanted to join this rebelling youth. Life in the capital was meant to be 'cool' and 'hip'. But here I was, about to enter one of the oldest, most conservative and traditional companies in the world. When I went for my interview with the P&O-Orient Line the men of the City still wore the uniforms of dark suits, rolled umbrellas and bowler hats. I was therefore somewhat apprehensive about how I would get on with my new colleagues and where I would have to go for training. The whole thing felt against the grain.

Bognor Boy

I also had the little problem of finding somewhere to sleep that first night and a bedsit for the next couple of months. Standing on a platform at Earls Court I decided to ask couple of likely-looking lads about my age whether they knew of a place to stay. One was tall with a sports jacket and the other was smaller and rounder but no less cheery. Following my question they looked at each other, nodded their heads slightly and then the smaller one said:

'Why not stay with us? You can sleep on the floor of our sitting room. I warn you though that it's a very small flat in a cellar and no sunshine comes into it!'

I was only too pleased to rest my head somewhere. The lads turned out to be BBC trainees, the tall one called Tom wanted to become a cameraman and the other called Piers hoped to become an assistant producer. They clearly enjoyed being in London in the mid-60s and were full of fun. But their flat at 37B Maclise Road, about half a mile away at the back of the Olympia in West Kensington, was certainly dark and damp. The narrow hallway which led into it was covered in green mould with the wall paper peeling off. I spent the night on a filthy carpet in a damp sleeping bag but nevertheless slept like a log, only too pleased to be in London at last.

Pete Norman in August 1964

After a few weeks on their floor, I managed to arrange with my old school friend Pete Norman, who was now living with his parents in Epsom and working as an insurance clerk in the city, to rent a ground floor bedsit in a slum tenement at 8 Sevington Street, Maida Vale, close to Paddington. Again it was a pretty awful place, with the old faded red lino on the floor and two rickety beds which had a deep furrow in the middle and made a terrible grating noise whenever you turned over. The 'kitchen' was behind a small partition with a couple of cooking rings. At night, I could hear mice running across the dirty floor and one morning a mouse fell out of the cornflakes' packet. This happened on two occasions! But I did not mind too much because I was excited to have my whole life in front of me. I had also started training with the P&O-Orient Line which would introduce me to many new parts of London.

I started off with six other Purser Cadets. One of them dropped out because he felt so homesick in a bedsit on his own, particularly at the long weekends. After reporting for duty at head office in Leadenhall Street in the City at the beginning of October our first port of call was the booking office – a grand neoclassical building at the bottom of the Haymarket and close to Trafalgar Square. It had a huge, cavernous, wood-panelled room at its entrance with row upon row of clerks sitting behind desks ready to serve passengers who came in to make bookings. It was before the time of cheap airline flights so they did particularly well with Australians and New Zealanders – 'Aussies' and 'Kiwis' – as well as with passengers who wanted to go on a cruise. My job as a Purser Cadet was simply to learn how everything was done so I was sent from one department to another, observing things and writing up my impressions in a large green journal.

On the first floor at the booking office at the bottom of the Haymarket there were countless clerks dictating answers to letters from potential passengers. I felt they were poor lost souls, trying to keep up appearances on a pittance, chained to their desks and forced to be polite. There was also an overflowing typing pool with young girls making a terrible din and bashing away at typewriters for all they were worth. I particularly felt sorry for the girls but at the same time excited by their curves, their perfume, their painted long nails, and their short skirts. Nearly all of them felt their work was temporary and were waiting for 'Mr Right' to pluck them out of the typing pool so that they could become mums in the suburbs.

I had read in a newspaper at the time that most men died within two years of their retirement at 65. I was determined therefore not to worry about getting a mortgage or a pension as I would soon die when I had paid them off. It simply showed that the suburban life of extended boredom and quiet despair was not for me.

The booking office was next door to Trafalgar Square with its lions guarding the fountain, and its worn stone steps going up to

Bognor Boy

the National Gallery and the National Portrait Gallery. I would often go into the square with my sandwiches – bought with Luncheon Vouchers – to sit on a bench in the autumn sunshine, surrounded by interested pigeons. I also ventured into the National Gallery where I saw some of the Impressionist and Post-impressionist paintings which I particularly liked.

Early in October 1964 I saw a play of the novel by Ivan Goncharov called *Oblomov*, starring Spike Milligan, at the Lyric Theatre nearby. The main character was a minor Russian landowner who thought there was no reason to get out of bed since life had so little meaning for him. Spike ad-libbed and acted the clown. It was a hilarious performance but had a serious message. The idea behind the play chimed with the opening of Camus' *Myth of Sisyphus* where he says that the great question of the 20th century is why a person should not commit suicide. His idea was to get people thinking about the meaning of their life in an absurd world and why they should live in the first place. I asked myself the question and felt that it was important not to kill oneself but to forge one's own set of values and destiny and not live as others would want you to.

That and Jean-Paul Sartre's short essay 'Existentialism is a Humanism' made me both an existentialist and humanist at this stage. I was particularly impressed by Sartre's idea that since God does not exist there are no God-given values. It only confirmed my belief that we have to create our own. I was also impressed by his argument that we are 'condemned to be free' in the sense that we always have to make a choice. We can choose to be dead like an inert stone pretending that we have no choice or we can try to lead an authentic life in the face of our own inevitable death. I was only just 18 but their writings left a deep impression on me.

Another influence at this time was going down on Sunday morning to Hyde Park Speakers' Corner. Here were all sorts of people arguing for all sorts of things, from Black Consciousness, Nihilism to Communism. Revolution was definitely in the air although I'd become part of one of the most conservative companies in the world with old traditions running back to the Age of Empire. Did not the words 'A1' (the best cabin on the top deck) and 'Posh' (Port Outwards and Starboard Homewards) come from the P&O? On the India run the coolest and most comfortable cabins were considered to be on the Port side of the ship in the shade going out to the old colony while coming back it was on the Starboard side out of the sun.

The talk and discussions at Hyde Park on Sunday morning were very heady for me as a young man and I heard ideas and opinions that had never occurred to me at boarding school which had been so Anglican and Conservative. It was indeed free speech in action. Although there were a few police constables in tall helmets around they never seemed to intervene.

The general attack on the Establishment, those politicians, bishops, judges, industrialists and aristocrats who had gone to Oxbridge and held power in the land, made me think anew. One man in particular I liked to listen to was Donald Soper, a Methodist preacher with white straight hair who wore an old black cassock and dog collar. He was a socialist, an opponent of blood sports and nuclear weapons and, above all, a pacifist. He argued for true democracy and equality. He wanted to see the upper house of parliament – the Lords – abolished as it contained a bunch of unelected old buffers ('proof of the reality of life after death', as he put it). He believed that the principal means of production, distribution and exchange should be nationalised. He was particularly critical of the British Empire and supported the new independence of the former colonies. The way forward, he argued, was to have common ownership rather than have private wealth in the hands of a few selfish individuals.

Listening to him and his agile mind, I realised that I was not only an existentialist but fast becoming a socialist too. He echoed the opinions of my old history master Arthur Lee at Steyning.

His argument for pacifism drew on his personal experience. He said that one day he was reading in his armchair behind a door when a rough man entered with a gun. It was like the Raffles' stories I had heard in the art room at school all over again. But he told the intruder quietly:

'I am behind the door but don't worry I am no threat to you. You can take what you want. It doesn't mean much to me anyway.'

Here was a man who set no great store by private property and personal possessions and was not frightened by a man with a gun. Having engaged the robber in conversation he managed to persuade him not only to throw away his gun but even to go straight in the future! It was yet another illustration for me that persuasion can be more effective than force, a view I had held and practised as a dormitory captain.

While living with Pete Norman in our bedsit in a slum in Maida Vale, part of Paddington, we started to gamble on the horses as a means of spicing up our life. I was bored observing people work in the P&O and he was even more bored as a clerk in the 'Sun Life' insurance company in the city. As young men we wanted the excitement and the intensity of living. We did not find it drinking bottles of brown ale in the Music Hall in a huge smoky room at the back of a local pub. The huge owner and MC celebrated the Empire by singing at his upright honky-tonk piano – in a Cockney accent – 'The Road to Mandalay'. Eating jellied eels and cockles from a barrow outside the pub or walking along the filthy canal in Paddington didn't seem like the height of entertainment or all that we could get out of life. After all, we were young, eighteen, all 'dressed up' and raring to go.

We therefore formed in our house a gambling syndicate which consisted of a Swedish would-be actor (who lived above our room and who paced up and down, reading out loud long extracts from Shakespeare); a red-headed Irish girl (who worked as a waitress at a chain restaurant); and an intriguing diminutive secretary in her late 20s (who always dressed in black and lived in the top garret).

My brother Michael was back from the sea doing his second mate's certificate and lived temporarily with his girlfriend Shirley in a bedsit opposite ours on the other side of the road. He also joined the syndicate and threw in a few pounds.

We persuaded them that they would get their return on their investment in the syndicate by us betting on their behalf each way on the second favourite horse at each meeting which had six races. If we lost a race then we would double up our stake on the next race but if we won we would stop there. Very soon we had a common kitty of £500, a fortune for us at the time.

With my brother Michael, we placed on 27 March 1965 a bet on our estranged father's horse 'Black Spot', ridden by Johnny Gamble in the Grand National at Aintree Racecourse near Liverpool. We watched the race on a small black-and-white television owned by the girl in the top bedsit.

'Black Spot' was considered a rank outsider, with the bookmakers offering about 100 to 1, but it ploughed through the high fences. To our amazement, it lay third at the second last fence from home and was coming up fast. We were all cheering like mad; it was the first time that something in our father's life had directly impinged and affected us. We were about to make a lot of money but the horse, to our unbelieving dismay, pulled up at the last fence – we never knew why. After that I didn't bet much on my father's horses, although he was going from strength to strength.

I noticed after a while that the hands of my friend Pete Norman shook in the local betting office whenever our chosen horse was moving towards the winning line. He was becoming too emotionally and personally involved. This culminated one afternoon when he broke our agreement and used all the kitty money on his own and bet on the first favourite rather than each way on the second as agreed; it lost. He did not want to tell me and the others so he borrowed about £500 from the lift man at work in the city who was also a gambling man.

Pete Norman then literally 'went to the dogs'. In this case he lost all this money at an evening meeting at White City – famous for its greyhound racing. He had no alternative but to admit his debt to his father and me. His father immediately came up from Epsom and paid off the lift man with a cheque but refused to pay us anything. Poor old Pete Norman had to return home to Epsom and slowly pay of his debt to his father with his monthly pay in the same boring job in the City. Needless to say, the members of our syndicate in our tenement were not too pleased but then several told me that they did not expect to get back their money in the first place.

I went to stay with Pete Norman in Epsom a few times at the weekend but he was not his old carefree self. His debt to his father was too much. He did not like staying at home but felt he had no choice. I gradually lost contact with him, particularly as he didn't come up to our bedsit again and I was soon to go to sea.

I got a letter from him on 23 May 1966 saying that he had sent two previous ones that I never received because I was at sea. Living in Reading, he wrote that – with two other partners – he had gone into the road transport 'business'. He added: 'Do not be noble and join the ranks of the unemployed.' I would rather be 'noble' than go into 'business' to exploit others. The company probably went bust for the last thing I heard about him was that he had become a travelling salesman and died at the age of 27 from lung cancer.

I had been brought up in Bognor and at school to think that 'class' was very important. My middle-class and socially aspiring grandmother had been horrified that the first girl friend of my brother had been the daughter of a local fisherman. No doubt partly by reaction and partly because of my new-found socialism, I was intrigued to find out how the 'other half lived'. In this case, the so-called 'working class'.

Bognor Boy

One evening I had a bit of a fling with the Irish girl in our Paddington tenement. She was returning from a day's work serving in the 'Happy Platter.' I liked her and we chatted on the stairs until it grew dark about her life in rural Ireland. One thing led to another, as they say, and we kissed each other. She was very willing and it was very beautiful but I found her auburn hair smelt badly of frying. It rather put me off. We remained friends thereafter but I did not want to go any further, especially as I was only there temporarily.

As part of my training to become a Purser Cadet I was sent to an evening class in Victoria to learn about accountancy. I was soon able to do a profit and loss account but the experience only confirmed for me that finance was a dismal science and that I had been right not to have become a provincial accountant as my uncle had wished. Having just done an A-level course in the subject, I was also sent during the day to attend a French conversation class at a language school in Oxford Street. Our teacher was a smallish young French woman dressed in black who I very rapidly had a crush on. I had recently seen the film *Jules et Jim* and she reminded me of the beautiful actress Jean Moreau. I did my necessary homework but also showed her the poetry I had been writing. I even wrote for her some French verses of my own. She said she was impressed but – being about five years older than me and probably having her own boyfriend – our relationship sadly remained Platonic.

This was not the case in early January 1965 at my brother's 21st birthday which took place in a flat of some Australian girls he knew in Green Park. I went with a fellow Purser Cadet called R.E.F Stemp who had been doing the rounds of the P&O-Orient offices with me. We tended to call each other by our surnames as we had done at school. His father had an aircraft factory in Manchester and although only 18 years old he had receding black hair and an 'afternoon shadow' on his chin. He had brought with him some champagne which – with a cigarette in his mouth – he duly opened. Someone took a photograph of him with my brother Michael, his girlfriend Shirley, an Australian girl and me.

A girl in the crowd of revellers soon made a beeline for me. She came from the East End of London with a pronounced Cockney accent. About my height, she had long brown curly hair, a dark blouse over small breasts, a dark-coloured miniskirt and tights with knee-high boots. I was dressed with a narrow tie, narrow

R.E.F. Stemp, an Australian girl, me, Shirley and Michael

trousers and started off with a light corduroy jacket. After dancing the 'Shake' together to the latest Beatles' records she became more intimate and we decided to go to the dark bedroom where people had laid their coats. We were soon kissing passionately on the bed. She started to fondle me. As another couple came into the darkened room she suggested moving to the toilet 'where we can be more on our own, like.' We continued to caress each other, with growing passion. It was not long before I realised she wanted to make love and I was certainly only too pleased. The upshot was that I lost my virginity with this strange, beautiful girl standing up against a wall. We both seem to have an explosive orgasm very quickly at the same time; for me, it was truly wonderful.

I learned the next day from one of the Aussie girls that she had told her that as I came through the door in the flat she had decided to 'ave me' that night at the party. I was extremely flattered by her as well as being elated that I had at long last lost my virginity. I tried to contact her by telephone where she lived in the East End but she would have nothing of it. I always regretted not seeing her again. Although she no doubt forgot me long ago, I could never forget her.

After spending some time at the booking office in the West End and at the offices of the P&O-Orient Line in the city, I was sent down to Tilbury Docks to see how the ships were filled with new stores and made ready to go back to sea again. I saw the old ship *Chusan* which my mother had been on for a cruise down to Casablanca in Morocco. It was comparatively small with beautiful wood-panelled rooms. At sea, it had Goanese stewards from mainly Catholic Goa (it had been a Portuguese colony) in India and some Chinese in the laundry in its stern.

I found the ships swarming with workers making them ready. They had been transformed from sleek ocean-going vessels to lame ducks wallowing in filthy and fetid water. I was warned not to fall in the dock which sent bubbles of noxious gas to the surface as it would mean having all my clothes burnt and being sent to hospital to have my stomach pumped out. The dock workers were still very well organised in their unions. Having been brought up on the Sussex coast and at boarding school it was strange to hear the East End Cockney accents and to see the flat caps all around me.

My journal in a large green ledger was complete for the year but it was full of the bald facts and unimaginative observations of a young man wandering around the offices and ships of the P&O-Orient Line. It did not give, however, any inkling of my real thoughts and feelings. While I already had misgivings about becoming a cadet officer on a cruise ship, I still wanted to travel around the world and visit as many ports as possible.

I had learned that a cruise ship was divided into three areas: the deck department, which navigated the ship from port to port and was responsible for the cargo; the engineering department which, as its name suggests, was responsible for the ship's engines; and the purser department which held the 'purse' of the ship, was responsible for the comfort and entertainment of all on board, directed the galley, ordered the stewards who served in the restaurant and who looked after the cabins. The pursers also had to link up with the shore authorities.

In fact, a cruise ship was very much like a floating hotel in which the pursers ran the hotel side and the deck and the engineering departments made sure that it got from A to B. Because they were primarily concerned with the paperwork I soon became aware that the purser department was the least romantic. It was also part of the rigid hierarchy of shipboard life where the word of the captain was virtually law and the officers of the departments could not be disobeyed however one might disagree with their decisions. You had to call a senior officer 'Sir', simply obey orders and never answer back.

In many ways it was just a continuation of the rigidity, authority and hierarchy I had experienced at boarding school. No wonder the company liked to recruit its officers from grammar and public schools where 'insubordination' would not be tolerated. If it had not promised the prospect of seeing the world, experiencing the 'exotic' and encountering the unknown, I would not have gone to sea with such a company. I had been trained for it but my new-found socialism and sense of justice and equality made me question it. The clash between the two world views would not only be painful but lead to an unexpected result.

My mother paid £100 for my uniform, having as she put it 'worked her fingers to the bone' doing hairdressing at home in Bognor. I was duly thankful to her. I did not like, however, the tailor of my uniform in the City who was very creepy and took too much time over measuring my inside leg.

We were to wear dark blue uniforms in the cool weather and then change into starched whites in the Bay of Biscay where the weather turned hotter. On the shoulders of my uniform I had epaulettes of gold on a white background and gold buttons which denoted me as an officer and a purser. Leading 'hands' of the crew only had silver on their uniform. The rest of the 'ratings' had nothing. Rank was defined by metal and it meant so much to a lot of the uniform-wearers.

For the last summer holiday before I went to sea I came home to Bognor. My Uncle Al, who liked to claim paternal authority, took me aside and said in no uncertain terms:

'That's it. From now on you'll not get a bean from the family. You're on your own.'

I was 17 at the time and shocked once again by his aggressive words but I never asked for money from my family for the rest of my life. In a way he did me a favour as from then on I was free and responsible for my own life.

About this time I read Sartre's autobiography of his early years called *Words* where he said that he was grateful for his father having died when he was two years old. He did not have to carry his father on his back as many of his friends did. Having not seen my father or being contacted by him since I was two I could see what he meant, especially when I saw how my friends had to come to terms with their fathers and were often crippled in their decisions and actions by them. I was determined to not carry my uncle on my back instead.

I stayed in Chideock in Bognor with my grandmother, mother and her new husband. His name was Oliver Townsend but everybody called him 'Sandy' because of the colour of his hair when he was young. I knew him when his hair was going grey – he had all his teeth out at 50. He had been apprenticed as a stone carver, with one day-release at an art college, and had worked in the churches of Devon. As a member of the Exeter Cycling Club – which went all over the county – he knew Dartmoor like the back of his hand. He was a self-taught musician on the accordion – the squeeze box – and knew a huge selection of songs and tunes.

During the war he had joined the Army as a soldier. Tragically, he had volunteered to try out a new mask against gas which they feared that the Germans might use. It made the men feel very claustrophobic; they pulled off their masks and were seriously gassed. He never fully recovered and was unfit to see action and after the war was unable – so he said – to return to his trade. He went to work in a conifer forest near Exeter planting trees as a forester in the hope that the air and life in the open would improve his lungs. After his first marriage broke up – because of an affair his wife had with a local shop manager – he left her and three boys and then drifted from one job to the next around southern England.

My mother had met him ballroom dancing in Bognor but she was adamant she would not get married until her 'boys' were settled in their careers. They got married in a registry office, had a reception in a pub nearby in Aldwick and spent the first night of their married life in the second best hotel in Bognor near the pier. She had had 'boyfriends' whom we were obliged to call 'uncles' in the past but they had never come to very much. Once in Paris with a friend she went out with the heir of Hermès (a luxury French store famous for its silk scarfs), and on one of her many cruises (during which she invariably won the deck quoits and table tennis tournaments) had a serious fling with a Portuguese man (she had a photograph to prove it). However, the idea of my middle-aged mother having sex was not an inspiring one and I quickly banished the thought.

I saw many girls on holiday that summer parading up and down the promenade in Bognor. They just further inflamed my desires. Despite my best efforts to 'get off' with them I was not very successful. Nearly all were working-class girls (who worked in factories or typing pools) down from the Midlands and the North

Not so Swinging London

on holiday for a week or two.

I was then invited out of the blue to what the French called a *surprise-partie* at the big house at the end of Victoria Drive where the previous summer I had sporadically worked as a gardener. I was meant to go out with Françoise once again but my eyes were on Jenny, a black girl who spoke very good English.

Jenny had originally come from Martinique in the Caribbean but – when she was ten months old – her father, a writer and French teacher at a *lycée* at Fontainebleau called Joseph Zobel, had brought her over to metropolitan France with her mother and two older brothers. She told me that she had grown up in Fontainebleau until she was ten and half years old and then went with her father to Sénégal in West Africa. He was meant to become the headmaster of a new school in the country but soon got fed up with it and moved to the capital Dakar to become the Director of Culture on the national radio. Jenny had been for a short while at boarding school with much bigger girls when her family was away but then had attended a *lycée* in Dakar. She was now at the university studying English. Her family, it seemed, had an old house called Moun Oustau (which means 'My House' in Provençal) near Anduze in the Cevennes in southern France where they went during the summer holidays. It had once been a small silk farm.

I had briefly met her brother Roland the year before on the beach milling around with the other foreign students. He was going out with a Swedish girl. One cold day I lent him a pullover and, taking off my 'L' plates, gave him a lift on my small BSA Bantam motorbike to where he was staying at the end of Victoria Drive. He seemed friendly enough although his English was not great. He was attending an art school in France.

I immediately felt attracted to his younger sister Jenny when she came over the following year. No doubt I had been prepared by my love of jazz, French culture and the exotic in general (at least for me, a provincial boy from a seaside resort on the Channel coast) to fall for a beautiful, lithe, vivacious black girl who lived in Africa. Whereas my family had little education, hers was French-speaking, well-educated and very different.

I had just passed my test and my grandmother and mother lent me their new, white Austin Mini and I drove, with Jenny, all over West Sussex, up on the Downs and down by the sea. It was a magical and heady time. Although we were together for only about

Bognor Boy

two weeks we fell, as they say, 'madly in love' with each other. We did everything but sleep together – to my chagrin and probably her relief. When she left London to fly home I saw her off and returned to sleep on the floor of a room in a Hammersmith bedsit which my brother was renting from some Hungarian refugees at the time. I was inconsolable and cried myself to sleep in my sleeping bag on the hard floor. We vowed to write and hoped to see each other again. But I was off soon on the SS *Oronsay* to go around the world as a Purser Cadet.

19

AT SEA AT LAST

Ijoined the passenger liner SS *Oronsay* in September 1965 in
Tilbury Docks. It looked beautiful, white, well-shaped and ready
to take on whatever the sea might throw at it. Its size overwhelmed
me as I went up the gangway in my blue uniform for the first time
and the 'leading hand' welcomed me on board. He called me 'Sir'
as an officer cadet despite being a middle-aged and experienced
man where I was a new innocent-looking boy just turned 19.

I could never get over this anomaly. But the thought of leaving
England and going round the world on the forthcoming voyage
and not coming back for at least nine months was heady indeed.
I had been longing for the day to come. Goodbye stifling Bognor,
goodbye the lost clerks of the shipping offices, goodbye England
with its damp weather, drab life and grey politicians. As I stepped
from the land onto the wood of the gangway everything was full
of promise and uncertainty. It was a momentous event in my
short life. I was stepping into the unknown and unexpected and I
revelled in it.

I sent a pretentious letter to Richard Collinson who had been a
cadet with my brother. We had become friendly after a visit to his
family in Norfolk. His mother put a rose in a vase and a copy of
Oscar Wilde's 'Ballad of Reading Gaol' by the side of my bed – I
had never been treated so well.

I wrote to him however from the ship SS *Oronsay*, still tied up in
Tilbury Dock:

> At the entrance to the Dock of Hell I write. Tilbury
> docks. In all its cesspit of tired suits, tired minds, and
> bloodshot eyes thrown together in one mute and inert
> pot. Outside the world circles and the leaves fall in
> dusty autumnal places, yet the incessant and effete
> conversations propagate, impervious to life's vitality.
> Surely this dockland is an aborted amorphous mass
> from the womb of an absolute evil being... There is
> nothing worse than the closed mind, the materialist,

In my Purser Cadet uniform

the despot... The White Collar and Cash Register which rule absolutely in England contribute the greatest portion of the English Death. The Necropolis which is the British Isles...

Meanwhile I shall experience the all-too-mortal, hedonistic pleasures of sea life. I have found that my entourage have the single ability of being able to say simply nothing on every subject of interest to me.

I was writing poetry at the time and intoxicated with the meaning and the use of language, especially with unusual words. And I was surely alienated from my work and fellow workers whom I considered like me to be wage slaves.

In the meantime, I learned that the SS *Oronsay* of the P&O-Orient Line had been named after a small island near Jura in north-west Scotland, the second Orient Line ship to be built after World War II. It was a passenger liner of about 27,600 tons and completed in 1951 in the Vickers-Armstrong shipbuilders in Barrow-in-Furness in the heyday of the British Merchant Navy. It was about 700 feet long with a beam of 94 feet and a draught of 31 feet. It could run at 22 knots with Parsons Marine steam turbines propelling two 'screws', that is to say, propellers. It was about to take me around the world – across the Atlantic, through the Panama Canal, up the coast of North America and across the Pacific Ocean to Australia and then home via the Suez Canal. The very names of the oceans and countries sounded beautifully exotic and faraway to me.

I soon realised it carried about 1,500 (1,471) passengers, of whom 668 were in first-class and 883 in tourist class (no second-class citizens in the 60s). It had a crew of 663, including Goanese stewards in the restaurant and galley. Before I could qualify as a full assistant Purser I had to go to all the different departments of the ship as part of my training at sea.

The ship had been used as a backdrop to the irreverent British comedy *The Captain's Table* made in 1958 which included the suave Donald Sinden, the curvaceous Peggy Cummins as well as the buxom Joan Sims. The film was mainly shot from the point of view of the newly appointed captain John Gregson who was an excellent seaman but without the necessary social skills to deal

Bognor Boy

SS Oronsay

with the passengers. They included amorous widows and young heiresses as well as an ex-army major who claimed to have the ear of the director of the shipping company. Most of the officers and crew, led by the chief Purser, were on the fiddle. Could I expect the same?

Entering the gloom of the ship after the bright sun outside, I was shown to my new cabin by a steward. It was at the end of a dark side corridor in the officers' deck. It was on the port side just above the waterline. A couple of bunk beds were opposite a day bed and the open porthole. This was to be my home for the next 9 months with another cadet.

Whilst I was unpacking my uniform and a few 'civvy' clothes for shore leave, a tall, handsome Goanese man in his late twenties came in. He introduced himself as 'Natty', not giving his Indian name. I presumed that he had been called that by previous officers who had found him neat and tidy and well turned out. I asked him his real name but he said he preferred to be called Natty. He was to be my steward for the rest of the voyage. His entire job was to clean the cabin and look after the well-being of the two young English cadets under his care. He laid out my uniforms on the day bed and polished my shoes.

Natty did the same for my fellow cadet and friend Stemp who slept in the bunk below me. He was the young lad who had been at my brother's twenty-first birthday party. He seemed to enjoy his work but I hardly ever saw him as we had different shifts and went ashore at different times.

After the Bay of Biscay, on the word of the captain, the officers and cadets were expected to change from their dark blue uniforms with gold buttons into their long, stiffly starched whites and white blancoed shoes. The change in uniform was meant to signify a change in the weather. In the evening, I wore patent leather shoes, dark trousers, a broad black cummerbund, a short white jacket and a black bow tie. At all times I had to wear a shirt with a separate stiff collar. Some pursers even had wing collars.

I was late reporting to the first-class office in the front of the ship and was introduced to the chief Purser R.C. Temple. He was a round man with balding hair. He welcomed me on board and then returned to his papers. I was pleased to see several women assistant Pursers amongst the busy men. I then went to the tourist class office where I was told by the senior assistant Purser Pike to man the front desk. He was as prickly as his name and no less aggressive than the fish. I could not help thinking that freedom for the pike is slavery and death for the minnows.

I was immediately in the thick of it with irate passengers complaining about their cabins. Since I knew very little about it I just passed them on to the other assistant. With a map of the ship in front of me I could at least explain where the swimming pool was on the upper deck and point the passengers in the direction of the restaurant below.

I noticed several young girls amongst the crowd and I wondered what chances there were of ever meeting them. I had been told that many of the officers decided which ones were for them as they climbed up the gangway. There were other girls who, if the officers had not accosted them on deck, could at least meet them at the captain's parties held separately for the first and tourist classes on the ship a few days out.

Captain Cowen's word was virtually law on the ship when she was at sea. He seemed to enjoy all the attention that the officers and passengers gave him. As a cadet, although the lowliest on-board, I was still an officer and had to form part of a queue at the captain's party. The queue moved slowly forward as the captain assigned one of us to a group of awaiting passengers. They loved it but I did not. They were no young girls amongst them and they seemed to consist mainly of rich Australian farmers with thick, lined necks, or American self-made businessmen, dominating their mousy wives who said as little as possible.

I rapidly found that I did not like my job of always putting on a friendly face to the passengers and getting on with the older pursers. I was a round peg in a square hole. I preferred French

novels to the type of 'Carry On' films in the ship's cinema. No
doubt I appeared as a pretentious little prig to my fellow pursers.
My main pleasures were reading literature, daydreaming and
staring out to sea. I loved to lie back on the top bunk in my cabin
and listen to the water constantly whishing along the ship's hull
through the open porthole.

Our first port-of-call was Le Havre but I could not go ashore.
We took about two weeks to cross the Atlantic, arriving at the
mountains and plains of the island of Trinidad which had linked
up with Tobago. It was hot and humid and I was now deep in the
Caribbean, close to where Jenny came from.

I did manage to descend the gangway in the capital Port of
Spain. The country had only recently become independent from
Britain. It seemed mainly to consist of low-rise buildings with
corrugated-iron roofs. It was very bustling, no doubt due to its
oil and gas wells. It felt very much in the tropics and the people
spoke Creole English which took me some time to tune into. I
noticed a lot of people were of Asian background, and among
the many churches were temples and mosques. They presumably
had been brought over to work as indentured labourers in the
sugar-cane plantations. The island was famous for its rum. There
were also some Chinese who had intermixed, especially with
Indians.

I heard some Calypso music coming out of a building; their steel
instruments called 'pans' had been beaten out from old oil drums.
Unfortunately the famous carnival was not on so I couldn't see
all the scantily dressed gyrating bodies in their colourful outfits.
Instead, I bought – from a plump black woman selling trinkets at
the side of the dusty, sandy main street – a finely made wooden
cigarette box with the name of the island and a palm tree carved
on its lid. It smelt very warm and exotic inside, rather like cedar
wood.

It was a short hop to the wide bay of Cartagena, Colombia in
South America. Again I got some shore leave, although this time
it was in the evening. Between Tobago and Cartagena, I plucked
up enough courage to ask an attractive American girl travelling
with her rich parents whether she would like to go ashore with me.
Contrary to what I expected, she readily agreed. But there was one
problem: I had virtually no money. So I decided to take her to the
local casino and see whether I would lose all the little money I had
or make some more to take her out to a restaurant for the evening.

She was dressed in a colourful frock, suntanned and fit-looking having spent much time around the swimming pool during our crossing of the Atlantic. That's where I first noticed her tanning herself in her scant bikini.

That evening ashore we went up the broad sweeping stairs to the bright lights of the casino. I bet my money on the black (*noir*) numbers on the roulette wheel and won. I doubled my stakes and bet on the same colour again. And again I won. I then decided to put all reason and caution to the wind and bet all my money on number 23, the date of my birthday. It seemed a complete miracle when the whirling, little white ball slowed down and the number came up. I therefore had about $500 in my pocket, a small fortune. I decided there and then to leave the casino and getting off with my girl was much more important to me than winning money.

I took a taxi waiting outside the casino and asked the middle-aged driver if he knew of somewhere to eat and dance. He said in broken English with a Spanish accent that he knew of the perfect place out of town. He took us some way along the coastal road to the 'hot spot' – where they ate at tables in the open air and danced on an adjoining floor to the South American rhythms of a brass band.

I asked the taxi driver to wait for us as money was no object at that time. It was pleasantly warm, with a balmy sea breeze. The full moon in the sky, crowding out the stars, created shadows amongst the palm trees along the beach. Between the musical numbers I could hear the surf of the ocean crashing on the sand. We grew closer together over the food and wine and even closer dancing. Our bodies were soon entwined as we swayed with the rhythm. I could not believe my luck again. I then asked her whether she would like to go for a walk along the beach. She agreed.

We walked across a long stretch of sand to the waters' edge. We took off our shoes but felt our feet sinking in the soft sand. The bright moon created shadows from our bodies. Behind us the bright lights of the dance floor lit up the dark, with brooding palm trees beyond the beach along the coastal strip. The music became more and more distant as we continued to walk. I listened to the surf as each wave rushed up the beach only to fall back and meet another one coming in.

I suggested that we sit down close to the sea and she agreed. We were soon kissing under the full moon. I touched her breasts, without any resistance on her part. I thought I might be able to repeat that magical and deep experience of making love which I had first felt at my brother's birthday party so far away in London.

I was completely involved with the girl until I heard a sudden movement above us. I looked up, my body on top of the girl's, to see a group of thin, wiry teenagers who had appeared over the high crest of sand created by the last high tide. They towered above me, about five of them, with the apparent leader holding a knife in his hand. It glinted in the brightness of the moon. I got up, full of adrenaline but with no wish to flee. I decided there and then to try to fight the boy with the knife; I judged that I was much stronger than he and the others would run away if I defeated him. I had won too many fights at school not yet to be a complete pacifist. If I went down they would attack me and no doubt grab the girl. I did not want to imagine the rest.

At the very moment that my assailant and I moved closer together I heard a tremendous shouting on the beach above us. The group of teenagers disappeared as quickly and quietly as they had come. It was my old, portly taxi driver, waving his arms and shouting in Spanish.

My girlfriend got up and brushed the sand from her disarranged frock. We walked back with the driver feeling very deflated. Our desire had vanished, just like the waves crashing on the shore. The old man said, still puffing, between breaths:

'Veery dangeroos walkin' on beach at night. Many banditas y ladrones, si, muchos. These boys kill you, rape girl. I see you come on beach from taxi and follow you makin' sure you all right. It ees very lucky for you!'

It was indeed a close shave and after being so enthusiastic about winning at the casino and full of desire at nearly making it with the beautiful American girl, I returned to our ship. I gave the driver a large tip for waiting for us and possibly saving our lives.

The experience which could have made us so much closer had ripped us apart.

I went to work in the morning feeling tired and bleary-eyed at the tourist Purser's Office. I felt even more miserable when I met the girl around the pool in the afternoon.

She said in no uncertain terms that she did not want to carry on with me.

'I want a quiet life! And I won't be getting that with you…'

After Cartagena we approached the Panama Canal which linked the Atlantic and Pacific Oceans. Thick mangrove swamps were on either side of the entrance to the wide channel. Dark, lithe men in loin cloths dived from their dugout canoes for small coins which had been tossed overboard by passengers. The passengers laughed at the antics of the divers; I was disgusted by the contrast between their wealth and amusement and the poverty and indignity of the divers far below the ship.

We slid slowly through the canal, almost silently, with thick tropical vegetation brooding on either side. It was under an overcast sky, with dark low clouds about to release heavy rain. There was a large lake called Gatun in the middle of the length of the canal which had to be reached and descended by a series of enormous metal locks. I had been through locks on English canals but this one was on an unimaginably grand scale for huge ships. About 48 miles (77 km) long, the canal had only been opened in 1914 on the thin strip of land between North and South America. It had been controlled by the French and Americans and was now run by the Panamanians. It meant that we wouldn't have to go around Cape Horn (experiencing the Roaring Forties) and it would take weeks off our journey.

We travelled along the canal very slowly and I watched alligators slipping down the steep banks of the thick jungle into the brown, fetid water. The climate was very hot and humid and I understood why so many of the diggers of the canal had died of tropical diseases. After about ten hours we reached the Pacific Ocean. The water was beautifully turquoise and at last there was a sea breeze. We had arrived in another world.

Our next port of call was Acapulco in Mexico. We anchored in 'Millionaire's Bay', so called because there were so many large and beautiful villas dotted around the wide green slopes of its semi-circular bay. I had some leave and went ashore in one of the tenders which ferried the passengers across the water. On shore, I met a young assistant engineer from Newcastle whom I had first met at the captain's party and with whom I had become friendly. The Geordie seemed much more interesting than most of the other pursers I had met.

With my friend we went to a restaurant overlooking the sea on a steep cliff. For the diners' entertainment, young men dived into a tiny creek below which was full of sea when the Pacific swell rolled in but was just bare rock when it retreated. It was like the slow breathing in and out of a huge monster. Again, I was put off by the contrast between the diners, including myself, who lived a life of luxury and wealth, and the poor divers who risked their lives for a few pesos.

My engineer friend then said that he knew of a club up in the hills which I would like. By the time we reached it by taxi it was already dusk. The club – set apart and overlooking the Pacific Ocean – had neoclassical columns and a central temple with very low blue lighting. Girls came to us dressed in white, flowing togas as I imagined they had done in ancient Greece or Rome. They spoke English with a strong Spanish-Mexican accent. I soon realised that my engineer friend had brought me to a 'high-class' brothel. One was meant to choose a girl and go with her to one of the neoclassical cubicles bordering the open air, sunken floor. My friend went with one of them but I chose to remain on a bench with a couple of girls for whom I bought expensive drinks.

I did not want to pay for sex and still believed that I could meet a young girl on board among the passengers to satisfy my burning, youthful desires. Many of the other older assistant pursers seemed to have managed it. Going out with the officers on board seemed to have a cachet about it for the girls and unattached women as they would be invited to the (allegedly) best parties.

Back on the great white liner, we travelled in hot weather on a glassy sea along the coast to Los Angeles. I saw the young girl I had taken ashore descend the gangway with her parents for the last time. She had deliberately avoided me ever since our experience together but I still felt a sharp pang at the thought I would never see her again.

20

POETRY IN
THE PACIFIC

In Los Angeles I was allowed to go ashore again but since my fellow cadet was working at the wrong hours I had to go alone. It seemed strange to be on American soil for the first time. I had seen so many Hollywood films and Westerns with my brother and mother at the old Odeon, Regent and Picturedrome in Bognor and here I was where they all had been made. But I did not want to go up to see Hollywood straight away and got in a taxi and asked the driver to take me to the centre. He said:

'There's no downtown, man. Where do you want to go?'

'What, do you mean there is no centre to the city. Where are the main shops?'

'They're all about. But as you are from England, I'll show you around.'

He was right – the sprawling city was laid out as a grid on the flat plain. There was one block after another.

Eventually I asked him to drop me at a busy crossroads. I thought I would have an American hamburger for the first time on American soil so I went into a likely café at the corner. Every table was full except for one old man sitting alone at a long table for six. I politely asked him whether he minded me sitting on the end.

'You're not welcome', he muttered in reply. 'You're not welcome!', he repeated, raising his voice.I got up and appealed to the young waitress, saying that it was my first time in the country and I wanted to try a famous American hamburger.

She replied in a drawl: 'I'm sorry sir but the man sitting at the table has the right to decide who sits at it. I can't do anything about it. That's the way things are.'

I said that I had come all the way from England again but it still cut no ice. Since there was no other table free, I had to leave. I felt like a pariah. It made me realise what black people must have felt. After many non-violent protests led by Martin Luther King all legally enforced public segregation had just been abolished by the

Civil Rights Act. But there were still cases of racial segregation.

'So this is America', I said to myself. 'The first thing I do is wrong. It's never happened in any other country!'

I caught another taxi after a while and asked the driver to take me to see Beverly Hills and Hollywood. Perhaps there was something else there to see and do. I saw some big houses set in even bigger lawns. He dropped me off at a theatre where various 'stars' had left a hand imprint in wet concrete. As I was not interested in the 'star' system or so-called 'celebrities' and finding the other gawping tourists rather sad, I decided to get another taxi back to the ship. That was Los Angeles for me.

It was a very different experience when the boat reached San Francisco. It was late 1964. There were hippies, the counterculture, rebellion and the smell of marijuana in the air. After my experiences at my boarding school and as a cadet on board a passenger liner this seemed far more the place for me. On my own once again, I had a meal at Fisherman's Wharf. I then went up to the top of a tall building in a glass lift on the outside. From the top I could see the Golden Gate suspension bridge spanning the wide bay and the waves crashing on the rocks of the small island of Alcatraz. The cold currents made the notorious prison there virtually impregnable and I shuddered to think what it must be like to spend the rest of your life in a stone cell.

It was late afternoon so I went to the City Lights Bookshop. On my way I saw a sign pointing to the district of Haight-Ashbury where the first hippies hung out, preferring 'to turn on, tune in and drop out' and 'make love, not war.' It was the beginning of 'Flower Power', much better than organised warfare.

At the City Lights bookshop, I bought Plato's *The Republic*. It was full of ancient Greek philosophy but I found his ideal society thoroughly authoritarian and hierarchical, particularly as he wanted to banish what I considered the most interesting people – musicians and poets. The book I bought on Socrates was much more to my liking. It explained that Socrates wrote nothing but was condemned by the State of Athens for 'corrupting the youth' . It described how he allegedly said that 'an unexamined life is not worth living.' I was clearly corrupted and I was certainly examining my life.

I also bought a copy of the poem *Howl* by the Beat poet Allen Ginsberg. Its famous opening lines declared:

> I saw the best minds of my generation destroyed by
> madness, starving hysterical naked,
> dragging themselves through the negro streets at
> dawn looking for an angry fix,
> Angel-headed hipsters burning for the ancient
> heavenly connection
> to the starry dynamo in the machinery of night…

Heady and subversive stuff indeed, especially for a Purser Cadet of
the P&O-Orient Lines. They were clearly about to lose me to the
starry night…

City Lights was the centre of the 'Beat Generation' in the city
and I felt I was at the centre of the world. Despite my background,
and what I was doing, I liked their rejection of materialism, their
stylistic originality and their alternative vision of what it was
to be truly human. Although I was travelling on a steam ship
round the world, I liked to think I was having similar experiences
to Ginsberg's friend Jack Kerouac in his novel *On the Road* –
although this was hardly the case!

By chance, I managed to listen to a reading of a poem by
Lawrence Ferlinghetti, who had founded the bookshop. In his
book *A Coney Island of the Mind* he declared:

> and I am waiting
> for the Age of Anxiety
> to drop dead
> and I am waiting
> for the war to be fought
> which will make the world safe
> for anarchy
> and I am waiting
> for the final withering away
> of all governments
> and I am perpetually awaiting
> a rebirth of wonder…

And so was I.

After hearing the recital in City Lights Bookshop I asked
someone in the audience where I could listen to some jazz that
evening. He told me to go to Basin Street West. It was dark by

now but the area was bright with neon signs. There were clubs dropping down steps from the 'sidewalks' in which I could dimly make out men playing around billiard and pool tables. Eventually I came across a jazz club which advertised my great hero, the pianist Thelonious Monk. Being so important and original in modern jazz and having played bebop with Dizzy Gillespie and Charlie Parker in New York I could barely believe my luck.

I went down into the smoky, dark club and ordered a drink at the bar. There were only a few black faces and the club was not packed as I had expected. I found a vacant table close to the stage which was just a raised dais with a gleaming grand piano on it.

It was some time before the great man I had been waiting for came in. He wore dark glasses, a black suit and tie, white shirt and balanced a single red rose on the piano. He was without any other musicians. He said nothing, opened the piano and then burst into his famous number 'Round Midnight.'

When he finished a hubbub was still coming from men at the bar. He looked disapprovingly towards them. He then played my favourite number 'Blue Monk' with its chunky notes and awkward rhythms. When he finished, there was some desultory applause yet the men continued to chat in low tones around the bar. It was enough. Monk suddenly closed the top of his piano, said nothing and walked off. I couldn't believe it that the men would be more interested in what they had to say in their half-drunken state than listen to the great and original musician. What a missed opportunity...

I had not only been the president of the Jazz Society at school but even had a copy of the cover of his vinyl disc *Blue Monk* along with *Miles Plays the Blues, Modern Jazz Quartet*, and *Erroll Garner* on the walls of my bedroom which I shared with my brother in Bognor. It had been so far away and on the other side of the world and now I was at the centre of West Coast Jazz, normally associated with the cool music of baritone saxophonist Gerry Mulligan and trumpeter Chet Baker. I left the club as disappointed no doubt as Monk and took a taxi back to the ship. It had been a magical day – despite the end – and left me more confused about my direction in life than ever. I was certain though of one thing: I was in the wrong job.

From San Francisco, it was a comparatively small hop to Seattle, situated after the ancient woodlands of Oregon on the North West

Pacific Coast and close to the Canadian border. It was beginning to feel cold in December and I only had time during my short leave to visit the virtually empty site of Seattle's World's Fair which had attracted almost 10 million visitors a couple of years before. It still had recently planted trees with their large leaves turning yellow.

There seemed very little to do there for a young man with limited time on his hands and I returned to the ship thinking that I would not return to Seattle. I was impressed though by Puget Sound on which the city was built and was pleased that it was named after the chief of the local Suquamish Native American tribe. Like so many other American Indians, they had received a bad deal from European settlers and had been obliged, at the point of a gun, to give up their land and live in a reservation. They used to travel up and down the coast, not recognising man-made borders, in dugout cedar canoes, very different from my massive passenger liner.

Our next port of call was Vancouver in British Columbia just over the border in Canada. It was beautifully situated as we sailed in, lying between an inlet to the north and the Fraser River to the south. It was protected from the wrath of the Pacific Ocean by Vancouver Island which was heavily wooded on its lower slopes with snow on the peaks of its mountains. Unlike Seattle, it had been named after a captain in the British Royal Navy.

Although it was meant to have one of the mildest climates in Canada when I arrived in January it was cold, wet and sleeting. I went ashore in the afternoon and saw men living rough and stretched out amongst empty bottles in doorways of a 'skid row' close to the docks. There were bars and a few seedy hotels.

I warmed up in a café but there were very few people about and there seemed little to do as the dark evening came in early. In the West End, I was told there were some old skyscrapers but I did not have the time to make it over there. I trudged back to the ship in the sleet, dreaming of the light, warmth and conviviality of San Francisco. I was surprised later to learn that Vancouver was considered one of the best cities in the world to live in; it clearly depended whether you had money and a warm place to stay in.

We took on passengers in Vancouver to head off across the Pacific Ocean to New Zealand and Australia. We soon found the going was rough for we headed straight into a gale. The 30,000 ton ship began to heel to starboard and I noticed amongst the passageways that ropes had been placed for people to hold on to. I was told that 'stabilisers' had to be put out to stop the ship rolling too much in the rough sea. The first-class restaurant that lunchtime was virtually empty. However, where the officers and cadets ate behind a curtain, it was full and bantering continued as usual. After several months at sea, we had found our sea legs.

In the tourist Purser's Office there were virtually no questions to answer that day; nearly all the passengers were keeping to their cabins. In the afternoon I went for a walk on one of the upper decks away from the wind. I was shocked to see how large the breaking waves were, with spray and spindrift forming on their crests and foam streaking down their backs. It must have been at least a Force 9 on the Beaufort scale. The brownish Pacific Ocean swirled and heaved and crashed. Then I saw something which I would never forget. It was a tiny yacht moving in the direction of the wind under bare poles. It was quite close, being tossed hither and thither. At any moment I thought it would be swamped. Yet it rose above each breaking wave and miraculously continued on its way. It must have been seen by the officers on the bridge but had refused any help through its small VHF radio. I was deeply impressed and thought it must be hell on such a tiny yacht in such terrible conditions at sea.

When it became calmer, I spent some time in the galley to learn how it operated. I was shown the cold rooms where the vegetables and fruit were kept and the refrigerators which contained carcasses of meat. I remembered an early experience of my brother on a ship. He had opened a fridge only to find a member of the crew swinging from a hook. The man had suffered a heart attack and was being transported back home. But no one had told my brother!

I was taught by the chief chef how to make a plain omelette, which consisted of three eggs lightly stirred in a jug with a little water added and then quickly cooked in a small hot frying pan containing bubbling oil. I also spent some time with the Goanese cooks and enjoyed their company. They cooked delicious curries, particularly using coconut, fish and prawns. I thought though how lucky I was in the upper decks to avoid the din and heat of the galley where people shouted at each other and were forced to live under artificial light.

I was invited by the Goanese assistant curry cook to his birthday party. He was a very dark man, small, thin, and wiry but with an irrepressible smile. He was probably in his early 30s, a little older than the steward 'Natty' who cleaned out my cabin and laid out my clothes every day. They came from a region on the west coast of India which had been a Portuguese province and had a substantial Catholic minority. The 'privilege' of being a crew member in the British Merchant Navy was passed down from generation to generation, despite the fact that they would have to spend a long time away from their families and their pay was paid at the local rate. It was however work which was greatly sought after.

On the evening of the cook's birthday I made my way into the dark bowels of the ship and found where the Goanese cooks lived. I could hear their merry making and music from afar. It was very dark down there and they had no portholes and their bunks were very close to each other. I did not think such a place existed on the passenger liner. They stopped their drumming and singing as I appeared and seemed surprised to see me, a young Purser Cadet in his white uniform. But they soon gave me a very warm welcome and found a place for me to sit. As they returned to the drumming I was handed a tumbler half full of whisky. They were allowed to drink alcohol because they were Christians and not Hindus or Muslims.

I drank the whisky fairly quickly and was immediately handed another. But I was aware that they wanted to get the British cadet drunk as soon as possible in order to see how he would react. I soon realised that I was going too far and refused another drink. I wished the cook a happy birthday and withdrew discreetly. Thereafter a good word must have got around and I was always enthusiastically welcomed by any Goanese crew. I don't know if I had made history but I certainly enjoyed listening to their singing and drumming and seeing them enjoy themselves.

My most interesting time however was spent with a Scottish assistant fish cook who worked on his own in a small room just above the waterline with humid sea air blowing through an open porthole. He spent his day cutting fish open on a wooden block and brushing the guts with a knife into a revolting dustbin which was full of heads, tails and heaving intestines. He was a thin man in his late twenties with red curly hair. The rims of his eyes were red from squirting fish juice. He spoke in a broad brogue and it took me a while to understand him. I asked him whether he liked his job:

'Och ay, it's not too bad a way to earn some money and I occasionally manage to go ashore an' see a bit of the world. I'm a poet from Glasgow and got this job as a means to an end. The end is beauty!'

Bognor Boy

I thought he must have a strong calling as a poet to work in such terrible conditions. I went to see him most days when I was down the galley. He showed me a blood-splattered, crumbled sheaf of his poems which were full of grace and hope. I never learnt what became of him. But he inspired me and I felt that one day I too would become a poet and a writer. I appreciated his enthusiasm for literature which seemed to be shared by no one else on the ship where power, money and sex ruled the day. What seemed important for the other crew members was their place in the hierarchy and even the lowest dish washer would dream of promotion.

When I was in mid Pacific, I wrote a poem called 'Summertime' recalling my short and loving time with Jenny:

> Every moment was a moment
> Not one awaiting another
> Or another regretting one
> Simple Joy
> Usually knowing
> Yet always full
> As any mountain stream
>
> Her eyes washed away
> The dirt of day
> Falling like leaves
> In a motionless autumn
> Upon my face.
>
> And too perfect solace
> When her hand slid into mine
> As certain as the sun in the sky
> Or the bitter taste of time.

Apart from the fish cook, there was a good-looking and tall man in his early thirties from the Home Counties and who had a degree from Oxford University in Philosophy, Politics and Economics. He had decided to live the uncomplicated life of a deck hand rather than a life of luxury and ease. He reminded me of TE Lawrence who became a humble airman after being 'Lawrence of Arabia.' He worked on the bridge steering the ship during his watches and had to call the other officers, including me, 'Sir.' But he appeared very self-sufficient and did not seem to mind his lowly place in the hierarchy, spurned by the other crew for his 'posh' middle-class accent and by the officers for his intelligence and knowledge. I found him very interesting and asked him what it was like to be a student at University.

'It's very good', he said, 'you can choose what subject you want to study and have all the time in the world to follow up your interests. I would recommend it for anybody. But I love the sea and I love ships so I don't mind much being on my own.'

'What did you learn at University?', I asked him.

'Many things. I can't go into them now. I liked philosophy best. The most important thing for me is not the pursuit of happiness, however defined, but the ability to distinguish between truth and falsehood. I would rather at the moment have little power or money and live a simple life. It suits me here for a while. I can see the world, at least some of it.'

I thought this was very profound; it seemed to me that everybody around me wanted to pursue happiness but mainly defined it in terms of pleasure, that is, in satisfying their desires. And yet very few people I met, including myself, seemed to be truly happy. Happiness, I concluded, was not an end in itself but perhaps something which crept up on you when you least expected it and you had another important goal, like doing the 'right thing' or finding out what was 'true.' Perhaps one day you would surprise yourself and say 'I am happy'!

There were rumblings in the Purser's Office against the 'gentleman deckhand' and they said he would not be signed on for another voyage. He gave the crew the wrong idea. I felt this animosity was fired by jealousy and merely demonstrated their crass ignorance. For me, it seemed that there was some mystique about university and you could not be fully educated and knowledgeable without having been a student. I wanted to enter this holy Temple of Wisdom to see what it was all about. I felt I could not go through life without having at least experienced it.

Unbeknown to my fellow officers I was doing again an A-level in French by correspondence in the hope that one day I too could apply to university. At different ports around the world I received, from my tutor, written notes about French books and poetry typed on rough green paper. I also had to write an occasional essay which I sent off to be marked. The whole thing seemed miles away from the work I did on the luxury liner.

Bognor Boy

Most officers and passengers only seem interested in distraction. For their entertainment, they were offered most days deck tennis and deck quoits consisting of throwing a rope ring on concentric circles drawn on deck; light music and dancing to the ship's orchestra; the daily Tote betting on horses; frog racing which involved jerking a wooden frog with a piece of string; diving for spoons in the swimming pool; the cinema which showed amusing films; or attending an 'interest talk' such as 'The Sea' or 'Ocean Currents'.

Before arrival in a port, there would also be a talk about the places of interest as well as the sale of tickets for an excursion. It was one of my jobs to sell tickets in a small office opened especially on the upper deck near the swimming pool. I enjoyed this not only because I was on my own in the small office but I could see the sea and eye up the girls, many of whom came to buy tickets in their bikinis. Despite my interest in poetry and philosophy, I was still after all a young man…

21
HOMEWARD BOUND

The Captain continued to have his parties with the new passengers who were taken on in Vancouver. The officers, as usual, were lined up in a queue to accompany a group of them for cocktail drinks. I had to do this in the first-class of the ship and found it both incredibly boring and a heavy burden. I had to make polite conversation with rich old men and their overdressed women who, on dry land, I would have avoided at all costs.

Several had vast farms in the outback of Australia. Their necks were not only deeply tanned but criss-crossed with lines. They ate huge breakfasts, often with a couple of eggs broken on a great T-bone steak. The first-class passengers that I was introduced to did not even have attractive daughters. I was sometimes obliged to sit at their tables in the first-class restaurant and just hear them bragging about their wealth and how much they had achieved in their lives. There was no talk of philosophy or poetry. It convinced me that I did not want to become a millionaire without any culture except that which money could buy.

One compensation, however, was that the ship called next at Honolulu in the islands of Hawaii in the middle of the North Pacific Ocean. The 50th State of the US had steep volcanic mountains covered in tropical vegetation and sandy beaches washed by clear, warm turquoise water. Coconut trees bent over the white sand just as in the posters: the archetypal image of a 'tropical paradise.' As the ship docked on the wharf in Honolulu a bevy of swaying brown girls dressed in grass skirts, bikini tops and flower necklaces danced the hula to the rhythm of the steel-stringed guitars of a local band. I thought at once of the English explorer Captain Cook, the French painter Paul Gauguin, the bombing of Pearl Harbour by the Japanese and then the beautiful young Polynesian girls who had become fodder for overweight tourists to gawp at.

I made for Waikiki Beach along the seafront of Honolulu – alone as usual as the other cadet had to stay on board. It seemed a wonderful place to be and I soaked up the sunshine and atmosphere. It was famous for its surfers and after viewing its

Bognor Boy

long rolling breakers I thought I would have a go myself and hired a long board. What I did not realise was that it was low tide. I paddled out in the low waves and tried to stand on my board but was rapidly thrown into the water. On about my fourth attempt, far out to sea, I was flung onto the coral reef under the surf and my back was badly scratched. I was horrified to see red blood mingle with the water and immediately thought of sharks. I quickly ran up to the sand and dried myself with my towel but found that the wounds were not deep and the blood soon stopped flowing. I returned to the ship.

I sent Jenny a poem called 'Surfing at Waikiki Beach, Honolulu':

> I was hard and clean
> As the igneous rock.
> The morning clouds
> Hit the mountain tops.
>
> I felt good and true
> As the naked rain.
> The fighting surf
> Hit the solid sand.
>
> I saw far and clear
> As the seagull's eye.
> The diving soul
> Hit the swirling foam.
>
> I knew the answers
> To the questioning seas.

Jenny called it one of my best poems, particularly as she felt it caught the very *cadence de la mer*.

I was about halfway round my world cruise and the next place we would visit was Suva, the capital of the island of Fiji. When we crossed the line of the Equator on 13 December 1965 (in the middle of the Pacific Ocean between Hawaii and Fiji) I participated in an age-old ceremony. As it was my first time, I was brought by the first-class swimming pool where a member of the crew dressed up as Neptune – holding a Trident and sporting a white beard – was seated on his throne. I was judged and then thrown into the swimming pool with some other cadets to the

Be it now Proclaimed by Call of Conch and Nautilus throughout the Latitudes and Longitudes of Our Oceanic Domain, that We, Neptune, Ruler of the Seven Seas, King of the Secret Currents, Lord of the Boundless Waves, Master of the Tides, High Constable of the Coral Caverns and Uttermost Recesses of the Deep, do hereby Sanction and affirm that Our Most Noble CROSS of the EQUATOR be bestowed on PETER MARSHALL who but a mere Mortal, hath, this 13 day of -- DEC 1965 on Board ORONSAY accepted with Good Humour and Withstood with Fortitude the most Rigorous Initiation into the Ancient and Moistening Rites of our Aquatic Court Sealed and Witnessed in the presence of

Captain

Certificate for crossing the Equator

delight of the passengers who looked on. Afterwards, I was given a colourful certificate signed by Captain Cowen with my name on it for accepting the initiation with good humour and fortitude.

During that long passage across the Pacific, my decision became clearer that – unlike the other officers – I did not want to go around the world for evermore, living a life of luxury and privilege, pursuing pleasure, looking out for the girls and women who came on board and having brief affairs with them and only going ashore to a smart hotel for drinks or a meal. They seemed to have no interest in the different countries, peoples and cultures they encountered. Rather than broadening the mind, their travel on a cruise ship seemed only to confirm their worst prejudices and their sense of belonging to a privileged class and race. While smiling and being polite to passengers or those 'above' them, they were in themselves insincere and hypocritical.

I wanted my life to be an open field of unexpected opportunities not a closed future in which I went round and round the world, experiencing the same things and going predictably up the hierarchy of shipboard life as I grew older, fatter and more cynical. I had realised that a sense of authenticity and doing the 'right thing' – whatever that might be – were more important to me than having material possessions and power over others.

Bognor Boy

I used to walk around the ship during my time off, and was always fascinated by the sea and the surf created by the great white liner. I spent hours leaning over the rails, watching the continuous play of the water below and listening to its swish and splash as the ship sliced through the waves. The sea was constantly changing but always remained the same.

In the stern of the ship in mid-Pacific, I also would look at the boiling wake of the ship. It was often followed by sharks which would criss-cross the turbulent water and leap in a wild feeding frenzy whenever waste food was thrown overboard from the galley. I was careful not to fall overboard as well. An officer cadet who had been a friend of my brother had disappeared one dark night at sea, either because he jumped or was pushed over by a disgruntled member of the crew.

There was a beautiful girl with short blond hair and a lithe tanned body who was travelling with her parents in first class from America to Australia. I tried to go out with her and saw her a few times but she preferred an older assistant Purser with a square jaw. He invited her to drinks and the parties of the officers who were the most sought-after on the ship. I was told by the young 'Writer' in the Tourist Purser's Office – a small Cockney boy in charge of passengers' cash and a leading hand – that she had voluntarily gone down to the stewards' sleeping area and been repeatedly made love to by stewards who queued up outside the cabin for their turn. I was shocked. I presumed it was to get back somehow at her wealthy, middle-class parents who wanted to control her life or else that she had become mentally deranged before or during the voyage. I found it difficult to believe that such a beautiful and well-educated girl wanted to be screwed by anonymous stewards one after the other. I had heard of gang rape but not of a girl deliberately seeking it out.

Suva in Fiji was our next stop. We were met by outriggers with triangular sails as we steamed in. I was granted a day's leave after seeing on board the pilot with a deck officer. Fiji was still a British Crown Colony. I liked the low rise buildings in the town after all the American skyscrapers along the waterfront in Honolulu. Apparently, no building was meant to be taller than a coconut tree. The air felt sultry and oppressive and heavy rain fell on the deep green tropical vegetation and thudded on the corrugated iron roofs. When the rain stopped and the hot sun came out from behind the low dark clouds, I wandered around the town. I noticed that the few policemen present wore sandals and long white kilts with deeply indented hems. People tended to smile at me and said 'Bula' which I took to mean hello. One young man even stopped and asked me 'how old are you?' I told him and he moved on.

I had in my rucksack a small towel and swimming trunks and since there was not much to do in town I strolled along the beach on the other side of the harbour to go for a swim. I walked for about an hour along the white sand under the leaning coconut trees. Having found a small bay where there was no one to be seen, I undressed and laid my clothes carefully at the foot of a coconut tree.

The water was delightfully warm and transparent. The small bay was sheltered by two arms which almost met in the middle. I assumed they were made of coral; the waves of the open sea crashed through the narrow gap. I settled down to a relaxed swim and began to look for the coral underwater. Many multi-coloured fish flashed by. When I surfaced to take a breather, I saw a middle-aged man in a grass kilt by my clothes shouting something and pointing manically out to sea.

I looked round and saw the unmistakable shape of three dorsal fins cutting through the water towards me. Sharks! I decided to freeze, not wishing to attract them although I felt my heart pounding wildly. They swam nonchalantly around me. I thought I was going to be killed; it would only be a matter of time before they attacked me and I would be done for. I recalled the sharks I had seen from the stern of the ship and shuddered. But after a short while, which seemed endless, the sharks left me in a leisurely way and made for the open water again.

'Phew, I'm alright' I said to myself and made for the shore as quickly as possible. My arms and legs felt like lead. I made it though and the man passed me my towel.

'You is almost killed, man', he said. 'No fella swimmin' in bay. I know, I fisherman!'

He pointed to his outrigger canoe which was pulled up on the sand.

'Come to my home', he said. 'You want hot drink!'

It was true that I did and I followed him through a coconut plantation to a nearby hut made from wood and grass. I took off my shoes as he did and entered the low, dark interior. When my eyes became accustomed to the light, I made out his large wife who was sitting on the dirt floor. She made me some tea over a small fire. She smiled all the time but did not seem to speak much

English. I noticed that behind her – in pride of place on the wall – was a framed picture of the young Queen Elizabeth. I pointed to the frame and the fisherman said:

'We love her! Our Queen and yours! She come here not long ago. She look after us.'

I didn't express my low opinion of the monarchy. It didn't seem fair to say that to my guests. Instead, I stayed and drank some hot tea and felt better after the chat. When I left it was beginning to get dark so I thanked the fisherman for saving my life and his wife for her tea and hospitality.

I walked back briskly along the seashore in the growing darkness towards the harbour and thought how lucky I had been. I also thought that the fisherman and his wife seemed very content with their simple life, so unlike my own with all its ambitions, to change the world and perhaps one day to go to university.

Nothing much happened to me after Fiji except that one day I was told to go a see a passenger in a first-class cabin who wanted to make a complaint. As I knocked on the door of the cabin a very attractive woman in her 30s invited me in. She shut the door behind me. She was in black evening dress with a very low neck line.

Although many years older than I was, I immediately felt very strongly attracted to her. She obviously felt the same, becoming quite coquettish. There was strong sexual energy in the air. I wanted to kiss her and imagined her lying down on her double bunk but I was inexperienced in these matters and she did not directly lead me on. I regretted later not having made the first move but I did not want at the time to cause a scandal, particularly with her boorish husband in mind. I withdrew as well as I could; she never did make her 'complaint' after all. Perhaps she just wanted some company and attention.

We eventually pulled into Wellington on North Island, the capital of New Zealand. What I saw of New Zealand – which was little – I found to be very much like the Little England of the middle class just after the Second World War when I was brought up. Most people of European descent clearly enjoyed a beautiful land, plenty of space and a good life. They did not seem to mind being called 'Kiwis' after the flightless bird with a long beak which was the national symbol of the country.

Thinking that I might one day apply there, I went to visit Wellington University which was on one of the hills overlooking

Homeward Bound

the harbour. Like the scattered villas with their gardens, it had many trees, shrubs and green spaces. No doubt it would be a lovely campus to wander around but I wasn't sure how intellectually stimulating and challenging it was at the time.

I also visited a Maori centre in Wellington and was pleased to see that their traditions and language were still alive. I looked at their wide canoes, some which were made from huge tree trunks and propelled by pointed oars. But I also learned that the first European settlers took much of their land and introduced many diseases. It was a pattern perpetrated by colonialists around the world. The warlike and tattooed Maoris themselves had been comparative latecomers to the islands, arriving from East Polynesia probably in the 13th century and displacing the local peaceful community which had made fine pottery and raised great stone monuments to the sky.

Australia seemed very different from New Zealand. We docked just under the Sydney Bridge at Fisherman's Wharf. The new opera house was being built with its vast interlocking 'shells' set upon a terrace in the centre of the wide bay.

We were in Sydney for about a week, disembarking many passengers and taking on new ones. During my leave, I went to a bar which I was surprised to learn closed very early. It seemed entirely functional and just like a lavatory, with no attempt at decoration. The customers were all male and all white, returning from offices or building sites or other places of work to drink 'middys' (about half a pint) or 'schooners' (a pint). It was appropriately called the 'six o'clock swill.' Their conversation quickly became raucous and loud. I drank a few 'middys' and left. I was principally interested in girls and clearly I could not find any here. 'Aussie' girls had a good reputation for enjoying themselves from what I had seen in London and from the hearsay of my brother. They definitely weren't all called 'Sheilas' just as English people were not all 'Pommies' (Prisoners of Mother England) – although some were.

I decided to take a ferry across the bay and to go to a small theatre where they were playing Samuel Beckett's *Waiting for Godot*. It seemed very avant-garde and fired my imagination and my appetite for more. It was described as a 'tragicomedy' in two acts but I thought it was more tragic than comic. It was set on a country road with a single stripped tree in the backdrop of a bleak moor. I did not fully understand what I saw of the two main characters, both washed-up tramps in bowler hats called Vladimir and Estragon. Then a pompous master called Pozzo appeared with his whinging slave Lucky with a rope about his neck. A boy announced that Godot may come tomorrow.

The two main characters seemed two aspects of the same person, since one was restless and thoughtful while the other was irrational, dozy and driven by desire. I certainly knew the relationship between the master and servant from school and even in the P&O-Orient Lines.

In the second act, Pozzo and Lucky suddenly reappeared but the rope was much shorter than the day before. However, Lucky guided Pozzo. For some reason, Pozzo had become blind and Lucky mute; indeed, Pozzo was no longer arrogant and he was humbled by the loss of his eyesight. The two characters thought about taking their own lives but were even incapable of that. Pozzo's departing line, quoted in the programme of the play, seemed to sum up our condition: 'they give birth astride a grave, the light gleams an instant, then it's night once more.'

The only hope in the play I could see came at the beginning of the second act where I noticed several leaves on the single tree. Perhaps spring would come one day and the tree of life burst forth again. Then perhaps not. Godot never appears. For me, the play raised many more questions than it answered and it lingered on my mind for a long time.

Waiting for Godot seemed to me like waiting for a God who is absent from this world but is vaguely sensed. I thought the play was both absurd and existentialist, questioning how to live in this world without a God. If there were no God then clearly we had to create our own values by which to live. I had already – under the influence of Existentialism – come to similar conclusions.

The audience seemed very enthusiastic as well as bemused. I would certainly have liked to get to talk to them more about the play. My fellow officers and passengers on board never appeared to think about or discuss any important or fundamental questions. I took the ferry back to the ship, gazing at the black water and wondered whether there was a Godot ever to be seen or discovered.

I decided the next day to hire a car in Sydney and drive up the east coast highway. I chose a convertible Ford Mustang, a newish American car. I wanted to experience what it felt like to drive a smart modern car so I could at least get the mystery out of my system. It had a bucket seat and with six cylinders drove very fast indeed. I can see why it had become so popular with those who could afford it. With a long front bonnet looking like a Maserati, it looked very sporty.

I drove fast along the coastal road to Palm Beach which was only about 35 miles north of the central district of Sydney. It had a beautiful, small, curving bay with white sand and a turquoise sea sheltered by lush green vegetation. On the northern headland was a lighthouse. I went for a swim in the warm Pacific Ocean and then, from a café, surveyed the waves as they relentlessly came in and broke on the shore. I wondered what I would do after the voyage. It was clear that I did not want to continue as a Purser Cadet but I wasn't sure what else I could do.

I was pleased to hand in the new Mustang to the hire company, realising that a fast, stylish car could not bring lasting happiness and did not change our existential condition of being born 'astride the grave.' It was like the passengers in the first class of my ship: rich and powerful but ultimately boring because they provided no intellectual stimulation and seemed mainly preoccupied with their status and wealth. I did not want to join their ranks but preferred the company of the Goanese, the poetic fish cook assistant, and the educated deckhand. At least, I could learn something from them.

Whilst in Sydney harbour taking on new passengers, I got my certificate to 'captain' a life boat in case the passengers had to abandon ship. This involved lowering a lifeboat by the davits on the side of the ship into Sydney Harbour. It had long oars as well as blocks of wood in front of the passengers which they could turn via a crank attached to the propeller, making the boat move forward.

I was supposed to take command of the lifeboat at the tiller even though there was a more skilled and older deckhand next to me. But he was a rating and I was an officer. To me it just showed the absurdity of the hierarchy of shipboard life which was not geared to the most skilled and experienced. After several days of telling people what to do, I received my certificate. It was drummed into me that in general the crew and officers were the last to leave a ship in difficulty.

Before we left Sydney I could not believe my eyes to see, on the wharf, the attractive young girl who had slept with many stewards, one after the other. She had come back for more.

Bognor Boy

The next port of call was Hong Kong, still a British colony. We docked in Kowloon on the mainland. I had heard much about Hong Kong. It was meant to be an ideal place to buy cheap cameras and watches and to get a suit made according to your size. And there were 'cherry girls' to meet in the bars which my brother had talked about so enthusiastically.

I was able to go ashore in the evening. I did not get a suit but decided to go to a bar in a district flashing with neon lights. I was disappointed by the bar-girls sitting on high stools who only seemed to want you to buy expensive drinks for them and nothing else. I left and asked my taxi driver waiting outside to drive me to a place for a massage – said to draw on ancient Chinese methods and to be a great experiences He took me to an apartment block and then took the lift to the third floor. We went into an apartment where there was an overdressed woman acting as a receptionist. The décor seemed predominantly silver.

I was then shown into a room where the walls were not only painted black but were covered in large mirrors. I also noticed there was a huge mirror on the ceiling. I waited and waited but no one came. I sat on the bed and soon realised that I was in a brothel and all the girls were busy. Just as I was about to leave there was a knock on the door and a middle-aged woman, who clearly had been found in the street, was ushered in. She was very ugly and old, with smears of make-up on her bedraggled face – clearly worn out. I fled.

I saw the taxi driver below waiting for me. I told him that I was interested in a traditional Chinese massage, not a prostitute. He drove me to another apartment block. I climbed some stairs and was shown into another flat, but this one was clearly of a poor family. It took me a minute to survey the scene: a father sitting down to eat with his two young children at a table and a line of chairs on which I recognised a couple of stewards from our crew. The man clearly was getting his wife to 'service' the waiting men in their bedroom. I was no less horrified and left immediately, going back to the ship by another taxi, knowing that paid sex was not for me.

I was not unhappy to leave Hong Kong the next day. The next port in our voyage would be Manila. During our voyage, I saw two American bombers pass over in the sky, quite close to us. The Vietnam War was raging at the time with horrific casualties and deaths on both sides. I had hardly read any newspapers and was preoccupied by my own teenage life on board but I suddenly became aware of major events which were taking place in the wider world.

Manila was the largest city of the Philippines, a country which consisted of many different islands. The water in the wide, open bay was beautiful and seemingly clean. The influence of the US was still strong however – it had been an American colony since the turn of the 20th century and a Spanish one before that. There were some skyscrapers in the centre of town but in the sprawling area around were small houses, often with corrugated roofs, full of people. I was told that anything could be bought in the city. American G.I.s serving in the Vietnam War would come over for 'R&R' (Rest and Recuperation) which meant bar girls and brothels.

I only had one afternoon and evening of leave and was asked to join some other officers for a party in the penthouse of a tall Americanised hotel. As I entered the door I saw many officers from the Purser's Department, the Engineering Department and a sprinkling of deck officers. I soon realised that this was a 'sex party' that I had been invited to. There was no escaping now and they wanted to see how the youngest cadets on board would react.

Beautiful young Filipino girls served us drinks and we were invited to sit in chairs in rows with the senior officers in the front and the junior ones at the back. Then a young couple came out in front of us, stripped naked, lay down on a bed and made love. They made no noise. It was quite surreal. The girl first rubbed the man's penis so that it became erect, then he penetrated her and when he had come he pulled out and they put towels on their private parts. They then got up, bowed smiling at the officers and then left. It was over in a few minutes. It seemed so clinical and unloving.

I will never forget the lined face and balding hair of a senior engineer as he bent down to get a better view.

We were then beckoned to go off with the girls into adjoining rooms. Some went. I left as soon as I could. I had only stayed that long because of not knowing what to do, whether to cause a scene and leave. No one else did. I felt no desire and I found the 'show' demeaning to the prostitutes who looked so young and vulnerable and must have lived in great poverty with their families. I walked back to the ship, low, sad, sullied and deflated.

On board I returned to leaning over the railings in my spare time looking at the bow wave and wake created by the ship as it sliced through the calm and warm Indian Ocean. I had finally decided, once and for all, after my experiences of meeting the other officers and passengers on board, that I would resign from the P&O-Orient Lines – despite them having paid for my training. It was almost two years since I had left home in Bognor during which I had explored London and almost rolled around the world. I had grown up and experienced more than most 18 and 19 year-olds. But the life of luxury and repetition on board a cruise ship was not for me.

But what should I do? I had occasionally kept in touch by letter with Jenny with whom I had fallen in love briefly but whom I thought I would never see again. She was still at the university in Dakar, Sénégal, studying English and American language and literature. On the off chance, I asked her whether there were any teaching jobs available. My plan, if I could, was to teach for a year and do an A-level in English by correspondence in the hope that one day I might be able to enter a university in England.

By a stroke of luck, her elder brother Francis – who had done a degree in English beforehand – had just decided as a teacher to move from the Collège St Michel in Dakar to another one. Jenny went round and saw the headmaster of the secondary school, a French Canadian called Frère Emmanuel, and asked if I could replace her brother. He readily accepted me and offered the large sum of 1000 New Francs a month. He even wrote out a contract for me there and then on his small typewriter in his office. I might have been English-speaking but I had only a bad A-level in Art at the time. I could not have been happier for now I had an alternative and I would see Jenny again.

We only stayed for a day and night in Bombay taking on passengers who wanted to travel to Britain. I was not allowed any leave this time so all I could see from a top deck of the sprawling and mysterious continent was the impressive 'Gateway to India', a huge monument with its four towers, built of yellow basalt. It had been erected early in the century to commemorate the visit of King George V and Queen Mary to their principal colony.

It was hugely frustrating not to join the milling crowds below me on the dock side and have a glimpse and taste of the country. It looked one of the most thrilling places to explore, particularly as my uncle had worked there in dispatches during the war and I had also read about the excesses of British colonial rule, including the 'Indian Mutiny' and the 'Black Hole of Calcutta.' At the very least, I wanted to savour a genuine curry.

One day after leaving Bombay I found an attractive young Indian girl looking over the railings at the sea in my favourite spot. I got chatting to her and it turned out that she was a Tamil girl who had been brought up in Kuala Lumpur but was going to Britain to become a nurse. Her dark face was pitted slightly – I presumed from smallpox when she was young. She was very pretty and vivacious. I enjoyed talking to her, learning about her life, and she seemed to like talking to me – particularly as the other passengers rather shunned her. I invited her back to my cabin for tea for a couple of times; my cabin steward 'Natty' from Goa was no doubt surprised to see his young charge talking to a fellow compatriot but he didn't show it.

We called to refuel in Aden in Yemen on the eastern approach of the Red Sea. Yemen had just won its independence from Britain. Again I was given no leave and had to stay on the ship. We then travelled up the Red Sea which was as calm as a millpond. The murmur of the sea, as it whished past below the open porthole of my cabin, was even more subdued than usual.

We then entered the Suez Canal, first opened in 1869. It meant that it was no longer necessary to travel around South Africa to reach India and the Far East. It had been nationalised in 1956 after the 'Suez Crisis' by the Egyptian leader Gamil Nasser who was still in power. Beyond some low mountains, yellow sands of the desert stretched out level beyond the banks on either side. It was uncannily still and quiet except for the muffled sound of ship's engines deep below. Occasionally, I could make out the minarets of mosques of small villages. A third of the way along the Canal we entered a large lake – the Great Bitter Lake. There was little traffic coming the other direction. Towards the end of the Canal, I could just make out the great Pyramids of Giza outside the sprawling city of Cairo. It was very tantalising indeed as I had not visited an Arabic country with an Islamic culture but it would have to wait for another day. I was not allowed to descend the gangway at Port Said at the end of the Canal where we had to pay our dues.

It was now April as we steamed across the Mediterranean. We called in at the Bay of Naples, where I had some time off. I caught a taxi up the hill to Pompeii, the Roman town which had been

covered by volcanic ash when Mount Vesuvius had erupted. I
wandered the streets at leisure and visited the well-preserved
forum, baths, houses and walls. Many were covered in graffiti
in Latin. There were plaster casts of actual people who had been
caught by ash as they went about their daily life. They seemed very
real. I was then ushered into an ancient brothel, which had wall
paintings of the inmates and customers performing sex. There
was also in a side room a small statue of the god Priapus with
an enormous erection. I was told that this fertility god was the
protector of merchant seamen.

Next we passed Gibraltar and went up the Portuguese Coast to
the Bay of Biscay. We were now back in the Atlantic. The officers,
including me, had to change from their whites into their dark blue
uniforms. It felt very strange; we were indeed coming home. We
finally travelled up the muddy estuary of the Thames to Tilbury
under a dark grey sky. As the passengers got off I leant over the
railing from a top deck and saw the nurse from Kuala Lumpur
who had given me a 'kukri', a knife used by Gurkhas in an ornately
wooden sheaf. It was curved and had a place near the handle
where the owner could cut their thumb and shed his own blood
before taking the blood of others. As Buddhists or Hindus, they
were meant to believe in *ahimsa* – no harm.

'I was given this by my father – it is originally from Nepal – to
give to a member of the family who is already in England', she
said. 'I know that the British Customs will not allow me to take
it ashore. I would like you to have it as a memory of our time
together. We will never see each other again.'

It was true and I felt a pang of disappointment. We did not
exchange addresses. I hoped she would fare well as a nurse and
find fulfilment in her life.

At sea I was not paid my usual salary and got an advance before
I went ashore. I therefore thought that I would have saved up
quite a bit. But I had to settle up my bar bill which covered drinks
and cigarettes. I had smoked about a pack of cigarettes a day and
often bought a round of drinks thinking that it would not add up
to very much. I simply signed a chit for them; it was all so easy.
I should have received about five pound a week but imagine my
surprise when I found that my advances and my bar bill cancelled
out any earnings. I left the boat as penniless as I had arrived. But I
convinced myself that I was at least rich in experience!

I also got back the large green-covered journal in which I had been asked to keep records of my time and activities in different departments on ship. It was mainly an account of bald facts and did not record my real thoughts and feelings. It had been duly signed by the Captain and by the Chief Purser. I thought they could have been more generous but no doubt they had got wind of the fact that I was handing in my notice to Head Office. They had to cover themselves. My resignation came into effect at the 'expiration' of my leave on the 27th April 1966. I received a reference letter later (dated 11th November 1966) from the Head Office of P&O-Orient Lines saying that I had received 'very satisfactory reports' from the Captain and Purser and that the management were 'sorry to lose such a promising young Officer.'

I said goodbye to the Purser assistants and the two Writers in the tourist office. Apart from leaving Stemp, my fellow Purser Cadet with whom I had shared my cabin throughout the voyage, I had no qualms. I had grown to like 'Natty' and gave him a big tip; he wished me well as I did him.

As I walked down the gangway of the ship and stepped onto English soil after nine months at sea I did not look behind. I took a deep breath. While the experience had been varied and unique, my childhood innocence was gone. I was only too pleased to start the next phase in my life.

From my time at boarding school and in the P&O-Orient Line, I had had enough of rules and regulations, of being told what to do by authority and working within a hierarchy. I would not be a subject of another man's system but work one out for myself. I wanted imagination, creativity, spontaneity and autonomy in my life. I would be free, taking responsibility for the consequences of my own actions, thinking and acting for myself. I would examine my own life and upbringing. No doubt I would make mistakes but at least they would be my own mistakes and not those of others. I would be free.

22
OUT TO AFRICA

After an eventful voyage sailing around the world on a ship, I realised the work simply didn't suit me. I was more interested in trying to understand myself and the world around rather than in endlessly circling the globe and laying passengers. I preferred reading Plato and Flaubert to selling excursion tickets and meeting ship's pilots, replying to passengers' enquiries and pushing pens. I did not want to be a fancy clerk or a hotel manager. I wanted to learn more about history, literature and philosophy.

My mother had moved with her new husband Sandy and her mother Nelly to a new bungalow on an estate overlooking Elbury Cove in Devon, halfway between Paignton and Brixham. It had a beautiful view through a large front window across some fields to an old farmhouse and then across the water to Torquay – far on the other side of Torbay. The cove was mainly of pebbles. On the western side there was a small ruin and a large wood which went up the cliff. There was a good walk along the coastal path through the woods to Brixham.

Torbay and Elbury Cove featured in the film *The System* (1964) – called *The Girl-Getters* in the States. It centred on a beach photographer (played by Oliver Reed) at the crossroads of his life and his affair with an upper-class girl who comes down from London for a holiday with her wealthy father. It shows how cynical the young men who work in Torbay in the summer are – particularly in their different ploys to 'pull the birds.' They have nothing but contempt for the 'grockles' who come down from the Midlands and the North for their annual holidays. It also takes a swipe at the 'Establishment' and class system of the day. But the working-class characters would rather break into it than abolish it by more radical means.

My Mater (she preferred being called that) and Nanna were pleased to see me but obviously worried about what I planned to do next. I told them that I would retake my exam for A-level French and find work. I would stay at Jenny's summer house in Anduze in the South of France before going out to Africa to become an English teacher.

My mother seemed more worried about my uniform than the fact that I was giving up life as a cadet.

'I've worked my fingers to the bone hairdressing to pay for your uniform and now you're giving it all up!' she said on more than one occasion.

I put my dark blue uniform with its gold and white epaulettes as well as my starched tropical whites in the cellar below the house where they went mouldy and were eventually eaten by mice.

During my voyage, I had written to Jenny at most ports sending my poems, and received her letters in beautiful French, full of love and colourful accounts of her daily life and studies in Dakar. On the 18 April 1966, she wrote to me, now newly installed in Elbury Cove:

'I think of you and love you, and I want you to be the same as I knew you, always; to be kind, clever, natural, happy and melancholic; to be against everybody and hate no one; to want to be given as much as you give, and to always ask "why?", even when you know the answer.'

After working hard revising and taking an exam I took on the job as an assistant Foreman of parcels in Paignton railway station. My job was to help the Foreman load sacks of letters and parcels delivered by lorries from the Post Office onto a waiting train. It was here that he asked me one day whether I knew my namesake Bill Marshall for whom he worked cleaning out the stables whenever he came to Newton Abbot races.

He arranged for me to meet my father in the Queen's Hotel where he was staying in Newton Abbott. I met him in the bar and afterwards walked many times around the adjoining park, learning much about his life, his work as fighter pilot during the war and why he had left my mother. At the end of the long meeting he promised to write. He never did and it was some time before I saw him again.

I had told my mother about our meeting as she drove me up to Bognor. She was intrigued but said that that she was now happy with my stepfather Sandy. We stayed overnight in a caravan in the forecourt of the Bridport Hotel where she had been brought up.

Before I left to go to Africa I said goodbye to my mother and caught the train to Newhaven where I crossed over by ferry to France and then travelled by train to Alès in the south of France. My gums were still sore having just had my wisdom teeth taken

out and my white handkerchief was flecked with blood but I
was pleased to be going to Africa to teach and stay with Jenny in
France beforehand.

When I arrived at Alès in the morning I was tired from my night
on the train and looked forward to going to Jenny's house to
relax and sleep. Her older brother Francis was meant to meet
me by car and I waited for him at the railway café sitting at an
outdoor table. I soaked up the French atmosphere, enjoying the
warmth of southern France and the blue skies, admiring the lines
of poplar trees with their white rings along the road. But Francis
did not turn up and I eventually got worried about whether I was
expected. No one answered at Jenny's home when I rang from the
café. I waited and waited and in the afternoon decided to catch the
bus to Anduze.

   It went through the dusty villages and then down winding bends
to the River Gardon, and crossed over a medieval bridge. I got
out in the bustling square of Anduze. It called itself *La Porte des
Cévennes* and I saw mountains covered in chestnut trees to the
North. I asked for directions in my best French – which wasn't
that good – to the valley where Jenny lived with her parents and
brothers in the summer. I had to walk back over the bridge and

*With my girlfriend Jenny and her two brothers
Roland and Francis (Zobel family archive)*

Bognor Boy

by the river Gardon along the side of a limestone mountain until I turned right up a track. I asked again an old peasant the way to 'Moun Oustaou'. He pointed me up a steep track. Near the top I saw a woman open the shutters of a window and shake out a yellow cloth; she had a light brown skin and wavy hair and was clearly Jenny's mother. I had arrived, exhausted but happy.

It turned out that Francis had got the time of my arrival wrong. Everyone gave me a warm welcome in the old stone house which had once been a silk farm like many others along the valley. Jenny's father, Joseph, was unlike his wife very dark and African-looking. He welcomed me in deliberate and formal French which was a pleasure to hear. He was a strong man dressed in corduroys and an old shirt, and held himself straight. He shaved his head. He gave me a kiss on either side of my face and I felt his stubble rubbing against mine. It seemed odd at the time but I soon learnt that this was a common French greeting between two men.

I was shown to my room upstairs which was lined with books and had a tiled floor. I shared it with Jenny's two older brothers. I had already met Roland in Bognor a couple of years previously. He and his brother Francis were particularly friendly towards me. Their younger sister slept in a small cubbyhole off the main room with the original walls made from rough-hewn stones. Small scorpions lived in the gaps and you had to make sure they hadn't gone into your shoes overnight. It was great to see Jenny again. I wanted some more work to pay for my boat ticket to Dakar in Sénégal and it was arranged that I should help in the *vendange* – the harvest of grapes – in a nearby farm.

It proved back-breaking work. The family of Spanish origin who ran the small farm wanted a *colporteur*, that is a person to gather in the grapes which were placed in a barrel by the pickers. With the help of an old peasant I had to collect the grapes in the hot sun along rows between the vines by hooking two poles under the metal protrusions of a large wooden barrel.

The great event of the day was the copious and tasty meal cooked by the farmer's wife which we ate on a rough table in the shade of a tree. About a dozen of us sat on benches and we could drink as much wine as we wanted. Afterwards, befuddled by the food, drink and the heat we had an afternoon siesta. We then returned to work about two hours later until about six o'clock. For each day worked on the farm we were given two bottles of the new wine of the harvest.

Washing in a tub in Moun Oustaou, Anduze, France

Bognor Boy

I enjoyed the camaraderie and the long lunches but the physical labour was exhausting. I returned home with my shoulders aching painfully. Jenny would give me a massage each night and I fell asleep almost immediately. It took me some time to get used to it, and the pain and ache in my shoulders remained.

I had in the meantime become an honorary member of a 'drinking club' consisting of friends of Roland. I was even issued a card, saying that I was *l'ambassadeur anglais*. It was really just an excuse to have parties at which we danced with our girlfriends – those who were lucky enough to have one – and of course drank too much. I was taught some old French drinking songs which were intended to make you throw back your glass and drink in one go until you rolled under the table. I would often declaim some French poetry in a bad English accent when I had drunk too much – to the delight of the other members.

I had earned enough money at the railway station in Devon and from the grape picking to buy a ticket on a new ship called the SS *Ancerville* from Marseille to Dakar on the 30th of September 1966. I would have to stay there for about a month before Jenny's family came out. The school where I was to teach began its term a couple of weeks earlier. I therefore caught the train to Marseille where I went on board the small ship which took passengers and some cargo down the West coast of Africa. It was very new, very white and looked like a huge motor boat.

I had bought the cheapest ticket available and travelled in so-called 'steerage' at the cost of 30 New Francs. I could expect to be at the bottom of the ship with the most basic amenities, no privacy, poor food and limited toilet use. I was warned by Jenny that I would be 'disgusted forever by boats and Africa'.

A few months before I had been an officer cadet on a large passenger ship which had been the pride of the British Merchant Navy but now was in the lowest of the low. I was led to the hold of the French ship where there was no natural light. We had to sleep in rows of bunks with a two-inch metal strip between each of us with a few blankets and a dirty pillow thrown on top. I was the only white man amongst the sea of black Africans who soon became very friendly and helpful. I learned they were mostly *ébouers* (dustmen) and *nettoyers de rues* (street cleaners) in Paris and other cities in France.

The men were mainly Senegalese workers going home to see their families. They were the invisible men who helped oil the cogs of the French economy. Apart from eating they mainly lay on their bunks for there was nothing to do. The light was not bright enough to read by. The only way to tell the time of day was to look at a watch if you had one.

In the centre of the hold where we lived was a large table with benches on either side. Food came down a hatch in a huge cauldron which was probably made from left-overs from the other two classes on board. The food seemed to consist mainly of a brown stew with a few bones.

We were each given a tin mug, a plate and a spoon which we had to wash ourselves in a large pot of greasy water. When the cauldron came down there was a huge rush to get something to eat. They were strong men and I had no chance against them but my neighbour in my bunk, who was a street cleaner in Paris, made sure that I got some swill on my plate and warm water in my mug.

I thought it was like a slave ship which took people from West Africa to the New World. The difference of course was that conditions were much better and we had to wait for only four days before arrival in Dakar instead of three or four weeks. We were also meant to be 'free men' and Sénégal had recently become independent from France.

After a day out at sea, I felt I could eat no more leftovers and craved for some fresh air on deck. Since I knew the layout of a ship, I climbed a gangway and found myself in the galley. I talked to a young French assistant cook with an auburn beard who agreed to give me some food in exchange for some English lessons. It mainly consisted every day of a cold Spanish omelette made with potatoes and peas but it was delicious compared to the food that we were habitually served down below in the dark hold. He also lent me a tie and showed me the way out into first-class accommodation. When I stepped through the metal door into the corridor I felt free again. When I made it on deck and breathed in the fresh air and looked at the distant horizon of the sea all around us, it felt wonderful. No one challenged me as I strolled around the decks.

Casablanca in Morocco was the only place we stopped in our four day 'cruise.' The city seemed white, with many alleys and souks amongst the tall French colonial buildings and palm-decked squares. I sent a card home to my mother in Devon to say that I was all right. I was used to the flies and inevitable poverty. I made a beeline for a little restaurant where the waiter spoke French in an Arabic accent and I ordered couscous (boiled semolina flour made from wheat) served with chicken, chickpeas and vegetable stew. It was marvellous to feel full up again! I knew that Casablanca and Morocco had once been the haunt of American and European Bohemians with its relaxed attitude to drugs and sex of different varieties. The Beat writer Jack Kerouac had visited and William S. Burroughs had written his drug-induced, episodic novel *Naked Lunch* there. But unfortunately I didn't have time to explore the city or plunge beneath its surface.

23
TEACHING IN AFRICA

It was already getting hot and humid but I wasn't prepared for the blast when I descended the gangway in Dakar. The French colonial buildings looked similar to those of Casablanca but it was clear from the faces that I was in a black African and not an Arabic country, the second one south of Mauritania in sub-Saharan Africa. The sky was overcast with low clouds and I was caught in a heavy downpour. I hailed a taxi to take me to Jenny's house in the district known as SICAP Liberté. It was a two-storeyed building surrounded by high walls with a sandy garden of sorts at the back.

The house was all locked up because the owners were away in the South of France. But I waited in the garden to meet Diallo, whom they called their 'boy', a short man in a white flowing robe who lived in a small hut at the end of the garden, sometimes with his young, small, chubby wife. When he turned up several hours later he was very surprised to find this young Englishman waiting there.

'I thought you were coming a few days later', he said apologetically in French with a strong African accent. He let me into a dark room in a semi cellar just below the level of the ground. There was a thin covering of gauze over the only window to keep out the mosquitoes. It smelt musty and damp.

'It's Francis's room. You'll be fine here', he declared, smiling sheepishly.

I was not so sure. I knew I would have to wait for a month before Jenny and her family returned. It was the opposite of the luxurious lifestyle that I had experienced as a cadet and the modest, clean and ordered house of my mother and grandmother. It was more like what I had recently experienced with the street cleaners and dustmen in the dark and sunless hold of the ship.

The house in Dakar was quite close to a large canal, Canal Quatre, which was an open sewer which gave off a pungent smell of rot, damp and decaying vegetables. The carcasses of dead dogs and cats were sometimes cast into it to rot under the sun. The stinking canal came out into the sea not far from the inshore fishermen. It was only washed out during heavy downbursts during the rainy season.

Bognor Boy

After a fitful night tossing in the humid heat and being eaten by mosquitoes, I was determined to make the best of it so I went into town on the back of Diallo's moped. He dropped me off and I explored the centre of town which had been built by the French with its ornate churches, smart squares and tree-lined boulevards. At the beginning of the century, the French had constructed the Plateau for themselves and forced the local African population into a new quarter called the Médina. The names still stuck although the areas were partly reclaimed by the local population.

I learned that Dakar was on a peninsula called Cap-Vert, with its back to the Sahel desert and its face to the Atlantic. It had won independence from France five years earlier and had a 'socialist' president Léopold Senghor. He was a great poet and advocate of *négritude* which took pride in African identity, culture and values. But since the city had been the centre of the French colonies, its administration was still overblown and many of its buildings grander than the size of the country required.

The main square called Place de L'indépendance could have been anywhere in a large town in the south of France. Despite this being a predominantly Muslim country a cathedral had been built nearby. I found my way down some streets to Collège Saint-Michel where I was to take over from Francis and teach English for a year. I would be paid well by my standards and have to teach for 22 hours a week with school holidays to myself. It was run by French Catholic Canadian brothers. The headmaster in a rather dirty white cassock with an old leather belt around his ample stomach welcomed me warmly into his room. His name was Frère Emmanuel. He spoke some English with a strong Canadian French accent but clearly preferred French.

Through his thick glasses, he said that when the pupils returned to the school I could live on the edge of town in a new monastery along with a group of French teachers who had chosen to work overseas as *co-opérants* rather than do their military service. I warmed to Frère Emmanuel straight away because he appeared so straightforward and clearly loved the children under his care.

Every day Diallo served me chicory coffee, a fresh baguette and marge for breakfast and a plate of white rice and liver for lunch and supper. The liver, probably taken from an ox, was a large lump, very tough with an awful taste. I had no money to buy vegetables or fruit. Diallo said that he had been given no money by Jenny's family to look after me. I had no alternative but to accept it.

While waiting to go to my new room at the monastery, Diallo took me around on the back of his moped to show me off to his friends. I went into the shantytowns and met people who barely spoke French, let alone English. They were handsome and dark and of the Woloff tribe, often dressed in flowing robes and colourful woollen hats despite the heat. I learned from them a few words. I was clearly a curiosity and I suspected that few white people had ever visited them in their huts.

One day Diallo took me down to the beach at Soumbédioune outside the city. Atlantic rollers came in one after the other on the long beach, causing a permanent cloud of light spray. There were many huts set back on the flat sand. Fishermen in long brightly-painted boats called *pirogues* – shaped like dug-out canoes with outboard engines – were bringing in their catches, skilfully negotiating the rollers, with many willing fellow fishermen rushing into the water to help them land and pulling the boats on rollers on the moving sand. Their wives or partners degutted the fish and sold them at the nearby traditional market, at prices enough to keep a family afloat. Portly women from the city came down dressed in colourful robes and sporting a turban (often with sticks in their mouths which they chewed to keep their teeth clean) and haggled over prices of the daily catch laid out on wooden tables on the sand. The stench was overwhelming, mixing with the revolting smell of the nearby sewage canal taking its untreated contents straight into the sea. The fishermen were already suffering from the giant Russian, Chinese, Korean and Japanese trawlers fishing just off their territorial waters.

I wandered off along the wide sandy alleyways between the huts and at a corner I saw two young girls who beckoned me over. They were very attractive, about my age, dressed in flowing clothes of many different colours. One deliberately flapped open her sarong several times, while the taller girl made the unmistakable sign of intercourse by putting one forefinger in and out through a circle made by her thumb and forefinger. They obviously wanted me to come and join them but I reluctantly declined, wanting to remain faithful to Jenny.

I eventually found Diallo again and he took me to a fisherman's hut owned by one of his friends. In a dark room we sat down on a mat on the sand around a tray brought by his wife from the adjacent kitchen. It was piled high with a fish simmered in tomato paste and onions in a bed of white broken rice. It was accompanied by vegetables which mainly looked like cabbage and carrots. It was called Thiéboudienne. I was told in broken French that it was the national dish of Sénégal and the fish had been caught that morning. We used our fingers to eat, taking morsels from the tray of food in front of us. It was hotly spiced and delicious.

During my stay in Francis' half-cellar room, I continued to be bitten by mosquitoes. I tossed interminably between damp sheets and was malnourished with white rice and inedible ox liver. It thankfully soon came to an end. Term-time at Collège Saint-Michel was about to start and I could now move in with the Canadian brothers in their new monastery on the outskirts. It was about five miles from the centre of town and would cost me half my wages. It was a functional two-storey, four-square building around a courtyard of coarse grass criss-crossed by two paths. I was shown to my room in the middle of the second floor at the back which had a concrete floor and a glass slatted window. In the centre was a single bed covered in a white mosquito net and against the concrete walls were a desk and chair and a little metal wardrobe for my few clothes. Its austere look suited me, especially as it was large, new and airy. Outside, I had a wonderful view of the flat sand stretching out before me, populated by a few shrubs and great baobab trees which had a wide girth. They had few leaves and looked upside down, like trees whose roots were in the air rather than in the ground.

In the evening, I met the other French *co-opérants*, and Richard Burchnall (an English VSO) and an American member of the Peace Corps. Like me they were all new lads, middle-class and eager to enjoy their year abroad teaching. I was the only one at Collège Saint Michel in the centre of town. All the others worked elsewhere.

I soon became friends with Richard. He had gone to Wykeham School at Winchester in Hampshire where his father was a housemaster and head of classics. In the following year he was going to Oxford – Jesus College, I think – to study classics himself. He was a good rugby player, round and strong, but not stuck up at all and threw himself into his new life. I often went to his room at the end of my corridor before supper and listened to the latest Beatles records. When he got a new EP of 'Strawberry Fields Forever' and 'Penny Lane', we played it over and over again until

Teaching in Africa

we knew all the words. They sounded very psychedelic.

The young man from the Peace Corps was much more cautious. He had gone to Amherst College and was heading for Princeton. He had been told on a course that the water in West Africa was not necessarily clean or reliable and therefore he refused to eat any food which had not been cooked. As a result he missed out on all the delicious salads which we were offered in our common refectory.

The refectory was on the ground floor and we sat on benches on either side of a long table. Every night proved a glorious uproar. We all had exuberant high spirits. Senegalese waiters brought in as much wine as we wanted and served several courses of wonderful French meals. The *co-opérants* really enjoyed their food and drink; one large lad from Brittany would often consume a whole Camembert at one sitting.

When term started at Collège Saint-Michel, I enjoyed my teaching. I was responsible for teaching English as a foreign language to pupils in the secondary school up to the Brevet, a diploma equivalent to O-Levels. They were mostly African, some Lebanese and a sprinkling of French. A few of the African pupils towered over me; they were in their 20s because they had only

My class at Collège Saint Michel, Dakar, Sénégal. I am on the left in the second row. The headmaster Frère Emmanuel is on the right.

begun their primary education at eleven years old. Some knew English very well since they had been born in The Gambia, a former British colony which cut into Sénégal on either side of a river. One boy in particular was very bright but he disrupted my class by reading comics at the back of the room. Finally being exasperated with him, I told him to leave my classroom after many warnings. The headmaster came across him in the corridor and banned him from school for a while. Afterwards he was very well-behaved, as most of my pupils were, since they saw the value of getting an education.

I bought an old mobylette, a moped with a tiny engine on the front wheel, to travel from the monastery, where I slept, to the college on the Plateau at the centre of the town. I had to get up at seven in the morning. Sand swept across the new highway. I had to stop at various lights where there were inevitably lepers begging from home-made boards on wheels on which they scrambled around. I gave them a few coins, but was careful – no doubt unnecessarily so – not to touch their hands which often had lost fingers. I noticed that men at the side of the road gathered together at tables to share their breakfast, which usually consisted of French-style baguettes and margarine, washed down with chicory coffee. I had been served the same by Diallo at Jenny's house before her arrival.

While I enjoyed teaching and discovering a new country, I spent most of my free time with Jenny. I was happy and wrote the poem at the end of October 1966:

> Am I part of all
> That I have seen:
> Flying fishes in
> Rainbows of seas?
>
> Am I part of all
> That I have touched:
> Smooth curves in
> The crevices of stones?
>
> Am I part of all
> That I have loved:
> Tender tears in
> Glances of eyes?

Jenny had come back with her family at the end of the rainy season and – despite being six months younger than me – attended her last year at the University of Dakar studying English and American literature. She lived at home with her parents since her two older brothers had left. Her mother Ennie had trained as a *patisseur* (pastry cook) in the island of Martinique in the Caribbean. Her father described his childhood in Martinique – living with his grandmother in a shack – in his moving autobiographical novel *Rue de Cases Nègres (Black Shack Alley)*. He had overcome the extreme poverty of his childhood through education.

Having been a French teacher in a lycée at Fontainebleau near Paris, he was now the director of the Cultural Programmes on the national radio. The house was full of African statues and masks which he collected. He spent most of his spare time when at home in his study writing and reading. He was composing at the time a short story called *'Le Chevalier Tombé'* based on his own experience of falling from a horse at the Police Academy.

One day parking my mobylette outside his house, I left my brief case strapped on the back. Imagine my surprise when I came out to find it stolen, with my wallet and all my money in it. On another occasion, I took my passport to renew my work permit and was surprised to have it back in a few days while it should have taken at least three weeks. Then I realised that I had put all my savings in notes inside it. They had disappeared. I was more careful after that.

Diallo did much of the shopping, helped in the kitchen and cleaned the house. He kept the garden tidy and lived most the week in the shack at the bottom. I had not changed my view that servants were both unnecessary and unjust, only perpetuating the class system, but Ennie retorted with the usual justification that she gave work to him which otherwise he might not get. I felt if you could do it yourself then you shouldn't get other people to do it for you.

One afternoon, when the rest of the family was out, Jenny and I made love for the first time in her shower in her small bedroom. Its walls were plastered with the world maps covered in plastic; it seemed an appropriate setting. She also occasionally came to visit me in my room at the monastery out of town. I would have to smuggle her out after dark to catch a taxi. I dreaded meeting a *frère* in the corridor or down the stairs but I never did.

I spent Christmas Eve with the family, having a dinner at home after midnight as was the French custom. After Christmas, Joseph drove us in the family car – with Ennie in the front and Jenny and me in the back – to Ziguinchour, the principal town in Casamance in the south of Sénégal.

We had to take a ferry to cross the river in the thin strip of The Gambia. It was disconcerting to see a Senegalese policeman at the border dressed in a *kepi* like a Frenchman, and a Gambian policeman on the other side dressed like a British bobby. They were from the same tribe and spoke the same traditional language, yet one would call his counterpart a '*sal anglais*' (a dirty Englishman) while the other a 'bloody frog' – such had been the overwhelming power of colonialism.

Before climbing back into the car, I was asked by a fit young Gambian for a sixpence. When I refused to give him one (I didn't carry any money on me at the time and he looked perfectly able-bodied to me) he called me a 'fucking Englishman.' Although I had travelled around the world, I had never been insulted in the same way. I'd never really thought that I was an 'Englishman' and if asked what I was, I would say British. But then I learned later that it was typical of English people not to worry about their country; such was their confidence in their own identity they never even thought about, let alone questioned it.

After Ziginchour in Casamance, we went to stay at a villa at Cape Skiring on a long beach. The vegetation was very luxurious behind us and the verandah looked out at the breakers rolling in from the Atlantic. It was superb to look out to sea but I found the weather very hot and humid which made me tired. We only stayed for a few days and then returned to Dakar on New Year's Eve. It was a long journey and when we arrived I could hardly keep my eyes open.

Jenny had arranged to join her friends for a dinner party at a restaurant overlooking the sea at the end of peninsula. I had agreed to pick her up in a taxi. But after I had changed for the evening I rested under the mosquito net on my bed in the monastery only to fall fast asleep. I awoke to hear banging on my door. It was Jenny, looking beautiful in a white silky mini-dress, reminding me that we had agreed to meet on this very special occasion. I was very embarrassed but could only apologise as we took a taxi, arriving late for dinner. At the restaurant in the smart hotel we stayed up all night for the New Year's party in 1967. I got my second wind, partied and danced and only felt exhausted again at the first red streaks of a dawn. The sea was at first grey but was slowly lit up by long red streaks. It was time to go back and sleep.

During my teaching at Collège Saint-Michel, I continued to study by correspondence for an A-level in English. I had already scraped through Art and French and was hoping with a decent grade in English to apply to university on my return to England. I took my exam in a room in the British Embassy. They had already invited me there for cocktail parties. I had studied hard, knew long quotes by heart, and felt that it was my last chance to get to university. If I didn't, I didn't know what I would do. I took it far too seriously.

I was supervised during the exam at the embassy by the third secretary. I had a glass of water and a packet of Craven 'A' cigarettes placed on my table. When I opened the paper to look at the questions, I realised I could answer them all. They were easy. But such was the huge pressure to do well my mind went a complete blank. It must have been 'nerves.' However much I tried, I couldn't get writing. I knew I could do it but I could not start. I left early, handing in a blank paper only with my name on top.

Jenny was waiting for me. Outside the embassy there was a sandstorm; the brown dust swirled through the streets, making everything dark and mysterious. It was in keeping with my mood. I could not hold back my tears any longer. I stumbled along like a blind man or like someone who had just heard some terrible news. I kept saying:

'I've had it. I'll never be able to go to university now!'

I rang up the embassy the following day to say that I would not be in to do the two following papers. But the third secretary rang me up soon after and said that I would have to come in to do them.

'You cannot leave it like this. You'll always regret not at least having tried. You deserve to do it just for your personal pride, if not for anything else! Come in and do the other two papers, even if you think you'll fail.'

I was persuaded and did the other ones to the best of my ability but was convinced that I would fail. I wrote easily this time with a flourish, showing off my knowledge and elaborate style.

When I eventually opened the letter with my result, I could not believe it. I had passed with a 'B' grade; I must have done brilliantly in the other two papers and got maximum marks. Or someone from the embassy unbeknown to me had written to the board of examiners.

Bognor Boy

Although I did not have two foreign modern languages at O-level, which were essential to go to London University, I was accepted into Kingston College of Technology to do an external degree in English, French and Economics. I was not obliged to have the two modern languages until I applied to the University of London in the third year in order to sit the all-important final exam.

It eventually came time for me to return to England. In August 1967, when my teaching was over at the college, I paid £80 for an air fare to get home, a small fortune in those days. I said goodbye to my new friends, particularly the headmaster Frère Emmanuel, who had encouraged me in all that I did. He wrote to me afterwards *'Je te le répète, je fus très content de ton travail et de ta conscience professionnelle.'* I got letters from several of my pupils regretting my departure. One even said he 'loved me like his brother' and felt the American girl who replaced me was nowhere near so good…

Richard, who was going up to Oxford, said we would meet each other again in England. Jenny had finished her degree and got a job as a French assistant teacher in Chatham Grammar School for Girls.

I was so used to black faces that the English at first looked very pallid and ill by comparison. I also found it difficult to get used to the grey skies and mild climate after waking up with bright blue sunshine and hot weather every day. But I loved the green English countryside, with its network of small fields and hedges, which I viewed out of the window of the train from London to my mother's house at Elbury Cove in Devon.

I went out to Jenny's house in Les Cévennes just before college to have a holiday with her and to celebrate my 21st birthday on 23rd of August 1967.

It was decided to celebrate my birthday in grand style by having an open-air banquet with all the friends round a long table with me at the head. The set menu was to have snails for starters and then roast a pig for the main course. And of course there would be copious amounts of local wine to drink.

Members of the club scoured the rough, prickly bush of the hilly and sun-baked landscape to pick up edible snails. Roland and his friends also chose a pig from a local peasant in the valley. It was called 'Napoleon.' It had had a reasonable life living off scraps from the family but the problem was how to kill it. Roland and three other, including me, led the pig out of its sty and tied it down on top of a table. We were instructed to each hold a trotter.

I noticed a large growth on its hind leg. Apart from its name, this somehow made Napoleon even more individual with its own personality. I didn't think killing a pig ourselves was necessarily a good idea but felt that I could not turn back now. Roland got a large kitchen knife which he plunged into the animal under its front leg hoping to hit its heart. But he missed and there was an almighty squeal from the pig which struggled to free itself from its bonds. Being spurted with blood, Roland put his knife in several times trying to kill the animal. It cried and cried like a baby. But slowly its kicking grew quieter and eventually it gave up.

I found the whole thing quite nauseating, particularly as it had been done for my sake. I felt nonetheless that one should be prepared to kill an animal if one wanted to eat it. I think the traumatic experience eventually contributed to my becoming a vegetarian in my late 20s. After killing the pig, I often felt guilty taking the life of another conscious being in order to have a fleeting burst of pleasure on the palate.

A few days later after the slaughter, death and murder of the pig – call it what you will – we had the grand banquet. I'd never liked snails but I knew that served with garlic sauce they were considered a great delicacy in France. I tried a few which tasted like rubber. After several glasses of rosé wine, I went on to a pork chop cut from poor old Napoleon which was being roasted nearby. More wine was plied to me and I knew I would have to make a speech in my best French towards the end of the meal. Everybody seemed in high spirits and I took off like a rocket only to fall all too soon down-to-earth, literally. I had drunk simply too much, fell off my chair and passed out. The 'English ambassador' had not excelled himself.

They threw me in to the back of a boot of a car. I woke up bumping along a track and felt terrible and claustrophobic. Somehow I was carried home by Roland and his friends. When I came to the next day I was immediately violently sick on the tiles at the side of my bed. Next time I managed to reach the bathroom.

As it turned out I had to remain in bed for about three days from a mixture of food and alcoholic poisoning. It seemed that most people who had attended the banquet had been sick as well. I learnt afterwards that you were meant to starve wild snails in a special cage for about a month so that they emptied their stomachs. We had only left them for a few days…

My 22nd birthday celebration in Devon was not as dramatic as my 21st in the south of France had been. I went with my mother, stepfather and grandmother to a dinner at the Casbah Hotel in Stoke Gabriel. Only the name spoke of the souks of Morocco. I remember they served my mother Brown Windsor soup and a fresh bread roll but when it came to the second course of half a roast chicken, she could not eat any of it.

Yet not all was quiet and uneventful amongst the retirees of Elbury Cove. My mother told me that a near neighbour had borrowed a gun from the farm below, saying that he wanted to kill the rabbits at the bottom of his garden. Instead, he turned it on his wife and killed her and then tried to kill himself. Having failed, he managed to drive himself down to the cove and threw himself off the rocks. He drowned in the sea. They were supposed to be 'a very happy couple.'

'You can never tell!', my mother observed.

24

COLLEGE LIFE

I was thrilled to be going into further education at last. I arrived in Kingston upon Thames at the end of September 1967 in an old jalopy – a beige Austin Hillman car. It was on its last legs and I had bought it for a few pounds; it was in such bad condition I could see the road through the rusting metal underneath the driver's seat. The accommodation department at the college told me that I was too late for them to suggest somewhere to live but they would let me know if anything came up. I was therefore officially homeless.

For a week, I slept fitfully for a few hours each night in my car parked in a quiet road behind the college. Or rather shivered, for it was very cold. I knew no one but was determined to make this opportunity to get a degree work, especially as I had had so much trouble at school and at sea where I did not agree with what most of my colleagues believed in and were doing. It seemed great to be able to devote three years of my life to studying subjects of my choice. And I had a free education and a grant which I would not have to repay – supplemented with holiday work, it would just about cover my costs. In those days, only about four per cent of young people did degrees in higher education.

Kingston upon Thames was, as it name suggests, on the bank of the river south west of central London. The college was a white stone building in front of the solid Town Hall. This had been built earlier in the century when the councillors and dignitaries of the town had an exaggerated sense of their own importance. Both buildings were functional rather than beautiful, built to impress rather than to delight.

Having lived in my old car for a week, I found a room in the small terraced house of a middle-aged grumpy Pole. The place stank of cooking and my dirty room was so small that I could hardly move around the single bed with its old, lumpy mattress. The old man lived alone, didn't look after himself or his house, and kept prying into the life of his new lodger. I worked in the library in the evenings and only used the place to sleep.

I immediately started looking for a new room which I found

after a couple of weeks next to a church down a cul-de-sac in Hampton Wick. The address was 28 St James Avenue, Hampton Hill, Middlesex. It was close to Hampton Court on the north side of the Thames. The room was dark and at the back of the suburban semi-detached house but at least it was clean and quiet. The owner was a man who dressed up every night in a tuxedo to work at a casino twirling the roulette wheel. His beautiful Scandinavian wife, who was much younger than he, stayed at home with a young baby. I occasionally met them on the stairs but they thankfully left me alone and just greeted me affably.

I worked hard all week on my own and had no real friends amongst my fellow students. But I got good marks for my essays. Jenny had started a job in Chatham Grammar School for Girls as a French assistant teacher and stayed with a 'Miss Lawrence.' Jenny was the sunshine in my hard-working life and I took the weekends off to be with her. She would occasionally come over to Hampton Wick and share my single bed. The landlord did not seem to mind me smuggling a girl into my room to stay overnight.

Michael wrote to me from Whitley Bay that he had been accepted at Newcastle University to study Physiology after getting good 'A' Levels at Paddington Tech. He was thrilled: 'Together we'll shake the world!', he wrote, adding that 'warm fire feeling is very binding.'

Despite my revolutionary enthusiasm, I was not opposed to enjoying the occasional luxury despite the fact I lived on my grant and holiday jobs. In Kingston, there was a little shop which roasted coffee, the aroma of which wafted down the street, where I bought Jamaican Blue Mountain, Mysore and Colombian coffee for my small Italian cafetière, as well as strong Java cheroots. I also prided myself on being somewhat of a connoisseur of teas, drinking smoky Lapsang Souchong and a minty 'gunpowder tea' from China which slowly unfurled from its pellet in hot water; mild Darjeeling and strong Assam from India; and light Nuwara Elya and medium Ceylon Orange Pekoe tips from Ceylon (the tea sellers preferred the old colonial name as opposed to the independent Sri Lanka). Apart from the taste and the slow ritual of preparing them, I loved the exotic names and was prepared to pay a lot for rare types and blends.

I also had a French curved pipe along with straight wooden British ones and a Turkish Meerschaum pipe, made from a soft mineral. Experimenting with different tobaccos I settled for tins of Russian Balkan Sobranie tobacco which had underneath its lid a girl in traditional dress, with the inspiring description 'a long cool smoke to calm a troubled world, an aroma to answer all life's worries too.' I sucked on my pipe while sipping my tea and thought all would be well. It seemed to add to my concentration as I worked, and mucking around with my pipe and tobacco provided a welcome respite.

We would sometimes go to a cheap Indian restaurant on the bank of the River Thames in Kingston where I would, after a few pints of beer, eat a hot Madras or Vindaloo, the hottest on the menu, no doubt with a small degree of machismo. On Jenny's 21st birthday I took her to the small, expensive French restaurant 'L'Escargot' (The Snail) in Soho and the grand opera at The Coliseum to see Gluck's opera *Orpheus and Eurydice*. I cried when Orpheus turned his love Eurydice to stone by turning round to see her while bringing her up from the Underworld.

My first great test at the college was the subjects I had chosen to do: English, French and Economics. I enjoyed the first two. Then it came to my third chosen subject Economics. I soon learnt that, as taught in the college, it was the most dismal of all sciences. I had hoped to learn how to reorganise society on a more equitable economic basis. I wanted to study the history and philosophy of the subject, especially Marx's analysis of capitalism and his concept of alienation and labour theory of value, and Keynes' mixed economy which had had so much influence on the Labour party in Britain. Instead the basic text was Richard Lipsey's *Economics* which explained the capitalism of the 50s in America as if it were the last word on the subject. It provided an introduction to 'macroeconomics' which celebrated economic growth and 'microeconomics' which was even more focused on economic growth, giving prominence to game theory. It was based on the theory of market capitalism which is to buy cheap and sell dear in order to make a profit. It contained no critical element and implied that this neo-liberal model of the economy would triumph forever. To open the book made me feel ill and to hear the lecturer outline the rest of the course made me even sicker. I had a terrible churning feeling in the pit of my stomach. After a week, I had had enough; I would look for another subject.

But what was there? Law, based on government rules and punishment and conveyancing private property, had only a small part devoted to protecting and extending 'human or civil rights.'

I had tried to escape the subject ever since my uncle wanted me to become an articled clerk to a solicitor or accountant in Bognor. History, as taught at the college, did not appeal. Apart from the great revolutions, it seemed mainly concerned with the story of kings and battles and with demonstrating how Britain had progressed towards the triumph of the empire and the modern state. Social history of working people, on whom the wealth of the nation depended, was not considered very important at the time.

The only alternative seemed to be to learn another language. It fitted in well with my existing subjects English and French. I had started an evening class in Latin so that I would have enough languages when I went into my final exam with London University but Latin was not on offer at degree level. I therefore chose Spanish which had a high profile at the college although I had never done it before. I had enjoyed going to Spain as a young man with my uncle despite it being ruled by the fascists and Franco.

I was very pleased with my choice and it was with a great feeling of relief that I closed Lipsey once and for all. The Spanish teacher was a small, affable man who welcomed me warmly into his fold. He said that I could learn Spanish from scratch and there was a large component of Spanish literature which required essays written in English. As a budding writer myself, I loved literature for the insight it gave into other people's lives and their relationships. I loved language not only for the words themselves but I liked to extend my vocabulary – the more obscure the word, the better. To learn another language also meant that you might understand another culture, traditions and experience and make your own life richer and deeper.

After one year of learning Spanish from scratch, I took an O-level and received an 'A.' I could now enter the final exam at the University of London.

I found that most of the students on my courses were girls and that most were three years younger than I was, having come directly from school. They probably did not have good enough grades to go to an established university and chose the College of Technology as second best. Unlike my fellow students, who seemed mainly intent on having a good time, I was very committed to my studies, particularly as I had had so much trouble studying part-time for my A-levels and getting into college in the first place. I no doubt seemed very boring to them and something of a 'swot.' My studies were certainly my centre of gravity at the time and I was determined to do well. Besides, I actually enjoyed them, being eager to learn about the literature of the past as well as French and Spanish culture and language.

Whilst at Kingston my studies made a permanent impression on me. In Spanish, the enthusiastic and kindly language teacher was joined by a man who was always brisk, had a crewcut, and was Head of Department. He taught us Spanish literature. I learned about the first true novel in Cervantes' *Don Quijote de la Mancha*, in which the voice of coarse common sense, represented by Sancho Panza, is pitched against absurd chivalry. Then there were the playwrights of the *'Edad de Oro'* (the so-called 'Golden Age' which coincided with the Spanish imperial conquests in central and south America) such as Lope de Vega; the mystical poems of St John of the Cross which seemed very modern; the realistic nineteenth-century novels of Galdos, taken largely from the perspective of the poor; and the symbolists poets at the turn of the century such as Antonio Machado.

Above all, I read Gerald Brenan's great history of Spanish literature and his *The Spanish Cockpit* on the social and political background of the Spanish Civil War. I learned from the latter that most of the Republicans who fought against Franco were anarchists who were betrayed in Catalunya by the minority Stalinist Communists who were strictly controlled by Moscow. Having read *Homage to Catalonia* by George Orwell, who fought on the Republican side during the Spanish Civil War, I knew I was on the side of the libertarian socialists and anarchists. He was shot in the neck and lucky to survive. But as a sniper at the front, he could not shoot a Fascist soldier in his sights because he recognised their common humanity when he took his trousers down to have a shit. I liked to think I would have done the same.

I also read Garcia Lorca's poems and plays and found that he had been killed by the fascists – under a tree in a remote village in the south – at the height of his powers. On reading his essay *'Cante jondo'* (Deep Song), I knew exactly what he meant when he described music and dance like the flamenco suddenly taking off as akin to the 'soul' of jazz.

In English we had a large Canadian man who taught Middle English and for whom we read Chaucer and the anonymous *Gawain and the Green Knight*. A world-weary but intriguing Jewish Londoner taught us Alexander Pope's 'Essay on Man' which encouraged a version of humanism since 'The proper study

of mankind is Man' but also a kind of cosmic conservatism –
'Whatever is, is right.' I enjoyed John Gay's *Beggar's Opera* (with
sweet Polly and knowing Macheath) which satirised contemporary
society for its social inequality, corruption and injustice mainly
by contrasting the thieves and whores with their bourgeois and
aristocratic 'betters.' I liked Swift's final part of *Gulliver's Travels*
to the 'Land of the Houyhnhnms' where rational horses live
in equality and simplicity in an anarchistic society while all-
too-human Yahoos fought each other in the dirt for gold. The
Houyhnhnms had no time for it.

We had an enthusiastic young woman with whom we studied
Shakespeare's *The Tempest*, with Prospero and Caliban showing
the new colonialism and reflecting 'nurture' versus 'nature, often to
the advantage of the latter. By contrast, D.H. Lawrence's *Women in
Love*, with its two sisters and their disparate lovers was a powerful
exploration of class differences, industrialism and sexual passion.
In her spare time, she encouraged us to read Arnold Wesker's play
Roots, a modern kitchen-sink drama. In their different ways, they
were texts which influenced me and I liked the lecturers who got
us to read them.

In French, there was a handsome, middle-aged lecturer with
wavy hair who was an enthusiast of the French Enlightenment;
I suspected he shared with Voltaire that Christianity is 'assuredly
the most ridiculous, the most absurd and the most bloody religion
which has ever infected this world.' With him, I studied Voltaire's
brilliant satire of Leibniz's optimistic philosophy *Candide* where
the anti-hero after a series of disasters around the world decides
that cultivating one's garden – one's back patch – is the best
way to keep oneself and friends from evil. I also loved Diderot's
Supplément au Voyage de Bougainville which gave a utopian view
of the Tahitians living in peace, harmony and free love which
contrasted with our own repressed 'civilization' in the West.

I shared Lamartine's view that *'La liberté, c'est mon pays'*
(Freedom is my country); enjoyed Balzac's sweeping novels
of society in nineteenth-century France which showed up its
hypocritical bourgeoisie; Victor Hugo's decision to go into exile
in the Channel Islands and write his poems *'L'art d'etre grand-père'*
rather than stay in France under the coup d'état of Napoleon III;
the powerful realistic novels of Zola who finally admitted that the
artist saw the world inevitably from his own corner and through
his own consciousness; the deceptively simple Symbolist poetry of

Verlaine and the *'bouleversement des sens'* (disruption of senses) of his young lover Rimbaud, particularly the poem *'Voyelles'* with its colours of letters; and of course Baudelaire who transformed 'decadence' into a fine art and was a great *'flâneur'* or stroller in the streets of Paris.

My French studies only confirmed my love of freedom; my belief in reason in the face of superstition, ignorance, and hypocrisy; and the power of the imagination to create something new and beautiful out of the old.

It was at the height of the so-called 'swinging 60s', with The Rolling Stones, The Beatles and the Kinks in the charts. But apart from dancing to their music I was much more involved with modern jazz. I was not interested in discotheques and 'mod' fashion, which was dapper and expensive, preferring the 'hippie look' based largely on second-hand clothes from charity or surplus shops. For the winter, I wore an ex-RAF coat dating from the Second World War.

However, the general air of loosening up and the pushing of boundaries in London affected me deeply. For once, I did not feel alienated from what was happening around me. I appreciated mini-skirts; seeing a girl's inner thighs and knickers seemed to be the norm. I was a direct beneficiary of the pill which meant you could make love whenever you wanted to as long as your partner agreed. Above all the general celebration of fun and joy was close to my heart.

Revolution was definitely in the air; the Establishment was on the retreat. Art no longer consisted of the Old Masters in stuffy galleries and museums but was more like a 'Happening', a performance event or situation which involved the audience. It was often spontaneous, creative and short-lived. The so-called 'counter-culture' or 'underground scene' was for me. I got *Time Out* magazine for its listings and radical articles. I enjoyed what was 'alternative' in London. I threw off the restrictions of boarding school and the merchant navy.

When I first went to Kingston I joined the Socialist Society and listened to some of the lectures. I was vaguely drawn at first to the International Socialists, a Trotskyist group which turned up at demonstrations and strikes in London. It espoused class struggle and wanted to end exploitation but like all parties seemed to have a strict ideological line, was organised in a centralised way and was still arranged from the top down. I did not hold to the old idea of a vanguard group leading and directing the Revolution. It meant that you were unable to think and act for yourself.

One evening a representative of the Marxist African revolutionary Amílcar Cabral from Guinea-Bissau and Cape Verde Islands came to give a talk at the Socialist Society. The lecture room was packed out. He was a real revolutionary ready to pick up a gun and fight the Portuguese colonialists for independence. He stressed the view that it was necessary to 'Destroy the economy of the enemy and build our own economy.' He undoubtedly reinforced my anti-colonialism and made me think that violent struggle was perhaps necessary in certain circumstances to gain national independence in Africa but it was not applicable to Britain.

Although I was never a card-carrying member of any party I felt sympathy with the so-called 'New Left' which emphasised the importance of community and the autonomy of the individual. It was much better, as Herbert Marcuse implied in *One-Dimensional Man*, to make love in a field than in the back of a car. And as Wilhelm Reich said in *The Mass Psychology of Fascism* (1933) sexual repression tended to give rise to an authoritarian character. Indeed, the traditional patriarchal and authoritarian family was the basic cell of the fascist state. I looked forward to a sexual revolution in which women and men would be considered equal and creative human beings and love was free as the wind. As if echoing my thoughts, the hippies in America declared in 1967 'a summer of love.'

In the summer of 1968, after visiting me in Elbury Cove (where I worked as a bus conductor), Jenny went to Anduze in the south of France for a few days in the middle of August to see her parents in their summer house there. She then got a job from the beginning of September as an assistant producer in the French section of the BBC World Service. After looking for a place to live, she eventually stayed with a small, plump Jewish American girl in a flat in Queen's Park on the north western side of London. I would sometimes catch the train and tube to visit her and share her single bed in her windowless room, divided from her flatmate by a heavy ruby velvet curtain.

In March 1968, I had joined in the mass demonstrations to end American aggression in Vietnam. I chanted 'Ho, Ho, Ho Chi

Jenny

Minh' as we danced down the Embankment in London. There was definitely a sense of carnival and joy in the air. However, a group broke away outside the US embassy in Grosvenor Square and there were hours of street fighting between police and demonstrators. Pennies were thrown at the mounted horses to upturn the riders. In the end, many people were injured and some 200 demonstrators arrested. It was beginning to get serious.

In April, Martin Luther King was assassinated having tried to end racial segregation in the USA by peaceful means and direct action. At the same time, the Black Power Movement, with its emphasis, like Senghor's *négritude*, on African values and Black pride was making itself felt in North America. They wanted to separate themselves from the whites. Soon after the Tory MP Enoch Powell made a speech against immigration and warned of race riots and 'rivers of blood' flowing in the streets in Britain.

Having a black girlfriend, I probably felt more than most the iniquities of racial segregation and every day prejudice.

'They (by which we meant racists) can't separate us, however much they may try', we would say to each other.

When students in London started to occupy art colleges and called for a new style of democratic education, particularly at Hornsey Art College in North London, I was in great sympathy. It was in this heightened atmosphere, that the May events in Paris in

1968 burst on the scene. I was still living in my bedsit in Hampton Wick and I listened all night to a French programme on my radio as the events unfolded on the streets of Paris. I really thought the Social Revolution had come. The media couldn't find a spokesman for the student movement very easily – the whole stance was against leaders – so they picked on Daniel Cohn-Bendit who was willing to play their game. Born of German Jews in France, he was only a year older than me and had joined the nationwide Fédération anarchiste only to leave for the Groupe anarchiste de Nanterre.

Starting at the suburban University of Nanterres, 'sit-ins' soon spread throughout France. Even the workers occupied their factories in solidarity with the students and called for a general strike. In the end about ten million workers in France took part. The Sorbonne was taken over and established a permanent debate on the means and ends of the uprising. Even the philosopher Jean-Paul Sartre attended and lent his support. Improvised discussions and assemblies took place throughout France. The state was reeling from the sudden onslaught; President De Gaulle was even ready to call in the French army to intervene.

I loved the upsurge of radical energy in France and was particularly impressed by the libertarian, imaginative and utopian spirit of the slogans inspired by Situationists which appeared on the walls of Paris. *'Il est interdit d'interdire'* (It is forbidden to forbid), they declared, *'L'imagination au pouvoir'* (Power to the Imagination), and above all *'Soyez réaliste, demandez l'impossible'* (Be realistic, demand the impossible). There was a simple equation for the brutal riot police (CRS) who attacked the students: CRS=SS. I had long believed that boredom reflected the nature of an empty and meaningless life; by contrast, I never felt bored as there was so much to know and do. It was therefore with pleasure that I read that *'L'ennui est contre-révolutionnaire'* (Boredom is counter-revolutionary). I also did not see the point of working for someone who only exploited you and alienated you from yourself, your fellow workers, and from nature itself. Why engage in such life-denying work? Surely there was more to life than *'Dodo, Métro, Boulot'* (Sleep, Metro, Work)?

But then the government offered a ten per cent rise to the French workers who, controlled by the Communist-dominated trade unions, accepted it and returned to work. The Revolution was over – at least for now. Students for the summer break returned to their

College Life

families or took holidays.

When the cobblestones of Paris were first thrown up into barricades, as generations of workers had done before them, students looked for the sand below as symbolizing freedom from the dead weight of oppressive civilization, the 'beach' and all its joyful connotations: *'Sous les pavés, la plage'* (Under the cobblestones, the beach).

Now they literally went to spend the holidays beside the seaside.

Although it did not become a political revolution, the events in

Slogan in Paris, May 1968

France succeeded as a social and cultural revolution. It left its mark on posters, songs, cinema, writings and the hopes of all libertarian revolutionaries who remained youthful at heart. As Wordsworth wrote earlier of the French Revolution: 'Bliss was it in that dawn to be alive, But to be young was very heaven!'

When Jenny got a job at the French section of the BBC World Service in that autumn she even arranged for me to be interviewed in order to explain the demands of the students in Britain for greater autonomy, democracy and freedom. The conservative broadcaster tried to get me to say that the students were prepared to use violence to achieve their revolutionary goals. I replied that if we were attacked violently then perhaps we might use violence 'in the last resort.'

I felt he was putting me in a corner. I was only giving my

opinion; it was for others to decide what they would do. I remained a pacifist of sorts, having been convinced several years beforehand by the arguments of the Methodist minister Donald Soper at Hyde Park Corner. The slogan 'Make Love, not War' at the time seemed to have a profound meaning for me: the more loving we are, the less aggressive we become.

The dangers of the Soviet Union and authoritarian communism were reinforced in August when the Russian tanks rolled into Czechoslovakia to put an end to the Prague Spring that had occured in the first half of 1968 following Dubček's attempt to move towards 'socialism with a human face' by introducing greater press freedom. In the same year in the United States the Democratic Party's National Convention in Chicago was disrupted by the Youth International Party ('Yippies') and thousands of other protesters who wanted to end the war in Vietnam. The mayor called up the National Guard and the US Army and this led to clashes in the streets which lasted for eight days. The worst was to come in October when during demonstrations in Mexico City preceding the Olympics, students were fired upon and over a hundred people were killed. The revolution had turned serious indeed.

25
AN END TO ALL THAT

In my second year at Kingston, I managed to stay in a bedsit behind the college. It was small, clean and had a Baby Belling stove to cook on, and a separate bathroom and lavatory down a dark corridor. I hardly ever saw the other tenants, but it seemed to be controlled by a self-appointed, bald retired man in one of the rooms. He seemed physically strong but probably had been a clerk whose wife had left him. He took the weekly rent and gave me the keys to the front door of the house and my room. He would complain about the curry smell of the cooking of the Asian family next door but did not seem to mind me smuggling in Jenny some weekends when I did not go to her flat in Queen's Park.

But I suppose that I was an ideal tenant, paying my rent, making little noise and spending most of my time in the college library. I was single-minded on getting good marks for my essays, making up for lost time at Steyning and proving to myself that I was not intellectually 'useless'. No doubt my fellow students, mostly straight from school and out to have a good time, considered me a 'swot'.

In the spring I went camping with Jenny to Castle Combe, allegedly the prettiest village in England with its old stone houses crossed by a river, which she said she loved: *'Chaque jour je revois nos escapades dans le Wiltshire et les moments extraordinaires passés ensemble.'*

In the holidays from college, I went down to my mother's house 'Magnolia' in 76 Brunel Road near Elbury Cove. Like the students in Paris, I too had gone at the beginning of July to *'la plage'* but not merely to rest but to work. I had already spent some time working as an assistant Foreman of Parcels at Paignton Railway Station before going away to sea. I got a job this time working as a bus conductor on one of the new buses which had folding doors and a spiral staircase up to the top deck. I got my license from the council to act as a conductor of 'a public service vehicle' on the 10 July 1968.

I was mainly on a number 12 bus which went from Brixham to Babbacombe. Although I had to start early, it paid well and had a good trade union which made sure we were given time and a half for overtime and twice our normal hourly wages if we worked on Sunday.

I worked closely with the driver. Generally, the passengers paid their fares. I wore a grey linen jacket issued by the bus company and kept their change in a well-worn leather bag on my side. I wound out tickets from a metal machine held on by two straps crisscrossing my shoulders.

Apart from the regular old ladies and young children, most customers seemed to be holidaymakers from the Midlands who didn't know exactly the name of the stop where they wanted to go. I rarely had any problem, except of course trying to get in fares when passengers filled the bottom aisle and I had little room to move. The worst was a run to a particularly notorious council estate at the top of the hills in Paignton; I was shocked by one boy playing truant who sat all over the seat and stank of grime and clearly did not wash. I hadn't before believed such people existed in Britain.

The last bus from Torquay to Paignton was also difficult since most of the men had drunk too much and were unwilling to pay their fares. One group of rough and shouting men at the back of the top deck simply told me – a young whippersnapper of a student – to 'fuck off.' I told the driver and he immediately pulled the bus to a halt, jumped out with me on the curb and closed the doors from the outside. He said:

'You'll see, the other passengers will sort them out. They want to get home!'

And it was true – when we opened the doors, they paid up reluctantly, grumbling all the time and we trundled off home.

I sometimes worked on the bus which went all the way from Dawlish on the River Exe to Plymouth. I therefore got to know the South Devon coast well, including the towns of Teignmouth, Totnes, Ivybridge and South Brent. There was a good bus café at Plymouth where I could get a large and cheap fry-up.

I also worked for a while in the evening in the public bar of the Harbour Inn. It was down by Paignton harbour which dried out at low tide and had a few inshore fishing boats and pleasure boats on their sides in the mud and sand. The pub was very busy with holidaymakers.

My fellow barman was very much a local Devonian, the son of a farmer, who spoke in a broad dialect sometimes difficult for me to understand. He was very brown from working outside on his family farm. He called the very old, badly shaven potman who gathered in the empty glasses for a few pints, a 'bibbler' because he liked his drink. He used to say 'ye' in place of 'you' and usually called things as if they were female: 'Bring she to me', he would say. He always called me 'thee.'

He lived near Elbury Cove at Churston and he sometimes gave me a lift home in his battered van to the top of the lane by the golf course. Despite our differences in class, education and upbringing, he took me under his wing. I learned from him how to pull a careful pint and became adept as a barman dealing with 'grockles' from 'up country.'

In the summer of 1969 my mother asked my brother Michael and me to paint the front of the house. He had come down for the summer holiday as he was now a student in physiology at Newcastle University. We duly did the fascia boards in white gloss, and then on the large triangle between them we scrawled in large letters 'End US Aggression in Vietnam.' We had some strange looks from the largely conservative passers-by on their way down the Cove and the cliff path through the woods to Brixham. When we then painted it over in white emulsion paint, we found at the end that our slogan still faintly came through – as it did many years after. My mother, who was a liberal by nature, dismissed it with the words 'Boys will be boys!' She probably didn't know where Vietnam was or that there was an American war against the Communist Vietcong.

One day, with my new-found radicalism, I announced to my Nanna, who must have been in her late seventies and who had been very good to me as a boy:

'I don't want any of your money. I don't believe in the right of inheritance. It is the main cause of inequality in our society!'

She was devastated:

'I have worked hard all my life with your Pop so that we could pass something on to your mother and Uncle Al, and through your mother to Michael and you. Now you say it wasn't worth it! I can't believe you want to disown us and all we stand for like that!'

But I was adamant about it and not to be diverted from my course. Was not private property a form of theft? Was not abolishing the right to inheritance the best way to bring about a more equal society?

I did not want to have anything to do with Tory politics and

Conservative beliefs. When my uncle heard about it he dismissed the idea:

'He might be a socialist now but later he will see the error of his ways and become a Conservative by forty! You mark my words.'

Michael also worked as a barman at a caravan park and would often come home the worse for beer after a lunchtime session complaining, as I did, about the leathery meat and two soggy veg which our mother steamed for hours trying to keep them warm. Taste, it seemed, was less important than having a hot plate. But she was undoubtedly doing her best and we were probably unfair.

Sandy, whom my mother had married when I was about to go to sea, made a great effort to get on with 'the boys.' He was a very good player by ear of the accordion (which he called 'the squeeze box'). He wrote ballads and had an enormous range of old songs. Having cycled with a club around Devon and worked as an apprentice mason in the churches before the War, he had enormous knowledge of the countryside, especially Dartmoor which he loved.

At Christmas, he put up decorations and got a barrel of cider in the cellar. He liked to go with us to the Manor Inn in Galmpton across the golf links or sometimes to the old manor house pub called Churston Court, an old haunt of Agatha Christie who lived nearby on the banks of the River Dart. We felt obliged though to listen to him talk endlessly in his soft Devonian accent, often opening his sentences with 'The thing is…' We felt that he did not want to hear too much about our lives and opinions, but then he probably did not usually have such a ready audience to speak to.

He was very welcoming to my girlfriend Jenny, who came down for Christmas and for a few days in the summer holidays. After I made some money in Torbay in the summer holidays, we would often go down to see her parents in southern France and then some times to Spain, sometimes hitching (including getting stuck on a motorway way outside Bordeaux until a long-distance lorry driver picked us up) and sometimes in my old jalopy.

In the summer of 1969, coming back to Calais from Spain in our car called POD (after its number plate), we set out in northern France early one morning after spending a night in a cheap pension. I noticed that a spider had got into Jenny's hair, and knowing that she hated spiders, I tried to remove it with my hand. Unfortunately, the road swung to the right and I carried on at slow speed straight ahead, ending up in a ditch, only to be halted by some saplings. When people came up to the car, they looked through the window and were horrified and immobilised by the blood. In fact, Jenny only had a cut on her wrist from a bracelet. Feeling as if I were being looked at as in a zoo, I eventually managed to push open the driver's door of the car which was lying on its side. A local mechanic came up with his car removal vehicle and wanted to be paid for taking it back to his village garage. But we had just filled up the tank and hardly had any money, thinking that we would be in Calais that evening. After much haggling, he agreed to take the old Austin Hillman with its new tyres and full petrol tank in lieu of payment. It was a write-off.

When we got to the local railway station and tried to buy some tickets to Paris we found we were short of some francs. We were lucky that a man behind us made up for the shortfall and we were able to continue our journey with a few belongings. When we arrived in Paris we stayed in the dark flat of an old friend of Jenny's father, Louise Bailly, who was a teacher of Greek and Latin in a local *lycée*. She was calm and soft-spoken and had worked in the French Resistance during the war. As a Jewess, she had been imprisoned and tortured in Ravensbrück Concentration Camp in northern Germany.

She was living with a radical lawyer called Antoine who had escaped from the colonels in Greece who had seized power in a military coup. I was fascinated by the amount of olive oil he poured over his boiled egg for breakfast. They lent us money so we could get home to London.

I studiously avoided all the hype about the Americans landing on the moon in July 1969. It was done partly to show their technological superiority over other nations. Only later did I realise it was a significant step, but not a 'giant leap' for humanity. It seemed mainly proof of some humans' wish to 'conquer' space as they had largely conquered the land and the seas. The blue photos of the Earth taken from space however were a reminder that two thirds of the plant's surface are seas. They encouraged many young people to think of the planet Earth as a whole spinning in space as well as the wider impact that humans were having on nature.

In the meantime, I had got friendly with Jeremy Gane – another participant on the English course at Kingston; his other subjects were history and law. His father had a private prep school in Bridlington where he grew up, and he had treated his three boys like any other pupil and almost as strangers during term time when Jeremy was obliged to become a boarder. The experience had a powerful impact on him. His mother, the daughter of a spy and diplomat in Russia, told me she had to curb her fun-loving nature and become the sober wife of a headmaster who was much older than she was.

Jeremy was then sent to The Leys single-sex, boarding school in Cambridge where he became something of a tearaway as I had done at my boarding school. At the age of 16 he had hitch-hiked alone to Morocco where he smoked hashish and slept on the beach. When I met him he was living with other lads in a rundown and rat-infested hut on the bank of the River Thames, sleeping in a damp bed with little creature comforts. He continued to go out with his childhood sweetheart Anne Davis who had lived with her younger sister and her divorced mother in genteel poverty in Bridlington.

Anne had become a student, studying French, at the Royal Holloway College, part of London University, a red-brick wedding cake of a building in its own grounds in Egham, Surrey. Its past students included the novelist George Eliot (I admired particularly her novel *Felix Holt, The Radical*) and the suffragette Emily Wilding Davison (whose call for equality between the sexes I espoused). The latter was arrested on nine occasions, force-fed many times and was eventually killed by colliding with the King's racehorse at Epsom. Anne was in a fine radical tradition, but the college remained all-female and generally conservative at that time.

Anne invited Jeremy as well as Jenny and me to a summer ball at Holloway. Jeremy and I reluctantly went in hired evening dress – 'like bloody Penguins', my friend said. It reminded me of being at sea in a uniform. At the grand dinner, during which we sat at a long table, we were meant to stand up and sing the National Anthem. Since Jeremy and I were both republican and estranged from the Church of England in which we had been brought up, we refused to stand and sing 'God save the Queen.' It was a small gesture of protest but I noticed that we – with our two girlfriends – were the only ones to remain seated and silent in the vast hall.

The college had hired many bands for the night but I found that the most interesting was a small jazz band in a side room. About 4 o'clock in the morning and the worse for drink and fatigue we went to hear 'Screaming Lord Sutch' with his top hat and preference for heavy rock with horror and death themes. He persevered despite there only being a few drunks talking loudly to each other in the room, ignoring the music. Like us, Lord Sutch was definitely the worse for wear.

Whilst at Kingston we also went to a summer ball at Senate House since we were studying for an external degree at the University of London. The Queen mother was the patron and each year had to have a dance with the head of the Students' Union. He wore a black polo-neck pullover and had long black, greasy hair. But he still had to wear white gloves to dance with royalty. The portly Queen mother, dressed in a long evening gown covered with sequins and a tiara on her grey hair, held him contemptuously at full length during their obligatory dance. I was dancing with Jenny at the time, and I told her to hold our ground and they moved around us.

I was also contacted by my friend Richard Burchnall whom I had got to know at the monastery in Dakar. He invited me to dinner at Oxford where he was a Classics scholar. In fact, it was to a private dining club with an ancient tradition in which an elaborate meal (with an endless supply of good wine) was served by grovelling servants. It was meant to be a great privilege to attend as members were allowed only one friend each. But I had had too much of privilege as a cadet in the P&O and thought I had left it all behind in my wake. He asked me to join him for a summer in Greece, but I said I was busy. I lost touch with Richard soon afterwards and I believe he went on to become a merchant banker.

In the last year at Kingston, from 1969 to 1970, I moved from my solitary bedsit to live with Jeremy in a seventeenth-century farmhouse rented from Oxford University down a track opposite Chessington Zoo. A portly, affable middle-aged antiques dealer who had thinning hair and a straight moustache sublet the farm to us. He came down from London for the odd weekend with a younger 'floozy.' We suspected he probably paid for her for favours. He slept on the ground floor, demanded a peppercorn rent and left us to our own devices. We hardly ever saw him.

Jeremy took a long room with a little bedroom off it and I took a small room next door on the first floor. His room with its old beams and whitewashed walls was used as a communal room and had a mattress on the floor at the far end. I worked hard studying in my room but in the evenings we would eat together downstairs in the kitchen, often preparing our favourite meal which was *chilli con carne* with rice. We then spent the rest of the evening listening to music, chatting or occasionally smoking cannabis in roll-ups. There was only a radio and no television. We made our own beer, with the occasional bottle exploding in a lumber room off the kitchen. Apart from going to college and seeing our girlfriends most times at the weekend, we led quite solitary lives together.

We used to like going to Kingston to buy our supplies. During one lunchtime session there we had too much to drink, stumbled into the market in the centre of town where Jeremy was attracted to a cage containing squeaking parakeets – he then bought one on impulse. He called it immediately Carrie. Not to be out done, I bought a blue budgerigar which I called George. I thought it would be much less trouble than a large bird. We decided to let them fly freely around our rooms at the farm. Carrie would fly from one end of the long room to the other, squawking and shitting wherever he chose. George in my room would sit on my shoulder when I was studying and nibble my ear. He became completely tame. He had a cage with an open door through which he jumped to have some food or water. He sometimes liked to stay in there although he could easily come out. When it was sunny he would like to peck at the white paint on the window. In the summer term I went one day into my room and found him lying dead on his side by the window; the old chipped paint must have contained some lead which poisoned him. We buried him near the house with great honours. Carrie continued to squawk next door.

One weekend we made a roast joint of a cheap cut of lamb's shoulder for Jenny and Anne. We then had a wild party during which we drank our strong home-made beer and danced the 'conga' around the house, through the bathroom and over the lavatory to the sounds of Captain Beefheart and Jimmy Hendrix and other of Jeremy's favourites.

A few times we went camping together for a long weekend, to the wildest places we could find in the countryside.

We also had a holiday together on the canals. I loved to open and close the locks as I had done as a boy with my uncle. On my birthday, the 23rd of August, the girls prepared a chicken for our evening meal. Jeremy was at the rudder. It was dusk and I had already been given a whisky to begin the celebrations. But as I was using a heavy metal key to pull up the very last sluice gate of a lock I didn't put it properly into the iron stop and suddenly the sluice gate went down, spinning the key which hit me in the lip. Blood

Jeremy, Jenny and me camping

poured out and splattered my white shirt. I looked terrible and Jeremy immediately thought that he should take me to hospital.

With a handkerchief held to my fast-swelling and bleeding lip, I stumbled down the tow path amongst high grass until we eventually came across the wooden door of an old cottage. We could hear within a man and a woman having a fierce argument in middle-class London tones. Jeremy knocked on the door; it was opened by a middle-aged man with a paunch.

'What do you want?' he said roughly.

'My friend has just hit his lip badly. Could you take us to the nearby hospital please?'

He took one look at me and said: 'No way!' and slammed the door in Jeremy's face.

So much for the milk of human kindness. We continued along the tow path until we came across a run-down cottage. The old countryman who came to the door was only too pleased to help us. He got out his old car and drove to the nearest hospital which was a long way away. In the distance, I could hear the rumble of traffic. We had to wait in the Accident and Emergency Department for about three hours. There had been a pile-up on the nearby motorway and all the doctors were busy dealing with the victims. When eventually I was inspected by a young doctor, she said that I would need some stitches as my lip had split over my teeth.

By the time this was done, it was in the early hours of the morning. A volunteer at the hospital agreed to take us back to the canal. The girls were still up waiting for us. They all enjoyed the meal, except me. I could only use a straw for the next few days, unable to open my lips. I have since had many birthdays which I can't remember, but that one I remember for the wrong reasons.

On the night of the general election in June 1970 Jeremy and I stayed up in the farmhouse to hear the returns from the constituencies, disappointed that the Tories under Ted Heath had unexpectedly got in, ending six years of 'misrule' by Labour under Harold Wilson. Although he backed 'white-hot technology' and supported nuclear weapons, Harold and his party had at least continued the process of decolonisation and had kept the country out of fighting in Vietnam. Despite our privileged backgrounds, we knew which side we were on in the struggle between labour and capital. The election seemed to mark a symbolic end to the possibility of any radical change in Britain. It ended my revolutionary hopes inspired by the events in 1968.

By the time dawn broke, we were tired and stoned, and after listening to the soprano Elizabeth Schwarzkopf sing the 'Nightingale Song', Jeremy put on the wild Captain Beefheart and his Magic Band. We danced manically on the stubble of the fields around the farmhouse – until our bare feet were bloody – with the loud strains of his blues and rock music coming from the open window mixing with the dawn chorus.

26
ANARCHY IS ORDER

I had seen on the walls of London the symbol of 'Anarchy is Order' as an 'A' inside an 'O' as well as the slogan 'Property is Theft' outside squatter communes. A few people started talking about anarchism as a third alternative to Soviet-style authoritarian communism and unfettered Western capitalism. It seemed to me very interesting.

To find out more I read in my spare time George Woodcock's *Anarchism: A History of the Libertarian Ideas and Movements*. I had come to agree with Godwin, that government was a 'brute engine' and I looked forward with him to its eventual 'euthanasia.' With Proudhon, I felt 'Liberty was not the daughter but the mother of order.' It turned out that he was the source of the slogans 'Anarchy is Order' and 'Property is Theft.' Was not Bakunin sensible when he wrote 'liberty without socialism is privilege, injustice; and that socialism without liberty is slavery and brutality'? And Kropotkin was undoubtedly right when he argued that mutual aid was a key factor in evolution and that we should break down the barriers between factories, fields and workshops. He emphasised that humanity needed intellectual as well as spiritual values; man (or for that matter woman) could not live 'by bread alone.' When I further read Emma Goldman's 'Love is free; it can dwell in no other atmosphere', I was hooked. I agreed with her that 'if I can't dance, it's not my revolution!'

But I could not agree with Woodcock's conclusion, first published in 1962, that anarchism was only a great idea and that after the defeat of the Republicans in the Spanish Civil War it had 'virtually cease to exist as a living cause.' The 1960s protesters with their libertarian enthusiasm – in America, France, Germany, Mexico and even Britain – were proving him wrong.

To clarify these views I further read Nicolas Walter's pamphlet printed by Freedom Press 'About Anarchism' in 1969. He had been active in the CND, of which I was a sympathiser, and in the protests against the war in Vietnam, in which I had also participated. He recognised that there was a considerable revival of interest in anarchism as 'a basis not for sectarian argument about the past but for good discussion about the future.' Given what I had observed in San Francisco and London, this seemed far more accurate than Woodcock's gloomy prognosis.

Walter covered topics such as what anarchists believe, how they differ, what they want and what they do. He saw it as an ideal type which demands at the same time 'total freedom' and 'total equality.' I wasn't sure what he meant by that either and how it would look in practice but it seemed reasonable to argue that the two were complimentary rather than contradictory.

Anarchism (which called for a society without government) was therefore a combination of liberalism (which concerned itself with liberty) and socialism (which wanted to establish equality). I liked its call for the abolition of authority and the expropriation of private property – however utopian it sounded – and the creation of free associations to manage the economy. In a simple, honest and clear way, Nicolas Walter distinguished between the historic strands of individualism, mutualism, collectivism and communism, stressing that the differences between them were not so different and had become less important in recent years. You could be an individualist in your private life as well as calling for a form of libertarian communism in society. Each strand was woven together. It seemed to me straightforward as well as possible.

At about the same time, I read Oscar Wilde's 'The Soul of Man under Socialism.' I had been a fan of Wilde for a long time, not only because of the hypocritical persecution of his sexual proclivities, but because I had read his sympathetic 'Ballad of Reading Gaol' about a condemned man. The essay argued that only a socialist society based on all sharing equally rather than accumulating things for oneself could encourage individuality, arts, sciences and the intellectual life. 'The true perfection of man lies,' as he put it, 'not in what man has, but in what man is.' This combination of libertarian socialism and individualism seemed a great affirmation of the 'joy of living.' I could only find it in what I took to be social anarchism.

Taken together with the events of May 1968 in Paris, these works convinced me that I was not merely a socialist; I was an anarchist. I felt it was certainly something to struggle for even if it would be difficult to be realised. Rather than being something in the far distance, I could try to transform my everyday life in an anarchist direction, here and now, without dominating others. Authoritarian communism, whether Leninist, Trotskyist or Maoist, with vanguard parties misleading the masses, was simply not for me.

Towards the end of my time at Kingston my French lecturer urged me to pursue my studies and I managed to get a place to do an MA on Jean-Jacques Rousseau leading to a Ph.D at East Anglia University. I liked Rousseau's argument in his 'Essay on the Origins of the Inequality of Mankind' that "The first man who, having enclosed a piece of ground, bethought himself of saying This is mine, and found people simple enough to believe him, was the real founder of civil society." They should instead have pulled up the fence and said that all the good things of the Earth are held in common and there is no 'mine' or 'thine', in other words, no exclusive private property.

I agreed with him also that we were naturally good but most of us were depraved by society or the State. I liked his reverberating slogan at the beginning of the *Social Contract* that 'man is born free and everywhere he is in chains' but I felt he lost his way in attempting to define the 'general will' and that one or a group of legislators could 'force people to be free.' His system of male education in *Emile* seemed progressive at the time, but lamentable in the education of girls, with 'Sophie' being brought up as a passive, weak, faithful and malleable wife to Emile.

Nevertheless I appreciated Rousseau's personal 'moral reform' in which he cast off his wig, representing the artificial conventions of his day; smashed his watch, preferring natural time measured by the Sun to the linear time of mechanical human contrivance; and broke his sword in two as a symbol of war and violence. His life and work were undoubtedly contradictory but well worth studying in order to clarify my own ideas on these subjects.

However, I finally chose an MA in the History of Ideas at Sussex University. I had always liked the literature of ideas and had read philosophy in my spare time. I thought it would be a good move coming from a course in literature and language to attend seminars on the methodology of the History of Ideas. It would also enable me to choose a horizontal strand in the history of political thought and a lateral strand in Romanticism. I would be able to pursue my interest in anarchism, particularly in its early forms amongst Romantic writers.

But my places to do an MA at East Anglia or Sussex all depended first on my final degree marks.

Bognor Boy

I could apply from the Polytechnic – it had just changed to offer its own degrees – to take the University of London exam. I had already passed two necessary languages at 'O' Level in French and Spanish. An external degree of London University, I was told, had a value which was no different from that of the internal degrees.

I had been due for a first class honours degree. According to the lecturers I was their best pupil – at least the most hard-working. But eventually I got an upper-second degree in English, French and Spanish from the University of London. I thought that I must have come down in the French exam. I had prepared carefully all the texts except for Molière's *Le Bourgeois Gentilhomme*, a satire on social climbing and the 'nouveau-riches', which had been chosen as a text for the two previous years. I thought wrongly that it would not come up again. It was my own fault for having tried to play the system. But then I noticed that the year I graduated there had been no firsts throughout the world in my subjects and only five upper seconds.

It was the end of an era and Jeremy and I parted soon afterwards and went our different ways. The parakeet Carrie was put into Chessington Zoo. We had assumed that it was male but it seemed that it later laid some eggs.

Jenny on a ferry from Barcelona

During the summer holidays of 1970, I went down to Elbury Cove in Devon to stay for few weeks with my mother and stepfather Sandy and to earn some money again as a bus conductor and barman and then went off to France and Spain hitching with Jenny. It was easy in those days for all young people to get a job if they wanted to – at least it seemed so for the ones that I knew.

We caught a boat overnight from Barcelona to Ibiza in the Balearic Islands where we had to wait on the docks. We then caught another small ferry to

the tiny island of Formentera. I shall never forget the sight of the
faraway islands at dawn, shimmering in the golden Mediterranean
light.

The capital of Formentera was called Sant Fransec Xavier in
Catalan but we called it San Francisco where it was 'all at.' At an
alternative café, which hired bicycles, we found out where to stay
cheaply. We ended up on the southern beach in a draughty shed
with a single rickety bed. It had once housed chickens at the side of
a small, rundown farm. But living rough in hot and sunny weather
seemed fine to us.

It was rumoured that the rock band The Who lived on a hill at
the far end of the island near the lighthouse. I got to know some
German hippies who lived on the beach. One of them, a small
man with a goatee beard and long hair, always carried around with
him a small doctor's bag. He said that they worked in the winter
in a car factory in Germany in order to earn enough money and
then spent the whole summer in the sun in southern Europe.
They had dropped out and turned on. They were the archetypal
hippies following the advice of Tim Leary, and I delighted in their
company and attitude to capitalism.

After the summer Jeremy and his girlfriend Anne went to
live in Paris. I was to go down to the Sussex coast to live for
the first term on the campus at the University which was set
in the rolling Downs. It was inland from the railway station at
the village of Falmer, roughly half way between Brighton and
Lewes. Perhaps Jenny, who was still working in the French
section of the BBC overseas department, would join me on the
south coast later.

I had by a quirk of history been fortunate to grow up in the 60s,
a time of widespread experimentation with ideas and feelings.
It was also a time of rapid change when the traditions of the
Establishment were being challenged and new ways of living and
seeing were being forged. It saw the explosion of feminism and the
demand for greater equality, not only amongst women and men
but between people of different racial and class backgrounds. I may
have grown up culturally poor in a declining seaside town but had
passed through several rites of passage in my travels around the
world and in Africa to realise the inestimable value of learning,
knowledge and freedom. My journey had taken me from the sunny

sands of Bognor to a vision of radical and peaceful change. And of course I had Jenny.

I felt I had disproved my uncle that I would be always 'useless'. Moreover, I had shown after the ritual humiliation by my headmaster at boarding school and the initial failure of my 'A' Levels that I was intellectually the potential equal of anyone. And I had become an anarchist, rebelling against authority and hierarchy, thinking and acting for myself in a wider community. I had followed Rousseau in his 'moral reform'. I was at last reasonably content in myself – at least for a while…

Mending a car in 1971

EPILOGUE

My slightly doubtful beginnings in Bognor ultimately led to a life which had many positive outcomes.

I did an MA in the History of Ideas at the University of Sussex which involved choosing a horizontal history of a particular subject, in my case the History of Political Thought, and a period of time, which for me was Romanticism. For my first paper, I chose the concept of Imagination in Coleridge's *Biographia Literaria* which was a collection of biographical sketches of his literary life and opinions. What I found most revelatory was his distinction between Imagination and Fancy, the first being an 'esemplastic power' or faculty by which the soul can perceive the spiritual unity of the universe, and the second which has only an associative power. It introduced me also to the philosophy of the German thinkers Kant, Fichte and Schelling. For my final dissertation, I considered the concept of the state held by Communist Anarchists in France at the end of the 19th Century, particularly the Russian geographer Peter Kropotkin who was in exile for his revolutionary beliefs. This only confirmed my belief in anarchism and encouraged me to look at its historical tradition.

I enrolled with John W. Burrow for a part-time D.Phil. on the 'Philosophy of William Godwin: Its Origins, Development and Influence'. Godwin was not only the first great philosopher of anarchism, an original moral thinker, a pioneer of socialist economics and progressive education, but an acute and powerful novelist as well.

My research was mainly done in the British Library which was then housed in the domed building in the centre of the British Museum. It was very inspiring – large, airy and quiet – and a perfect place to study. The line of desks were formed like spokes of a wheel around a central hub and any book could be brought to your seat. I was shown the place where Karl Marx spent twenty years of his life studying and writing *Das Kapital*. Kropotkin had described it as an example of anarchist society organized on a free, equal and voluntary basis without a central authority and in which every person receives according to his or her needs.

My thesis was eventually accepted with a distinction and I was duly awarded a doctorate. I reshaped it as an intellectual biography of Godwin's life and works and it was eventually published by Yale University Press. As my first book, it was very well received by the critics and encouraged me to become a writer which I had long wished for.

While living with Jenny at a shared house in Barnes I became friends with Graham Hancock who later became a well-known writer. He and I attended with my old friend Jeremy Gane the last Windsor Free Festival in 1974 and dropped acid together. The festival, dedicated to peace and justice, was smashed up by the police in riot gear who came at dawn. Graham and I broke into print, he in an article in *New Society* magazine, and I with a piece in *The Guardian* newspaper called ironically 'A Constable Landscape'.

I became vegetarian, realizing the unnecessary cruelty to animals in eating dead flesh and the need for a diet for a small planet. The experience of killing a pig for my birthday in France caught up with me and I've remained a vegetarian ever since.

I developed my own courses for the Extramural Department of London University. These included courses on Anarchism and Existentialism (including Kierkegaard, Nietzsche, Heidegger, Sartre and Camus) as well as 'The Makers of the Modern European Mind: Darwin, Marx and Freud' and 'Doubt and Anxiety in Modern European Literature' (which covered Dostoevsky, Tolstoy, Thomas Mann and Simone de Beauvoir). I also became a part-time tutor at the Chelsea School of Art and the Open University. Having been a 'mature' student myself, I was keen to help others to learn at different stages in their lives.

But doing all this work took its toll. I very nearly developed an ulcer and had to slow down. It was only by taking an allotment and practising yoga which I had learnt from Jenny's father that I managed to cure myself. Sitting under an old plum tree outside a hut and digging my allotment in the evening and at weekends, I realised once again how Nature brings relaxation and ease to a busy and troubled city life.

When Jenny announced to me that she was pregnant I was over the moon but I did not want to form a nuclear family in a small damp flat, so we joined a group that were planning to create a commune in the country.

We attended meetings with a mixed bunch of other potential members in a flat in Victoria. What united us all was an opposition to the mainstream society and the state, and a wish to create an alternative way of living close to the land based on sharing and participatory democracy. Just after Christmas 1977 we moved into Redfield which had been a country house near Winslow in Buckinghamshire. It had 19 acres of land, including a large field, mature woodlands, and a derelict walled garden with an old orchard and collapsed greenhouses. In those early days there were about 20 adults and 16 children.

We thrashed out together the principles and customs by which we wanted to live. It was a very fraught period, very much I imagined like the speeches in the assembly in the early part of the French Revolution. We managed to agree that we should proceed by consensus on a voluntary basis, having communal meals on the ground floor every evening while the rest of the large mansion was divided up into 'Units', the size of which depended on needs. We signed our names on a rota board to do an evening meal or two each month and generally cleared up the ground floor on a Sunday morning. There were no fixed laws or overreaching rules.

Despite its beliefs being very different from the mainstream Redfield Community was so organed that it still thrives to this day – more than 40 years later. I think this is largely because it is based on consensus and voluntary and libertarian principles. There are no charismatic leaders, and the age range varies from zero to over 60.

Our first child Emily was born in the first year at Redfield. I enjoyed living in the community, but Jenny, who did not share my ideological fervour, was less happy. Although I was keen on developing a Study Centre at Redfield, there was always a conflict between continuing my writing and working on the stable block roof! Writing is predominantly a private and lonely activity and clashed with the communal work and living.

I had, at this stage, not finished the book on Godwin so Jenny and I decided to rent over winter a two-storey stone house in Gwynedd, North Wales from Richie Williams-Ellis.

Called Garth-y-Foel (meaning 'Enclosure on the Hill' in Welsh), it was surrounded by 90 rough acres of small stony fields, woodlands, and mountainous ridges covered in bracken. It looked south west to Tremadog Bay and the Irish Sea beyond. It was backed by Cnicht, called the 'Welsh Matterhorn' because of its triangular shape, and the mountain ranges of Snowdonia National Park. It was just below the tiny village, little more than a hamlet, of Croesor which had developed to shelter nearby slate miners and still boasted a chapel and a small primary school of about a dozen pupils. However, there was a community in our valley. Since each homestead was at least ten minutes away, we could get on with our lives as we wished. We eventually decided to leave Redfield Community in 1981 completely and move permanently to Garth-y-Foel.

My next book was a novel, a rite of passage of a young man, largely based on my experiences at sea. Whilst completing it, I was telephoned by my friend Graham Hancock who had gone to Somalia and was then a 'stringer' living in Nairobi. He said he had been given a two-week trip free to Zanzibar and mainland Tanzania with no strings attached and that he could not go but would I take his place. Jenny urged me to take the opportunity as it would not come a second time. On my return I wrote six articles, one each day, for the national press and magazines. Every one was published.

Some time later Graham again rang me and asked if I would like to make an illustrated book called *Journey through Tanzania* with the photographers Duncan Willetts and Mohamed Amin. I set off on a three-month trip throughout the country with Duncan, including the game reserves and the national parks as well as along the coast of Tanzania in a dhow, the traditional sailing boat. I also climbed Kilimanjaro with Mohamed which was a high point in more ways than one. The book *Journey through Tanzania* was published by Bodley Head. I later wrote a *Journey through Maldives* with them on the coral archipelago in the Indian Ocean where I learnt how to dive.

Having studied independent socialism according to the Tanzanian president Julius Nyerere in the 'Third World', I turned to Cuba and its revolution. After travelling through the country, I wrote *Cuba Libre* for Victor Gollancz with the sub-title *Breaking the Chains?* I concluded that it had broken from the dictatorship of Batista and American domination, it had made strides in education and medicine and reduced sexual and racial inequality, but it was still ruled by Fidel Castro in a rigid one-party state. It had little room for freedom of expression, travel and sexual differences.

The success of my book, which went through three editions and was translated into Spanish, led me with Graham to form Zena

Publications and publish an illustrated book with the photographer Barry Lewis, eventually called *Into Cuba*. It went into two editions and four languages.

Zena went on to publish half a dozen books or so afterwards by different writers. I realised that I could earn a living by my pen (or word processor) and also occasionally publishing.

We brought up the two children Emily and Dylan who was born in 1982 and I loved their company, partly because it brought me down to earth, the 'here and now'.

Jenny and I befriended Lucy Rees who had a couple of horses and a donkey grazing in the fields surrounding our house. She was a 'horse whisperer' and had written a book on the horse's mind. Our children and I learnt to ride on her horses and I bought a Welsh cob, called 'Black Jack', from her.

In 1984 my brother and I plus two of his friends sailed across the Atlantic from Palma in the Canary Islands to Barbados where my father had lived. Afterwards we sailed on to Martinique where Jenny had been born.

Back in Wales I joined the local Sailing Club and took up sailing myself with a small gaff-rigged dinghy with yellow cotton sails and then a large wooden GP 14 (General Purpose 14-foot). I taught my children to sail and 'riding in the winter and sailing in the summer' became one of my mottoes.

I continued my own evening classes in philosophy under the auspices of the Extramural Department of Bangor University from 1980 to 1990.

With the architect David Lea I wrote a pamphlet in English and Welsh on the possible effects of a nuclear war in Gwynedd and Wales. As active participants in the Campaign for Nuclear Disarmament (CND) we went on protests against Trident in Cumbria and against nuclear weapons in South Wales.

Whilst living at Garth-y-foel, I wrote my monumental *Demanding the Impossible: A History of Anarchism*. It was the culmination of studying and lecturing and practising anarchism for over two decades. Ever since the May events in France in 1968 I had genuinely believed in the Situationist slogan 'Be Realistic: Demand the Impossible' for one self and society.

I also wrote a short book on William Blake, calling him a 'visionary anarchist'. While Blake had lived in a cottage in

Felpham, part of Bognor Regis, he had been charged with treason by a drunken soldier who broke into his garden.

After writing *Demanding the Impossible* for Harper Collins, my growing concern with environmental issues and what humans were doing to the planet led to *Nature's Web: An Exploration of Ecological Thinking*, first published by Simon & Schuster. When asked what would be my next book, I happened to say off the cuff: *A Voyage around Africa*. They immediately wanted to take it!

I had previously been involved with two programmes for HTV about our valley and the fall-out from Chernobyl in the area. I mentioned my proposed book casually to the director and immediately he became interested. He then told his commissioning editor who said he would like to broadcast six 45 minute programmes. I was sent on a course to learn how to use a camera and then had to make a short film. It was accepted and I was given a high 8 video camera. A team consisting of a woman sound engineer, a young cameraman and the director would meet up with me at six places for about a week during my travels around Africa. I therefore became a cameraman, writer and presenter of the TV series.

My plan was to start in Portugal, where the explorers and navigators had first left to go round the south of Africa, and try to find a boat to take me at different stages. I wanted to consider the relations between Africa and Europe in the last five hundred years, which partly reflected my own situation with Jenny coming from Martinique and growing up in France and later West Africa. As it turned out, the voyage by fishing boat, new container ships, old coasters, a yacht and a dhow took about 9 months to complete. I came back and wrote both the book and made the TV series. I gave the Christmas talk about my experiences and was 'guest of honour' at the Royal Geographical Society in London, and was later elected a RGS fellow.

But there was a heavy toll on my private life. On my return, I could see that I was estranged from Jenny – it had been too long – and she wanted a separation. Two years later, I left Garth-y-foel and took a winter let down by the sea in Borth-y-Gest. I moved out with my books and fondest memories. I met a mysterious woman crossing a deserted farmyard on the way who saw me crying and said: 'You're a fledgling now. You will have to learn to fly'. I never met her again.

It was the most difficult time in my life as I loved the children

Epilogue

and the family. My daughter had previously decided to do her 'A' levels in Bangor town but it was particularly hard on my twelve-year old son Dylan who was now a pupil in the comprehensive school in Harlech. I still saw him each week when he came to stay which was wonderful.

The following summer I decided to buy a small yacht – a Westerly Centaur appropriately called Celtic Gold – to learn how to skipper it and clear my head at the same time by circumnavigating Ireland. I then came back in the autumn and wrote another book and edited a radio series about my experiences and adventures.

Just before my fiftieth birthday, I gave a weekend course at Dartington Hall near Totnes on my philosophy of *Nature's Web*. I was thanked after the course by Elizabeth (Liz) Ashton Hill who was a senior lecturer in media studies, mainly in film and photography, at a college in Plymouth. I invited her to come sailing and, as they say, one thing led to another!

I had just agreed a deal with Macmillan to write a book on alchemy and we travelled together for research in China, India, Egypt, Spain, France and the Czech Republic. The result was *The Philosopher's Stone: A Quest for the Secrets of Alchemy*. An offshoot was a book on *World Astrology* and another called *The Theatre of the World* on the court of Rudolf II, the Holy Roman Emperor of the Austro-Hungarian Empire. In the late sixteenth and early seventeenth centuries he gathered around him in Prague not only artists but practitioners of alchemy, astrology and magic, who helped lay the foundations of the Scientific Revolution. I was particularly interested in him because he was prepared to lose his empire and yet encouraged free thinking and expression.

Having spent so much time on the wilder shores of speculation, I felt it was time to state my own views on environmental philosophy and wrote, partly in North Wales and partly in the small cottage of my new companion in Cornwall, *Riding the Wind: Liberation Ecology for a New Era*.

After my son Dylan had gone to university at Warwick, we then decided to buy a place together with some land just over the border of the River Tamar in Devon near Tavistock. I wanted to practise ecology in action. Here we planted an orchard of local varieties of apples, pears and cherries and developed a large organic vegetable plot and soft fruit run on organic lines. We kept a pony and my old Welsh cob in our two small meadows and rented some fields nearby for the winter. The wood below provided us with logs and I would sometimes shower in the cold, limpid waters of a trout stream at the bottom of a wooded hill. It was full of wild flowers in spring.

Ever keen to combine sailing with writing, I travelled with Liz and wrote a work called *Europe's Lost Civilization: Exploring the Mysteries of the Megaliths*, involving a four-thousand mile voyage in our small yacht from Scotland to Malta. From here we sailed into the Aegean and up to the Black Sea. This resulted in the book *Poseidon's Realm: A Voyage around the Aegean*, particularly looking at Ancient Greece.

Having turned 70 and had a tumultuous life and written 16 books translated into 15 different languages, I decided to write my early memoir to make sense of it all. And here I am with a second-hand Sadler 34 yacht called Monabhar (meaning 'Murmur' in Gaelic, the sound of the yacht sailing through the sea) kept in the Aegean. I intend to spend six month's sailing in the Med. while living for the rest of the year in a small house with a garden and allotment by the sea. I will not give up my poetry and writing. We can also enjoy our four grandchildren, two of each belonging to my daughter and son, who have both Ph.Ds and become teachers of the next generation.

Although I consider myself a citizen of the world I am a Bognor Boy at heart. I am as a radical as ever and would still call myself a liberation ecologist and anarchist…

Lightning Source UK Ltd.
Milton Keynes UK
UKHW02f0008120918
328751UK00007B/224/P